Soviet and Post-Soviet Politics and Society (SPPS)   Vol. 278
ISSN 1614-3515

Soviet and Post-Soviet Politics and Society (SPPS)

ISSN 1614-3515

Founded in 2004 and refereed since 2007, SPPS makes available affordable English-, German-, and Russian-language studies on the history of the countries of the former Soviet bloc from the late Tsarist period to today. It publishes between 5 and 20 volumes per year and focuses on issues in transitions to and from democracy such as economic crisis, identity formation, civil society development, and constitutional reform in CEE and the NIS. SPPS also aims to highlight so far understudied themes in East European studies such as right-wing radicalism, religious life, higher education, or human rights protection. The authors and titles of all previously published volumes are listed at the end of this book. For a full description of the series and reviews of its books, see www.ibidem-verlag.de/red/spps.

Editorial correspondence & manuscripts should be sent to: Dr. Andreas Umland, Department of Political Science, Kyiv-Mohyla Academy, vul. Voloska 8/5, UA-04070 Kyiv, UKRAINE; andreas.umland@cantab.net

Business correspondence & review copy requests should be sent to: *ibidem* Press, Leuschnerstr. 40, 30457 Hannover, Germany; tel.: +49 511 2622200; fax: +49 511 2622201; spps@ibidem.eu.

Authors, reviewers, referees, and editors for (as well as all other persons sympathetic to) SPPS are invited to join its networks at www.facebook.com/group.php?gid=52638198614 www.linkedin.com/groups?about=&gid=103012 www.xing.com/net/spps-ibidem-verlag/

Recent Volumes

269   *Izabela Kazejak*
Jews in Post-War Wrocław and L'viv
Official Policies and Local Responses in Comparative Perspective, 1945-1970s
ISBN 978-3-8382-1802-1

270   *Jakob Hauter*
Russia's Overlooked Invasion
The Causes of the 2014 Outbreak of War in Ukraine's Donbas
With a foreword by Hiroaki Kuromiya
ISBN 978-3-8382-1803-8

271   *Anton Shekhovtsov*
Russian Political Warfare
Essays on Kremlin Propaganda in Europe and the Neighbourhood, 2020-2023
With a foreword by Nathalie Loiseau
ISBN 978-3-8382-1821-2

272   *Андреа Пето*
Насилие и Молчание
Красная армия в Венгрии во Второй Мировой войне
ISBN 978-3-8382-1636-2

273   *Winfried Schneider-Deters*
Russia's War in Ukraine
Debates on Peace, Fascism, and War Crimes, 2022–2023
With a foreword by Klaus Gestwa
ISBN 978-3-8382-1876-2

274   *Rasmus Nilsson*
Uncanny Allies
Russia and Belarus on the Edge, 2012-2024
ISBN 978-3-8382-1288-3

275   *Anton Grushetskyi, Volodymyr Paniotto*
War and the Transformation of Ukrainian Society (2022–23)
Empirical Evidence
ISBN 978-3-8382-1944-8

276   *Christian Kaunert, Alex MacKenzie, Adrien Nonjon (Eds.)*
In the Eye of the Storm
Origins, Ideology, and Controversies of the Azov Brigade, 2014–23
ISBN 978-3-8382-1750-5

277   *Gian Marco Moisé*
The House Always Wins
The Corrupt Strategies that Shaped Kazakh Oil Politics and Business in the Nazarbayev Era
With a foreword by Alena Ledeneva
ISBN 978-3-8382-1917-2

Mykhailo Minakov

THE POST-SOVIET HUMAN

Philosophical Reflections on Social History
after the End of Communism

ibidem
Verlag

Bibliographic information published by the Deutsche Nationalbibliothek
Die Deutsche Nationalbibliothek lists this publication in the Deutsche Nationalbibliografie; detailed bibliographic data are available on the Internet at http://dnb.d-nb.de.

Bibliografische Information der Deutschen Nationalbibliothek
Die Deutsche Nationalbibliothek verzeichnet diese Publikation in der Deutschen Nationalbibliografie; detaillierte bibliografische Daten sind im Internet über http://dnb.d-nb.de abrufbar.

Cover picture: "Red Mother and White Baby" by Alexander Blank from his album "Pain", Kyiv, 2021 © copyright 2024 by Oleksandr Blank

ISBN (Print): 978-3-8382-1943-1
ISBN (E-Book [PDF]): 978-3-8382-7943-5
© *ibidem*-Verlag, Hannover • Stuttgart 2024

Printed in the United States of America

I dedicate this book to the generation that lived through
the caesura of 1989–1991, the post-Soviet era,
and that era's catastrophic end.
May the force be with us and with those who come after.

Contents

List of Figures..9

Acknowledgments...11

Introduction..13

1. Key Concepts in Post-Soviet History..19

   Human Beings, the World, and History...................................20

   Political Creativity and Imagination.......................................22

   The Framework of the Post-Soviet Period...............................31

2. The Logic and Stages of Post-Soviet History..............................43

   Perestroika and the 1991 Revolution......................................44

   The Post-Soviet Diffusion, 1992–1994....................................58

   Stabilization, 1995–2000..66

   New Century, New Conflicts, 2001–2008................................73

   The Period of Conflicts, 2008 On..79

   Concluding the Era...85

3. The Evolution of Perceptions of Post-Soviet Development...89

   Stage 1: Living through the Caesura and Revolutionary
   Change, 1989–1994...93

   Stage 2: Humbled Conceptualization, 1995–2003....................97

   Stage 3: Questioning Post-Soviet Progress, 2003–2022.........103

   War and the Interrupted Transition......................................110

4. The Achievements of Post-Soviet Political Creativity..........113

   The Democratic Outcomes of Post-Soviet Political
   Creativity..114

      Division of Supreme Power into Branches and Levels.119

      Refounding the State and the Nation...........................121

      The Liberal-Democratic Potential of European
      Integration..124

      Rule of Law...125

Autonomy of the Judicial Branch 127

Elections as a Right and a Practice 128

Democracy as a Unity of Electoral, Liberal, and
Deliberative Practices 132

The Autocratic Outcomes of Post-Soviet Political
Creativity 141

Unified Supreme Power and Neopatrimonial Rule 144

Post-Soviet Sovereigntism 150

The Autocratic Effects of War 154

Conclusion 159

Bibliography 163
Index 181

List of Figures

Figure 1. Division of Power Index: Estonia, Russia, Ukraine, and Uzbekistan, 1989–2022 120

Figure 2. Legislative Constraints on the Executive Branch Index: Estonia, Russia, Ukraine, and Uzbekistan, 1989–2022 121

Figure 3. Rule of Law Index: Estonia, Russia, Ukraine, and Uzbekistan, 1989–2022 126

Figure 4. Judicial Constraints on the Executive Index: Estonia, Russia, Ukraine, and Uzbekistan, 1989–2022 128

Figure 5. Voter Turnout by Election Type: Estonia, Russia, Ukraine, and Uzbekistan, 1989–2022 130

Figure 6. Electoral Democracy Index: Estonia, Russia, Ukraine, and Uzbekistan, 1989–2022 131

Figure 7. Comparison of Electoral, Liberal, and Deliberative Democracy Indices by Country: Estonia, Russia, Ukraine, and Uzbekistan, 1989–2022 133

Figure 8. Freedom of Expression and Alternative Sources of Information Index: Estonia, Russia, Ukraine, and Uzbekistan, 1989–2022 135

Figure 9. Mobilization for Democracy Index: Estonia, Russia, Ukraine, and Uzbekistan, 1989–2022 135

Figure 10. Core Civil Society Index: Estonia, Russia, Ukraine, and Uzbekistan, 1989–2022 138

Figure 11. GDP Per Capita (Purchasing Power Parity): Estonia, Russia, Ukraine, and Uzbekistan, 1990–2022 142

Figure 12. Homicides per 100,000 Population: Estonia, Russia, Ukraine, and Uzbekistan, 1990–2022 143

Figure 13. Neopatrimonialism Rule Index: Estonia, Russia, Ukraine, and Uzbekistan, 1989–2022 149

Figure 14. Ideology Index: Estonia, Russia, Ukraine, and Uzbekistan, 1989–2022 152

Figure 15. Mobilization for Autocracy Index: Estonia, Russia, Ukraine, and Uzbekistan, 1989–2022 156

Acknowledgments

This book was conceived during a series of discussions held at the School of Civic Education (London) in recent years. I am sincerely grateful to Lena Nemirovskaya and Yuri Senokosov, Inna Berezkina and Marina Skorikova, Lev Gudkov and Frank O'Donnell, Ivan Krastev and Nikolai Petrov, John Lloyd and Michael Sohlman, Pavel Viknyansky and Denis Semenov, Alexander Shmelev and Yegor Chizhov for our spirited discussions, as well as for the truths and fallacies we achieved in them.

I am vastly indebted to Maria Grazia Bartolini for her encouragement and constant support in the darkest of times. Without her inspiration, I would not have completed this book.

The book was written at the Institute for Human Sciences (IWM) in Vienna, to which I am indebted for the opportunity to work in the quiet of its library and engage in spirited debate at the Institute's workshops and lunches. I owe to Misha Gleny, Ivan Krastev, Katherine Younger, and all the other fellows of the IWM's Ukraine in European Dialogue Fellowship Program for insightful conversations that strengthened many arguments put forth in the book.

I am deeply grateful to the Wilson Center's Kennan Institute, which funded the editing of this book. Special thanks are owed to Marjorie Pannell, William E. Pomeranz, and Izabella Tabarovsky, who supported me in this endeavor and ensured that my research turned into a book.

Introduction

The post-Soviet era in Eastern Europe and northern Eurasia began in 1991 with the signing of the Belavezha and Alma-Ata Accords and ended in 2022 with the launch of Russia's full-scale invasion of Ukraine in February of that year. Even though armed aggression — and hence the early phase of the current war — in Ukraine had started eight years earlier, it was the combined air and land assaults by Russia on a sovereign neighboring state in February 2022 that put the closing punctuation mark to the post-Soviet period.[1] That period, between the fall of the USSR and the invasion of Ukraine, was a significant time of change for the post-Soviet states, change that was driven by major developmental tendencies rooted in the collapse of the USSR in 1991 and expressed in the creation of new nation-states in Eastern Europe and northern Eurasia. Vladimir Putin's decision to launch the February 2022 invasion dealt the final, decisive blow to the post-Soviet order.

This opening statement is the starting point for the linked arguments about Post-Soviet Humans and their historical habitat that unfold in this book. If I am correct that the post-Soviet era has reached its terminus, then the era can be considered substantially complete for the purposes of scholarly research while phenomenologically open for philosophical reflection. For this reason, and unlike before 2022, post-Soviet studies may finally enjoy some distance from the object of their investigation. With the declining role of scholarly ideological engagement and identity bias, research on the post-Soviet era now has a chance to become an academic discipline.[2]

For the purposes of my argument, the post-Soviet period is bookended by its beginnings in the simultaneously destructive and

---

1   The current war in Ukraine started with Russia's seizure of the Crimean Peninsula in February 2014 and the installation of the pro-Russia Aksyonov government there.

2   An ideological commitment and identity bias were two main drawbacks that were obvious in studies in this area conducted over the past thirty years, including my own.

creative processes of 1989–1991 in the Soviet Union and its terminus in another set of military and revolutionary events that acquired avalanche force in early 2022. These simultaneously destructive and creative processes of 1989–1991 and 2022 emerged in the historical caesuras that separated the post-Soviet period from what it succeeded, the Cold War era, and what has succeeded it: a new, as yet unnamed time kicked off by the big war in Eastern Europe.[3]

As a historical period, the post-Soviet era had its own logic and dialectics. The logic of its evolution is connected with what I call the post-Soviet tetrad, a set of four socioeconomic, cultural, and political trends or tendencies that can be concisely summed up as democratization, marketization, nationalization, and Europeanization. Many initially thought these tendencies were conjoined in such a way that each would support and imply the others, and that if a country realized one, the probability was high that the others would follow. That was the logical expectation. It turned out not to be the case, for each tendency had its counterpart, its oppositional value, so to speak, that was also always available, and how the different tendencies and their counterparts might combine turned out to be unpredictable. Thus the dialectics of the era manifested in the way these four trends combined in contradictory ways. Emerging market economies, for example, could choose to support antidemocratic actors, which would thenceforth limit their free market aspirations; the former socialist republics, now nation-states, could turn hostile to common European norms and practices and continue on a modified Soviet path. The individual trends themselves were the sites of struggles among countervailing forces as they sought to establish themselves. The post-Soviet democratization process had to compete with the pull toward autocratization. Efforts to establish free markets had to struggle with oligarchical control over competition. Nation building was constantly being torn between ethnonationalist, civic nationalist and individualist models. The Europeanization process in the former socialist republics

---

3   Thus the post-Soviet period can be seen as the second interwar interval, after the interval between the two world wars (1918-1939), in the recent history of Eastern European and northern Eurasian peoples.

was weakened by ambiguity in how common legal norms and political practices were to be adopted, as well as by negative social reactions to those norms and practices in the emerging nations.

The post-Soviet development in all its complexity was imagined—and not only by scholars but also by politicians and citizens—mainly in terms of the post-communist transition, as a movement from totalitarian darkness into democratic light. But this post-Soviet imaginary was changing fast, and by the 2000s, transition studies had changed their tone and focus: no longer espousing a vision based in optimistic expectations, they now offered up pessimistic assessments of the post-Soviet transition period. Growing skepticism around how the transition was evolving in different post-Soviet states reflected the growing autocratization that was taking place; and together, observers' skepticism and swelling on-the-ground autocratization began to shape the political imagination of Eastern European and northern Eurasian peoples, preparing them for the tragic events of 2022 and the launch of new historical caesura.

This book takes up many political, social, and cultural issues, but at its core it is about the Post-Soviet Human, a cultural-anthropological type that was shaped during the caesura of 1989–1991 and found expression in the political creativity of the post-Soviet interwar interval, prior to the invasion of Ukraine in 2022. My conception of Post-Soviet Humans and the world they created, then inhabited, stems from idea that one should judge human beings according to the connection between their actions' aims and achievements. Accordingly, I interpret the post-Soviet period as an unprecedented historical environment in which Post-Soviet Humans expressed themselves in the creation of new social worlds, economies, and political and legal systems. The post-Soviet era provided the once Soviet Man with a chance to overcome himself, to enjoy freedom and to realize his creativity without Marxist-Leninist shortcuts.[4] And in

---

4   Among other theories, Vladimir Lenin (1870–1924) offered an idea of how to make a proletarian revolution in Russian society, which at the start of twentieth century had a very small worker class. The vanguard (Bolshevik) party, the Soviets, and a number of other "tricks" had to speed up history in Russia. Thus

this book, I demonstrate the collective and institutional outcomes of Post-Soviet Humans' seizure of this chance and how they used it.

This book was written in three languages—English, Russian, and Ukrainian. Each version of the book differs slightly from the others as it addresses a different audience. However, the structure and arguments as laid out above are the same. Before finalizing the book, I tested its major arguments in a series of articles published in 2021–2023.[5] I collected both critical and supportive comments expressed by readers of these publications, sharpened the argumentation, and brought in more evidence, which found a place in the four chapters that follow. The work has gestated adequately and is ready to meet the post-post-Soviet world in published form.

Organization of the Book

The first chapter is dedicated to philosophical reflections on the foundations of the concepts of the Post-Soviet Human, political creativity, historical periodization, and the post-Soviet tetrad: democratization, marketization, nationalization, and Europeanization. Readers already at home with such theoretical deliberations may wish to move directly to the second chapter, where I describe the sequence of stages and the common rhythm of the post-Soviet nations' development—those fifteen independent states, including the Russian Federation, that were once socialist republics and part

---

Leninism offered a shortcut in the historical development and Marxist revolutionary practice.

5   The third and the fourth chapters advance arguments based on previously published articles. The third chapter is an expanded version of my article "The Transition of 'Transition': Assessing the Post-Communist Experience and Its Research," in *Meandering in Transition: Thirty Years of Identity Building in Post-Communist Europe*, edited by O. Kushnir and O. Pankieiev and published by Rowman & Littlefield in 2021. The fourth chapter is a further elaborated study of an article I wrote, the earlier version of which was published in 2023 as "Political Creativity and Its Democratic and Autocratic Outcomes: The Case of the Post-Soviet Period, 1989–2022" in *Ideology and Politics Journal*. This use is made with the permission of the copyright holders.

of the USSR.[6] The third chapter looks at how observers and political leaders in Eastern Europe and northern Eurasia, as well as those outside this broad region, imagined the post-Soviet development and its ends. The fourth chapter provides a sort of a balance sheet, listing both the democratic and the autocratic outcomes achieved by Post-Soviet Human. The conclusion takes a final look at Post-Soviet Humans' historic mission, fitful attempts at political creativity, and, often, a ragged return to Soviet-style power practices while under pressure to achieve democratization and Europeanization.

It is important to note that this book was written from the depths of another historical caesura, the one that started engulfing Eastern Europe and northern Eurasia beginning in early 2022. A new historical era is emerging in the unpredictable fragmentation of this region, where political creativity is no longer determined by the Soviet experience and the countering anti-Soviet sentiments. The thirty-year post-Soviet experience, though, is likely to be formative for the foreseeable future, and this book is precisely about its lessons. Which makes it a Post-Soviet Human's testament to the next generations, doomed to live in Eastern Europe and northern Eurasia in what remains of the twenty-first century.

---

6   The fifteen post-Soviet, independent states are Armenia, Azerbaijan, Belarus, Estonia, Georgia, Kazakhstan, Kyrgyzstan, Latvia, Lithuania, Moldova, Russia, Tajikistan, Turkmenistan, Ukraine, and Uzbekistan.

1.   Key Concepts in Post-Soviet History

A human being is an existential hope and, concurrently, an ontological catastrophe. The Post-Soviet Human, a cultural-anthropological type that dwelled in the post-Soviet social worlds, is no exception. Although Post-Soviet Humans' catastrophic nature is particularly evident because of the exaggerated expectations to which
they were subjected in the early 1990s and the ensuing disenchantment with their achievements in the 2010s. This book is about the
gap between those expectations and achievements, the origin or
seed of the tragic contradictions that shaped Post-Soviet Human.

The original meaning of the Greek καταστρέφω, "catastrophe," is a turning and overturning, which I interpret as an overturning of the original ontological order, the original order that was
initially established by Being as such. But even in this overturning,
a human being may still derive hope, for a human establishes a new
order every time the previous one is overturned — or, as the term
καταστρέφω was used in reference to Greek drama, ends in disaster
(a disaster for the initial order, but a hope for a new beginning).
This is how the order of culture is created out of the overturned
order of nature, or how the order of civilization is established out
of the natural state. Phrased differently, it is how one's choices define one's destiny, even though the choices are made in the context
of having been thrown by Being as such into the world, that is, into
some biological and sociohistorical context that in turn predefines
one's opportunities and choices.[7] This hopefulness of human existence, arising out of catastrophe, out of turning and overturning, reveals itself in the human capacity to create something new in a
world that was shaped well before we were thrown into it. To be a
human being means to exist both in rebellion against the original

---

7   Being as such, the central concern and the concept of ontology, has a long his-
    tory of investigation, from the Presocratics, Plato and Aristotle to Martin
    Heidegger and contemporary objective ontologists. In contemporary thought,
    Being as such is the initial ontological category referring to the foundation of
    everything that is/exists/is present and from that foundation everything pre-
    sent derives/grows/develops.

order and in a return to an order reestablished by our efforts at seeding new, often unprecedented beginnings. This "creative destructiveness" is humans' mode of existence in the world. It unites our theomachic response to being thrown into the world and our almost divine ability to participate in never-ending creation.[8]

Human Beings, the World, and History

Our creative destructiveness evinces a specific tension, at once ontological and performative, of human existence. The ontological tension lies in the divine ability to create something unprecedented, on the one hand, and on the other, the certainty of mortality: the animal finitude of each human individual's life, which places a terminus on our godlike creativity. The performative tension lies in the gap between the fact that a human being is present in the world as someone thrown-into-it whose trajectory is always directed toward the termination of life and the no less definitive fact that humans live though their efforts to define their own ends, to destroy or to create the lives of others, and to communicate with other human and nonhuman existences and things in this world. In all these manifestations, human beings constantly transgress boundaries established by Being as such, others and themselves. These ontological and performative perspectives reveal a human existence as a creative-destructive, catastrophic and ordering state of presence.

The catastrophically destructive creativity of a human lies at the heart of history, in an ongoing transpersonal experience consisting of at least four elements. The first element includes events that are individually and commonly experienced and preserved in the anonymous structures of the world usually referred to as tradition, language, community, and archetype. Those commonly experienced posits are all gifts of human existences that preceded our own but that cannot be linked to specific names, dates, and places of their formation. The second component comprises events either individually or commonly remembered in the form of written or

---

8   Theomachy (in Russian, *bogoborchestvo*): godfighting, a human (heroic) effort to establish equality with the God/gods or take over them.

orally transmitted histories. Here we can tie events to concrete facts, persons, and times. The third element consists of situations that we experience right now and that may in the future become either anonymized posits (element 1) or remembered histories (element 2). Finally, the fourth element of history embraces the openness of the future. These possible future events not only may befall individuals and communities in some prospective future (assuming that humanity continues to exist), they also encourage us to make choices now and to turn opportunities in acts and facts, realized and possible.

Thus history — as transpersonal experience vested in all four above forms and our ways to narrate them — began long ago, with the existence of the first humans and the origin of humanities.[9] This history is multidimensional and lasts as long as humans continue to be thrown into the world, to change it and to make sense of it. With that perspective in mind, we can also consider history as a multifaceted term encompassing an indefinite plurality of eras, periods, times, collective destinies, and individual outcomes of being present and of becoming in the world. The history is so complex that the word itself must be conceptualized, ungrammatically, as existing in the plural, *histories*, to respect the multitude of experiences and situations open to comprehension and transmission through storytelling and retelling, through remembering and forgetting.

The history consists of atomic events through which once-and-for-all contradictory human existences have manifested their presence and their becoming in the world.[10] And even after the end of the history, when no human presence inhabits the orphaned world, the history will remain an irreplaceable event of events and a story of stories.

As a destructive-creative existence, a human being participates in the constant change of the world, its continual redefinition,

---

9   The history of humanities is a rather new discipline; more on it can be found in Bod et al. (2016, pp. 1–2).

10   One-and-for-all contradictory human experiences refer to the fact that human existences are permanently in the grip of ontological and performative tensions.

and in the seeding of new beginnings in the wreckage of previous ones or, alternatively, in their continuation. Every human presence in the world is limited to the time span of individual life, from birth to death. However, a human being, through its presence, continually transcends these limits through becoming, through the intersubjectivity of human existence and the interobjectivity of the material changes that result from its actions. As human beings, we are born into a world that exists before us (stemming from both human acts and nonhuman accidents) and we leave it changed by us, augmented by our choices, achievements, and failures. Human beings are an important part of the multitude of forces involved in the creative interplay of history and the destruction and re-creation of orders in an ever-changing world.

Political Creativity and Imagination

The above ontological provisions are not merely theory: they are present here and now, evident in the various practices through which we manifest our presence and becoming in the world, for example in politics. Politics is one of the many realms in which the destructive-creative human existence leaves its trace in history. The study of politics entails introspection into what a human being is through research in political creativity, political actions, and their outcomes.

Dominance and obedience, dispute and consent, war and peace, dependence and freedom, crime and justice, allegiance and citizenship, personal gain and common good—these and many other political phenomena stem from our intersubjective co-presence in the different forms of order. In this ordered co-presence, human beings are condemned to connect, to interact, to enter into a communication fellowship, or *koinônia* ("having together," "sharing publicly," "participating in the commonwealth"), when we make decisions and accomplish them together.[11] This koinônia is the communication that entails a multidimensional process

---

11   This political koinônia—κοινωνία πολιτική—was written about as early as Aristotle (in *Politics*, II.1.1261a18, III.1.1275b20). See also Brill (2020, p. 27 et seq.).

allowing individuals with their private interests to become fellow citizens, members of the same political community, once the *polis* and nowadays the republic, the nation, the people, or any other political community. Becoming a citizen means to gain a status in each political act, each act of the political community, that can be characterized in terms of an active or a passive position and of the acceptance of or resistance to a central or marginal role in koinônia. Each such act is a deed of political creativity that changes human behavior and material conditions of life, that is, everything that constitutes a social reality.

From an ontological point of view, political creativity is the capacity of human existence to launch new beginnings in the political sphere. In that sphere, human actors cooperate and struggle to attain what Aristotle would call the *highest common good*. The novelty of such beginnings in politics can be absolute or relative. Absolutely new beginnings involve the creation of some unprecedented political practice, institution, organization, or ideological concept.[12] Relatively new beginnings involve the political outcomes that are new for some politically relevant group but have precedents in the experience of other groups. Whether absolute or relative, political creativity is about the manifestation of human presence in the world through the seeding of new beginnings in the form of political ideas, processes, and material or institutional outcomes.

The creativity of human existence is one of many other, equally genuine human capacities, among which can be mentioned destructiveness, passivity, participation as an equal actor in a network with other actors, or the radical rejection of such participation in the almost impossible choice of solitude. Human existence is present in the world simultaneously in chaos and in a variety of orders, also called networks (Latour, 2007) or systems (Luhmann et al., 2013). In these variously understood orders, humans live through conducting creative and destructive acts.

---

12 Hannah Arendt (2006) discusses this further in describing the specificity of "revolution": the seeding of new beginnings in the life of our political communities. See also the interpretation of human creativity in the political and ideological senses in Minakov (2022b).

Thus creativity is only one of many human capacities, but one that specifically manifests in seeding new beginnings in our political communities through activity that can be described as "sketching a project" – an act comparable to hurling the lasso of a plan into Nothingness and filling that plan with the living human energy that turns this Nothing into Being-present-in-the-world. In this way, human presence becomes becoming, and vice versa. This understanding of the existential character of creativity offers a compromise position or perspective vis-à-vis the competing phenomenological views on human existence of Hegel, Heidegger, and Sartre and removes the fundamental ontological contradiction between presence and becoming (Hegel, 2018; Heidegger, 2010, 2014; Sartre, 1960).[13]

This understanding of creativity does not contradict, and indeed is also acceptable in, a posthuman ontology, such as an actor network perspective. To be an element of an actor network means to be co-present and to interact in many different ways with non-human and not-entirely-human elements (Jensen, 2003; Latour, 2007; Murdoch, 2001). In actor networks, a human being manifests her or his specificity – but neither centrality nor a dominant position – in initiating a series of new situations and processes whose realization is possible in interaction with other elements of the

---

13   Georg Wilhelm Friedrich Hegel (1770–1831) is a German philosopher who saw a human being as an active participant in historical development in which history streams toward its end, the event in which Absolute Spirit recognizes itself as the Absolute in full collection of its past formations (*Gestalts*). Despite their active role, humans, at least before Hegelian philosophy, were not aware of the general goal of history and of the cunning of history. Martin Heidegger (1889–1976) is a German philosopher who taught about human existence (*Dasein*) as a unique existence able to understand and express Being as Being-in-itself and as Being-present-in-the-world. Heidegger also pointed to the specificity of a human existence as one that lives oriented toward its death, and in this life-stream *Dasein* fulfills existential projects that turn Nothing into existence. Jean-Paul Sartre (1905–1980) is a French philosopher who, among other concepts, developed the idea that a human being is present in history as a free actor, which means that a human through his or her choices can participate in changing the world and, together with other human beings, in making projects that fill the world with human sense and meanings. Despite many differences in their teachings, for all three philosophers, presence and becoming, as well as the tensions between them, are among the key issues to be addressed by philosophy.

network. From such an open perspective — one that respects existentialist ontology and posthuman philosophy — human creativity can be understood in terms of intersubjective and interobjective differences, connections, and productivity.

Human creativity is a capacity that has only recently begun to be appreciated in philosophy and the social sciences. In their short history of the concept of creativity, Vlad Glaveanu and James Kaufman correctly stipulate that "creativity is a modern concept and a modern value" (2019, p. 9). Although creativity was also known to philosophers long before modernity, and in other cultures with their own understanding of chronology, it was predominantly seen as a capacity with ambivalent significance if applied to a human being: this faculty was associated with divine, not human, functions. In the hands of nongods, creativity was a transgressive act of participation in the universe's creation — and thus prohibited (for humans) and punishable. It was only the Enlightenment, with its focus on rationality and individualism, that legitimized human creativity and sparked interest in its two main characteristics, novelty and originality (Glaveanu & Kaufman, 2019, pp. 14–17). So the collective force of creativity was transformed into the progress driven by the daring acts of Newton and Einstein, Chagall and Picasso, Tesla and Faraday, Gagarin and Armstrong, Faust and Danko.[14]

Over the past three centuries, since the launch of the Enlightenment in Europe and the spread of its intellectual and philosophical precepts around the globe, philosophers, psychologists, and anthropologists have categorized human creativity in four ways: (1) as a productive force of reason, (2) as some kind of unconscious process, (3) as a pragmatic force of problem solving, and

---

14 Faust, the protagonist of the German legends and Johann Wolfgang von Goethe's (German poet, 1749–1832) poem of the same name, is a great scholar who dedicates his lifetime to research and who, as an old person, makes a pact with the Devil, bargaining his soul for full knowledge of all the universe's mysteries and access to worldly pleasures, whereby he brings down disaster on the lives of fellow humans. Danko (from the Romani, "youngest son") is the protagonist of Maxim Gorky's (Russian writer, 1868–1936) short story "Old Izergil." According to the story, Danko rips out his burning heart to lead his people from cosmic darkness into worldly light. In doing so, Danko sacrifices himself for the happiness of others.

(4) as a process of mental associations generating new content (Brown, 1989, p. 4). Much more recently, the same four categories of creativity have emerged in discussions among geneticists (Barbott & Eff, 2019, p. 132) and evolutionary biologists (Feist, 2007, p. 16).

These four ways of understanding human creativity can also be seen in longlasting debates over its role in politics. For example, international peace has been seen as a product of human creativity, achieved through the application of human reason and the construction of modern, rational political institutions (e.g., Kant, 2008; Pinker, 2011). The political behavior of the masses has often been interpreted as the result of unconscious processes (e.g., Adorno, 1968; Freud, 2012). American pragmatists tended to describe political judgment and action in terms of problem solving or the prevention of problematic situations (Dewey, 1998; Honnet, 1998; Rorty, 1999). The fourth approach, which holds that creativity is a process of mental associations, can be seen, for example, in research on social and ideological processes (Etkind & Minakov, 2020; Freeden, 1996; Oakshott, 2011; Simmel, 1949). Whatever conceptualization of creativity is adduced, the existence of creativity in the political sphere is widely accepted in contemporary studies of politics.

The above interpretational differences notwithstanding, in general, political creativity should be understood as a transgressive, synthetic capacity that links individual human presence and the intersubjectivity of existence, personal interests and collective action, an actor's free will and determinacy by network capabilities. This transgressive, synthetic role of political creativity has been well expressed by Gerald Berk, Dennis Galvan, and Victoria Hattam:

> Political creativity [is] a concept intended to capture both the pervasiveness of change as well as the deeply embedded nature of social action. Political creativity is at once not determined by background conditions and yet constituted through extant social relations. . . . Political creativity jettisons the duality of free will and determinism (or necessity and contingency) for an investigation into the relationships and processes that situate creativity and are, in turn, reconstituted by it. . . .
> Political creativity blurs the analytic boundaries intended to keep order, agency, and change from mingling. (Galvan et al., 2013, pp. 3, 5)

In contemporary political philosophy and political theory, there is an ongoing debate as to which political conditions are best for unlocking and supporting the human creative faculty.

The classic liberal-democratic position is best expressed by John Dewey (2021), who holds that the adaptability and survival of the human species related to the intellectual faculty of resolving problematic situations in the context of a social reality. The social reality of a democracy is equally capable of creating problems for humans as the social reality of a dictatorship, but these two forms of governance offer radically different conditions for solution seeking. The democratic freedoms create the arguably best-known conditions for seeking solutions through open discussion and experimentation, while the multiple limitations of a dictatorship constrain human creativity in problem solving. Thus for Dewey, even though human creativity can be seen in the context of all forms of governance and all types of political regimes, the best options for the survival and evolution of humankind are provided by political institutions that support individual and collective creative problem solving, that is, by liberal democracies. Later, Karl Popper's "open society" concept, John Rawls's theory of justice, and Ulrich Beck's model of an enlightened "risk society" enriched the liberal-democratic perspective with an understanding of how life, freedom, and rationality reciprocally support each other in individual and collective creative acts (Beck, 1992; Popper, 2012; Rawls, 1971).

The socialist approach to political creativity tends to move the focus from its rational and normative foundations to social action itself. For example, Karl Marx, Jürgen Habermas, and Hans Joas, despite serious differences among their positions, aim at discovering social structures that direct human creativity and alienate human beings from the results of their creativity (Habermas, 1981; Joas, 1996; Marx 2004). Their theories of capital, communicative action, and the creativity of action establish firm foundations for practices engaging individuals and groups in common action to fuel social progress and group emancipation.

Many conservative theories and practices around politics, in general, share a common perspective on political creativity: they look at it as at a *longue durée* process whose historically rooted subject is a *tradition* or a *people*—a collective transgenerational subject that supersedes the "imperfection" of an individual and the limitations of historical events. Conservative optics in the West and East perceive creativity as a spatially widespread and temporally continuous process collecting the sociopolitical achievements of past generations into a single structure with one unchangeable identity stemming from some ideal past event, such as divine revelation or a sage's inspired decision, leading to an ontologically embedded, authentic, and just order that must either be restored or serve as an example for political action (see, e.g., Chateaubriand, 2000; Dugin, 2002; Huntington, 2000; Khomeini, 2001; Lübbe, 1981). The permanent dialogue between past and living generations of some religiously, ethnically, racially, or otherwise identified group occupies the center of attention for conservative thinkers, whichever position they take—reactionary or revolutionary—in this highly diverse assortment of ideologies.

Political creativity is also an issue for the theoreticians of revolution. The diversity of opinions within this perspective stretches from Vladimir Lenin's understanding of revolution as the "creative, living activity of masses" to Hannah Arendt's interpretation of revolution as "a coincidence of the idea of freedom and the experience of a new beginning" (Arendt, 2006, p. 29; Lenin, 1974, p. 57).[15] Despite obvious contradictions between their polar positions, both perceive revolution as a time and space where existing structural obstacles (social, economic, political, etc.) are destroyed and the creative human energy thereby released—whether of individuals, revolting groups, or mass movements—has a historic opportunity to launch an unprecedented beginning leading to a new expression of human existence in the sociopolitical sphere (Arendt) or a historic change in the direction of the fuller emancipation of humanity (Marx, Engels, Lenin). So revolution itself is seen as an event of great political creativity, a creativity that is ordinarily limited or blocked by political-economic and ideological structures.

---

15   Hannah Arendt (1906–1975) was a German American political philosopher and theorist, a student of Heidegger, and a researcher of the human condition, revolution, and totalitarianism.

Finally, political creativity is at the center of attention for thinkers who work on the idea of development (Calder, 1995; Gaidar, 2022; Huntington, 1965; Keynes, 2010; Sen, 2001). Unlike theoreticians of revolution, these thinkers attend to political creativity in times of social order rather than during moments of revolutionary chaos. As Pavlo Kutuev (2016, p. 61) rightly mentions, their theories look at the state as an agent of progress that would create conditions for and direct *modernization*, a transformative creative process uniting individual endeavors, small-group projects, and national development programs and bringing change to all spheres, including the social, political, economic, and cultural.

The differences among these diverse perspectives in relation to understanding political creativity are symptomatic of its significance for human — individual and collective — life. The transgressive and synthetic character of human creativity provokes debate on what it truly is, but it also offers a solution: human creativity is able to reveal itself on different planes and under different conditions, in theory and practice, in universal value systems and in particular ideologies. If one aims to study a given historical period from the point of view of human creativity in the political sphere, as I do for the post-Soviet era, it is essential to look at the creative outcomes under both democracy and autocracy, in connection with personal rights and with collective autonomy, in revolutionary moments and over the course of gradual development.

However, political creativity and its achievements are related not only to changes in the materiality of social reality but also to its imagery. Participation in politics and the horizons of human political creativity are connected with the social imagination, which unites thinking and practice, individuals and groups, ideal and real plans of existence. The human imagination is a complex cognitive factor. It integrates various human capacities in achieving stable cognitive and existential positions — ideas, decisions, beliefs that drive our behavior — and changing reality. By creating images and causing changes in the world, the human imagination becomes a key element of the human capacity to create.

For more than two thousand years, philosophers have regarded imagination as a cognitive function, combining fantasy

(Plato, Aristotle) and productivity (Kant) to make sense of others' existence and of one's own (Heidegger, Ricoeur). Paul Ricoeur offered a summary of the long evolution of philosophers' understanding of the imagination.[16] He specifically noted that in the history of philosophical thought—from Plato's and Aristotle's debate on ideas through the phenomenological and hermeneutic debate on the ontological conditions of understanding and interpretation—contemporary philosophy developed the concept of imagining as an act that can be used simultaneously in three ways: (1) to think of things that are not present in the current perception but can potentially exist; (2) to create images of things or situations that do not and cannot exist in actuality, but can in the imagination; and (3) to bring about images representing things, persons, situations, and ideas that are known to exist in actuality (Ricoeur, 1994, pp. 120–125).

By combining the modus operandi of possibility, fantasy, and virtuality, imagination allows a human being to *solve problems*, that is, to manage situations of uncertainty by combining work with the past (memory), work with the future (possibility), and work with the present (intellect) (Dewey, 1998; Rorty, 1998). But a far more important aspect of imagination is its power to combine the cognitive, emotional, social, political, cultural, and other elements of human existence into a single experience. From the imagination is derived the power of human existence to make existential projects in which we bring something new into the world.[17] Thus imagination is an important human faculty to participate in changing the world and in co-constructing social reality. Imagination turns out to be the source of the meaning of social life, providing individuals and collectives with a framework for interpreting and practically changing their realms of existence, their social reality.

---

16 Paul Ricoeur (1913–2005) was a French philosopher and hermeneutic phenomenologist who studied human understanding, culture, and interpretation.

17 This imaginal force has been studied by phenomenologists and hermeneuticists, including Edmund Husserl (1859–1938), Martin Heidegger, Jean-Paul Sartre, Alfred Schütz (1899–1959), and Cornelius Castoriadis (1922–1997).

From the perspective of political theory, imagination is a synthetic force that can unite different dimensions of time, space, and human existence:

> The process of imagination extends not only to how we anticipate the development of our personal lives, but also to how we envision the future of our social groups, be they micro-groups such as families, or macro-groups such as nations or even the fate of humanity itself. (de Saint-Laurent, 2018, p. 4)

Political imagination gives meaning to human creativity and morally engages participants of the political koinônia in common projects, both socially real, morally accountable and affectively perceived.

Political imagination is one of the important sides of political creativity, and that is why, when evaluating the results of such creativity in certain historical periods, it is necessary to consider not only the materiality but also the imagination of this period. In political action, we not only destroy and construct, we also legitimize these actions themselves, using meaningful concepts and stories. And the closer we get to modern times, the greater the role of social and political disciplines in this legitimization. Chapter 3 of this book is devoted to how we came to understand the post-Soviet period and the terms we use to describe it.

The Framework of the Post-Soviet Period

The transgressive, synthetic power of creativity and therefore of the imagination is especially evident in moments of significant political events that involve all human existences in a common process of thought and practice and move them toward some common destiny. For example, crises — tectonic political, social, or economic changes — can become *historical caesuras*, that is, pivotal moments in which we witness how a destiny acts by "rolling the dice" — by radically changing the conditions for the human collective presence according to the combination fortuitously rolled out on the playing table. In other words, a caesura is a hinge point that ends some long processes of a certain period, instigates the collective meeting of human existences with the Nothingness hiding behind the orders of social reality, and, for a short time, reveals the ontological, existential, and political structures of history.

A recent example of such a caesura is the revolutionary era of 1989–1991. For communities living between the Black and White Seas, from the eastern spurs of the Alps to the Kamchatka hills, these few years constituted an event of rethinking their recent history, of rejecting the political systems and ideologies associated with Soviet Marxism and the power practices of the Eastern Bloc, and, most important, of sketching new political projects and hurling them into the Nothingness of the future. Altogether, this caesura opened the opportunity to seed new beginnings for a new, post-Soviet era.

So the post-Soviet period began with the caesura of 1989–1991. It lasted for roughly thirty years, until the caesura of 2022 took hold, kicked off by the Russian invasion of Ukraine, which delivered the final blow to the post-Soviet social reality and relevant political orders. From a spatial perspective, the post-Soviet period applies to the countries and societies that took shape after (but not necessarily because of) the collapse of the Soviet Union.

Since the appellation "post-Soviet period" includes a central reference to the preceding Soviet era, it is important to point out its temporal and spatial frameworks as well. The Soviet era stemmed from another caesura opened by the terrible events that in the literature are usually described as the Russian revolution (1917) and the Civil War (1917–1922), which prolonged the violence of World War I and spread it around the lands of Eastern Europe and northern Eurasia. This period was brought to an end by perestroika ("restructuring"), the political and economic reform movement under Mikhail Gorbachev that unleashed the forces of civic, religious, entrepreneurial, and ethnonational emancipation. These forces led to the defeat of Soviet-style development and the caesura of 1989–1991 opening.

Perestroika was truly a catastrophe (some even called it "catastorika," catastrophic restructuring) for Soviet practices, values, and institutions. It culminated in the collapse of the political system, the mass rejection of values rooted in Soviet Marxism and power practices, and the inability of the power elites to retain control of the country. For people living in the USSR, the period 1989–1991 was a revolutionary event that opened up opportunities for democratization, nation-state building, the establishment of market economies, and the reorientation of nascent societies toward interaction within a pan-European regional project.

The post-Soviet period lasted for roughly thirty years, between 1991 and 2022, providing individuals and communities in Eastern Europe and northern Eurasia with the opportunity to exercise their destructiveness and creativity, their power to imagine and to act; to express their love for and fear of freedom; and to practice their ability to think and to betray the cause of thinking in a unique sociocultural context.[18] The following chapters examine how human presence and becoming have manifested in the form of a Post-Soviet Human, who has been given unprecedented opportunity to build free societies, states, and economies after the experience of living under the prolonged, almost omnipresent subjection of the Soviet system.

The term "post-Soviet" still elicits an aversive reaction from many of us, now that the war in Ukraine and the preceding autocratic wave have revived certain Soviet-style practices in some countries on the European and Eurasian continents in the past fifteen years. The more the societies of Eastern Europe and northern Eurasia fall back into a regime of ideological monopoly resembling the Soviet political regime, the harsher our reaction to the term "Soviet," even with the prefix "post." The end of the "Soviet'" did happen indeed at a certain level of social reality in the time span between 1989 and 1991. But at other levels, Soviet society continued to exist in different economic and political formations. In my opinion, with the collapse of the union, Soviet society did not disappear; instead, it divided into fragments and became more numerous, developing in separate new states. In a number of countries, these fragments of Soviet society survived in the form of local communities or as suppressed social strata (as happened, for example, in the

---

18   The cause of thinking is a philosophical concept meaning to remain true to responsible thinking, to not allow magical reasoning or other types of mental acts to infiltrate our thoughts and practices.

three Baltic republics, Moldova, and Ukraine). In other countries Soviet society—in its local shape—almost completely preserved itself despite the new socioeconomic and political conditions, thereby continuing on its historical path; examples here are Belarus and Transnistria. In yet other countries Soviet society has faded into the past, leaving only a trace in the collective memory of the fast demodernizing societies (as has happened in Azerbaijan, Tajikistan, Uzbekistan, and Turkmenistan).

When I use the term "post-Soviet" in this book, I am focusing not on the second part of the word but on the first. "Post-Soviet" refers both to a historical period and to a social experience based on *the rejection of Soviet practices and values*. This experience is constituted by attempts at self-overcoming by late Soviet individuals, communities, and entire societies. This self-overcoming began with the strange actions during perestroika, for example, public acknowledgment that alcoholism was a pervasive problem, the granting of permission for small cooperative entrepreneurships, and approval of the resumption of different religious confessions. The "post-Soviet" has continued in a mode of alienation from the Soviet experience. And out of all this emerged the anthropocultural type of the Post-Soviet Human.

Post-Soviet Human is a generic name for several generations in the societies whose collective experience of self-overcoming was linked to the destruction of the Soviet social world and to the revolutionary attempt to build new social worlds in Eastern Europe and northern Eurasia between 1991 and 2022. The post-Soviet period was a time of overcoming the Soviet communist legacy, of trying to do away with the totalitarian (and post-totalitarian) Soviet experience, and of striving to escape the "historical ruts" of both imperialism and colonialism. The tragedy of Post-Soviet Humans is that they shaped their future by pursuing the past, thus betraying the new beginnings they had sown in the caesura of 1989–1991.

This conceptualization of the post-Soviet period heads off the sort of prejudices and predispositions that have dogged scrutiny of the period while it was ongoing. In light of the many social traumas and political biases associated with the Soviet and post-Soviet legacies in Eastern Europe and northern Eurasia, turning recent historical experience into a subject of investigation requires a huge effort to put aside bias and take a sober look at the events and pro-cesses — social, political, economic, cultural — that constituted the post-Soviet period. But by undertaking this difficult task, we can focus on the practices and processes in the societies of Eastern Europe and northern Eurasia in terms of the outcomes of political creativity. That creativity manifested in two tendencies. First, it was inextricably linked to the desire to get rid of the Soviet totalitarian and authoritarian legacy. Second, it seeded new beginnings in the form of institutions that crystallized fundamental structures of post-Soviet political societies, economies, and states.

This sort of approach opens up the recently concluded post-Soviet period for scrutiny from a perspective in which ideological stance yields to a hermeneutic gaze: we can look at the past thirty years as a world in which Eastern European and northern Eurasian individuals and societies have lived and made their presence felt through social destructiveness and political creativity, the power of imagination and the capacity for action, a commitment to freedom and a fear of it.

This conceptualization of the post-Soviet period is based on a philosophical approach that envisions history as a combination of continuities and caesuras. I defined caesuras earlier, so let's look at what is meant by the continuity of a historical period. *Continuity* is an aspect of history that provides space and time for human creativity to grow and possibly to flourish. A continuity is filled with, and constituted by, the collective human efforts to live through time in the presence other, nonhuman actors — ideas, things, technologies, institutions etc — in the historical events of those periods until a caesura ruptures such processes.[19] Continuity is the historical element supplying space and time for human creativity to be realized, while a caesura is the historical point at which one continuity comes to an end and a new one has a chance to begin, exposing new opportunities and challenges for human creativity.

---

19 This conception of nonhuman actors comes from actor-network theory as developed by Michel Callon, Madeleine Akrich, Bruno Latour, and John Law, among others.

Understanding history as a constellation of continuities and caesuras allows us to look at the post-Soviet period as a continuity between the two caesuras of 1989–1991 and 2022 and beyond. Spatially, the post-Soviet period encompasses societies and communities that formed after the collapse of the Soviet Union. The post-Soviet period can be narrated as a time that unleashed human creativity in terms of political, civil, religious, entrepreneurial, and ethnonational emancipation under the strong influence of Western developmental models. In the smoke of the 1989–1991 caesura and in the fire of the revolutionary period that coincided with it and followed in 1992–1993, the idea of Europe became the guiding star for the development of the peoples of the region. It served as a kind of constitutive idea and a binding process that supported three other tendencies of the post-Soviet continuity: the establishment of functional democracies, market economies, and new nation-states.

Insofar as the caesuras bookending the post-Soviet period were both connected to wars, the post-Soviet period should also be understood as an interwar period. The first interwar period lasted between the two world wars of the twentieth century. The second interwar period stretched from the end of the Cold War to the Russian invasion of Ukraine and the spread of a militarized *Zeitgeist*, a special type of context for political creativity and social imagination where peace and freedom matter less than security and discipline.

In terms of political creativity, the post-Soviet interwar period was constituted by the four tendencies (or the *post-Soviet tetrad*) consisting of democratization, marketization, nationalization, and Europeanization. Each of these tendencies, however, developed in the constant fight against opposing traits. Democratization faced attempts at establishing an autocracy. The development of post-Soviet economies was constantly torn between a commitment to an open global market, national industry and local oligarchic control. Nationalization vacillated between the temptations of ethnic and civic nationalism. And Europeanization evolved from a process of pan-continental harmonization of different national political and legal systems into the competing integratory projects like the EU, NATO, AUKUS, the Eurasian Union, and the new Silk Road. These four discordant tendencies, pulling in support and against each other, structured, in one way or another, the post-Soviet continuity from beginning to end.

More specifically, the process of democratization directed the political creativity of post-Soviet societies toward the construction of new political cultures, systems, and regimes founded on the division of power between autonomous branches, as well as among central and local governments. Furthermore, democratization relied on the rule of law and the leading role of human rights and civil liberties in the political-legal systems being built. Democratization meant opening politics to ideological pluralism, diversity of parties, and competitive elections. Finally, democratization involved former Soviet populations in politics as citizens who would participate in free elections and deliberations during decision-making, in which capacity they were presumed to be supported by independent mass media and well-organized civic associations (Dryzek & Holmes, 2002; Gel'man, 2003; Gunitsky, 2018; V-Dem, 2023a, b). Even though the spread of democracy in the post-Soviet countries was a part of a wider global process, sometimes referred to as the "third wave of democratization," it had its own specificity: the former socialist republics had to reinvent political freedom and democratic institutions without any firsthand experience of such liberties and under the strong influence of Western political models and social imagination.[20]

The process of marketization directed the creativity of post-Soviet societies toward the establishment of new economies oriented toward the neoliberal market model and participation in the global economy. The economic transformation was expected to be accomplished through the privatization of state-owned assets (the economic legacy of socialism), the creation of an entrepreneurial

---

20   On the third wave of democratization, see the classic work by Samuel Huntington (1993) and its recent reevaluation by Stephan Haggard and Robert Kaufman (2016). On the post-Soviet specificity of democratization, especially on its inclinations toward "patronalism" and "bad governance," see Gel'man (2003), Hale (2011), and Magyar and Madlovics (2022). See also the methods adopted by the Varieties of Democracy research team to measure democratization (V-Dem, 2023a). They specifically measure five layers of democracy: electoral, liberal, participatory, deliberative, and egalitarian. Only together with these five elements can the development of contemporary democracy be measured.

class, and the formation of a middle class of economically self-sustaining citizens who would not be reliant on the government for sustenance and would at the same time demand respect for political liberties. The new social structure with its new classes was expected to be a bulwark against the communists returning to power and to provide an appropriate socioeconomic apparatus to support a democratic politics (Aslund, 2013; Horvat & Evans, 2011).

Nationalization was the process of the new post-Soviet states' "nesting" in the new nations. In the 1990s it was commonly believed by many in the West, and indeed among the political elite in the former socialist republics, that some form of nationalism – civic, ethnic, or of some blend of them – would create a stable majority of the population whose identity would be supportive of, or at least not hostile toward, liberal democracy and a market economy (Brubaker, 2011, pp. 1786ff.; Tismaneanu, 2009, pp. 16ff., 107ff.). A nation is usually understood as a large, historically stable entity that emerges among a population on the basis of common social and cultural experiences. But in the post-Soviet condition, state building coincided with the processes of destruction of Soviet society – which lasted much longer than the formal dissolution of the USSR – and the emergence of new national societies. The new nations did not have time to form in advance of state building but emerged either hand in hand with it or, often, in competition with the institutionalization of the core state organizations. Hence the complex, non-ethnonational states (such as the USSR, the Yugoslav Federation, and Czechoslovakia) could neither continue to exist nor provide governance of a democratic nature. The post-Soviet populations found themselves not only divided along income lines into rich and poor, as Brubaker rightly concludes, but also fragmented into majority and minority groups by tensions between three new social categories: (1) national states with their imagined majorities, (2) new ethnic minorities that were thenceforth to exist in the interstices between the majorities, and (3) external homelands with which these minorities identified themselves (Brubaker, 1996, pp.

7ff.).[21] Thus the outcomes of the nationalization project in different former socialist republics both supported and challenged democratic governance. The divisions into majorities and minorities that had neighboring nation-states and stateless minorities usually did not support *demos*, liberal norms, and equality before the law.

Finally, Europeanization was a regional integration process that aimed to ensure that political, legal, and economic systems, as well as societies themselves, would be able to unify considerably around common norms and values, leading to a long and peaceful coexistence and cooperation among Eastern European and northern European nations. The project of a common European home was strongly influenced by the imagination of the Gorbachev-Kohl—or Habermas-Yakovlev—generation.[22] According to this idea, future Europe was to be a space of peace and cooperation between peoples from Dublin on the Atlantic side of Europe to Vladivostok on the Pacific side of the continent (Avladiani, 2019; Minakov, 2017; Sakwa, 2021).

In the early 1990s, these four post-Soviet tendencies, along with the ideas and models associated with them, were pursued and imagined as if they were reciprocally supportive.[23] Quite often, however, they contradicted or undermined each other. The post-

---

21   The rich as a class did not exist in the USSR, while existing socioeconomic inequality was almost invisible.

22   Mikhail Gorbachev (1931–2022) was a Soviet and Russian politician who initiated perestroika and served as the leader of the Soviet Union and its Communist Party from 1985 to the USSR's dissolution in 1991. Helmut Kohl (1930–2017) was a chancellor of Germany (1982–1998) who oversaw the end of the Cold War, the German reunification, and the creation of One Big Europe. Jürgen Habermas (b. 1929) is a German philosopher and social theorist in the tradition of critical theory who influenced the European dialogue between the West and the East in 1980s and 1990s. Alexander Yakovlev (1923–2005) was a Soviet and Russian intellectual, politician, and diplomat who was behind Gorbachev's reforms of glasnost and perestroika, as well as the European dialogue. Their and their generation's ideas were expressed in the Charter of Paris for a New Europe (adopted by most European governments, the USSR, and the United States in Paris in November 1990) that established the foundations of security and cooperation for a united Europe from the Atlantic to the Pacific.

23   For more on this interdependency of practice and imagination, see Minakov (2022a). Here it is important to stress that our imagination directs us toward fulfilling imagined plans, thus making them part of reality. Through our behavior, imagination empowers practice, and practice fulfills the imagined

Soviet nationalization of states, the privatization of economies, the equality of citizens before the law, and promotion of the rights of national majorities were rarely in harmony with each other. These and many other discrepancies, as well the weakening of these four post-communist tendencies in the second half of the post-Soviet period, sharpened when the post-Soviet nations entered the era of "the third wave of autocratization." To unpack this phrase, autocratization is an overarching concept that includes a gradual democratic recession and the sudden breakdown of democracy, with or without autocratic consolidation, the whole process "resulting in less democratic, or more autocratic, situations" (Lührmann & Lindberg, 2019, p. 1099). An autocratic tendency does not simply connote the lack of democracy, however. Autocracies are products of political creativity, just as democracies are. Similarly, the third wave of autocratization, which began around 2008–2012, does not merely fill a gap created by the decline of the third wave of democratization.[24] The third wave of autocratization is an ongoing global political process during which "the number of countries undergoing democratization declines while . . . autocratization affects more and more countries" (ibid., p. 1102).[25] The internal and international conflicts that had been growing in the post-Soviet region since 2003–2008, including conflicts between countries where the color revolutions happened (Georgia in 2003, Ukraine in 2004, and Kyrgyzstan in 2005) and Russia have sharpened under the influence of wider autocratization. This has led to the start of Russia's war

---

24   In political science and the history of international relations, the waves of democratization are the surges of democracy among nations that have occurred in the most recent two hundred years. The third wave started in 1970s and 1980s with the democratic transitions in Latin America, in Eastern Europe in the 1990s (after the collapse of the Soviet Union and the Eastern Bloc), and in sub-Saharan Africa in the 1990s. The energy of this wave was exhausted by the beginning of the twenty-first century, which created an opening for the current global surge of autocratic transitions. For more on this, see Huntington (1991) and Lührmann and Lindberg (2019).

25   Compare with the data provided in Ágh (2022, pp. 74ff.) and Sato et al. (2022, p. 3ff.). Altogether the data show that in recent decade, more than half of world's population started living in nonfree states, while the number of autocratizing countries is growing for a second decade.

against Ukraine, a massive military conflict in the east of Europe, and put an end to the post-Soviet period in 2022.

Just as the democratization process—globally, and in most post-Soviet states—was disrupted, partly or fully, by autocratization, so the free market could transform into an oligarch-run market; the nation-state, instead of adhering to liberal democracy, could experience a demand for "managed" or "sovereign democracy" (and not only in Belarus or Russia but also in such EU member states as Hungary or Poland, though with a lower level of manageability); and the European common space, launched around inclusive organizations such as the Council of Europe and the Organization for Security in Europe (OSCE), could see its ideal tottering as it began to fragment into the EU and non-EU regions, the eurozone and extra-zonal financial systems, NATO members and partner states—as well as potentially adversarial countries. In this regard, the post-Soviet tetrad should be understood as a set of four trends that had many contradictions and challenges within them: democratization was challenged by autocratic processes, the markets oscillated between economic freedom and oligarchic control, the nation-states swayed between liberal inclusivity and ethnocentric exclusivity, and Greater Europe developed from the geopolitical harmony of the "Dublin-Vladivostok" axis to the catastrophic "Belfast-Magadan" axis. Thus what was once Greater Europe is being torn between the imaginary poles of Belfast, which signifies falling back into the dark days of ethnoreligious conflict, and Magadan, the capital of Stalin's gulag system, which symbolizes possibility for totalitarianism's return.

The post-Soviet period ended with an unprovoked attack on Ukraine by the Russian Federation. This event marked a rupture of the post-Soviet continuity and set in motion the catastrophic processes that finalized the disaggregation of the post-Soviet region and fragmentation of the global rules-based order. From that moment on, the post-Soviet tetrad— democratization, marketization, nationalization, and Europeanization—ceased to influence the political and economic situation and lost sway in the social imagination of Europe's power elites and populations. Russia's assault on

Ukraine put a terminal punctuation mark to the post-Soviet period, the Post-Soviet Human's habitat. In its wake we are left in a profound caesura, awaiting the emergence of a new historical era from καταστρέφω, a turning and an overturning.

2. The Logic and Stages of Post-Soviet History

The post-Soviet period grew out of the caesura of 1989–1991 and terminated in another caesura that enveloped the social worlds of Eastern Europe and northern Eurasia in 2022. Between these two turning points, the political communities that emerged from the ruins of the Soviet Union and the sites of construction of the new states evolved through five stages. The first stage was associated with the rise of the trends that made up the post-Soviet tetrad (democratization, marketization, nationalization, and Europeanization) as expressed in the opening up of opportunities for political creativity after the continuity of the Soviet era in 1989–1991. The second stage saw the realization of revolutionary opportunities as new power elites emerged in the former Soviet republics, the launch of new states and open market economies, and a search for rules of coexistence among the new nations, which rules were subsequently enshrined in the December 1994 Budapest Memorandum on Security Assurances (1992–1994) and the following bilateral agreements on friendship and partnership.[26] The third phase was a time of stabilization of the new political and economic systems when the populations of the defunct Soviet Union had to accept the new realities and participate in the newly created social, political, and economic structures (1995–2000). The fourth stage coincided with the beginning of the twenty-first century and provided an opportunity for post-Soviet peoples to assess the results of their

---

26 The Budapest Memorandum, or the Budapest Memorandum on Security Assurances, included three political agreements signed in Budapest on December 5, 1994, to provide security assurances by its signatories relating to the accession of Belarus, Kazakhstan, and Ukraine to the Treaty on the Non-Proliferation of Nuclear Weapons and their giving up those the parts of the Soviet nuclear arsenal situated on their territory. All three documents were signed by the Russian Federation, the United Kingdom, and the United States. Also China and France gave their assurances in separate documents. The memoranda prohibited the Russian Federation, the United Kingdom, and the United States from threatening or using military force against Belarus, Kazakhstan, and Ukraine. These documents have also opened the processes of signing off the bilateral agreements on friendship and partnership among the post-Soviet nations.

development in the first decade after the collapse of the Soviet Union and the creation of new social worlds; at the same time, the norms of the 1990s and their contradictions began to be institutionalized, which intensified the struggle for power, property, and recognition within post-Soviet societies and for the boundaries of their sovereignty and their place in the world-system (2001–2008).[27] Finally, the last stage saw the strengthening of autocratic tendencies and deepening differences between more versus less free and more versus less rich post-Soviet countries. These tendencies helped amplify conflicts between post-Soviet nations and marked the beginning of the trajectory that would lead to the conclusion of the post-Soviet period (2008–2022). This chapter considers each of these stages in detail.

Perestroika and the 1991 Revolution

Whether by the will of its initiator or despite it, perestroika saw the end of the Soviet utopia, more attention paid by the Soviet peoples to their social reality, and the rise of *chernukha,* or a "dark aesthetics" phase characterized by deep and widespread skepticism.[28] This overwhelming skepticism, it seems to me, was born out of the moral trauma of late Soviet society: memories of shocking events in

---

27   A world-system is a key concept of world-system theory, developed by André Gunder Frank (1929-2005), Immanuel Wallerstein (1930–2019), Giovanni Arrighi, Georgi Derluguian, and others. A world-system is a socioeconomic system that encompasses a large part of or the entire globe as the aggregate result of the sum of the interactions between related cultures, societies, economies, and polities. Historically, there were always multiple world-systems; however, in the late twentieth century, with the fall of the USSR and the Eastern Bloc, the world for the first time in history was covered by a single world-system, constituted by the Western countries at its core and the other countries at the periphery. The status of core or periphery was measured by a country's gain from international economic exchange, influence in international relations, and so forth. The post-Soviet region existed in the framework of this one world-system mainly on the periphery.

28   *Chernukha,* or Soviet *noir,* was a particular skeptical style and worldview focused on dark aspects, imbued with doom and hopelessness, of Soviet social reality, past and future. *Chernukha* also developed in early post-Soviet times, when it was in opposition to the creative energies of the 1991 Revolution. For more on that style and imagination, see Isakava and Beumers (2017), Pocheptsov (2017), and Vorobiyova-Ray (2010).

Soviet history that had previously been repressed from public mind into the collective subconscious were allowed into the daylight, where they appeared centrally in public debate and public awareness. The totalizing Soviet ideology denied everyday individual experience, and its language was based on referentially free-floating expressions: the words had meanings within sentences but almost no reference points in the actual state of affairs. Vladimir Sorokin in his pre-perestroika novels *Norma* (1983) and *Marina's Thirtieth Love* (1984) successfully captured the widespread ordinariness of the rupture of meaning from words said not only in public speeches but also in everyday small talk and intimate situations.[29] The same disconnect of words and social reality was evident in the dual structures of Bulgakov's novel *The Master and Margarita* (1940), publication of which in the USSR was permitted only in the mid-1980s, and in Chingiz Aitmatov's new, piercingly honest novel, *The Execution Scaffold* (1986).[30] Both novels expose gaps between a visible social reality and other, invisible realms — whether narrativized as Satan's coming to Stalin-era Moscow or as a wild animal's observations of the human society — and in doing so dismantle the Soviet myth. For the literature-oriented Soviet peoples of the time, these texts were symptomatic of a growing awareness of the chaotic nature of the world, the lack of connections between different Soviet social strata, the presence of hidden levels of social reality (state terror, organized crime, corruption), and the deliberate falsity of the visible layers of reality, smothered in Marxist blabber. The Soviet lifeworld was disintegrating into loosely connected elements, which created even more obstacles for a person looking for moral integrity and authenticity. Whereas in the *mid*-Soviet postwar lifeworld (1950s–

---

29   Vladimir Sorokin (b. 1955) is a contemporary Russian postmodernist writer and dramatist, one of most influential cultural figures. Among his many novels are the anti-utopian and dystopian sagas *Their Four Hearts* (1994), *Ice* (2002), and *The Blizzard* (2010).

30   Mikhail Bulgakov (1891–1940) was a Russian, then Soviet, writer and dramatist. His novels *The Master and Margarita* and *White Guard* are regarded as among most influential literary works of the twentieth century. Chinghiz Aitmatov (1928–2008) was a Soviet Kyrgyz writer who wrote in Russian and Kyrgyz. He was one of the influential late Soviet writers, and today is one of the best-known figures in Kyrgyzstan culture.

1960s), with all its cynicism and doublethink, it was crystal clear where the path of authenticity led and what it would cost a person to look for it, in the *late* Soviet situation (since 1970s), the social chaos offered too many branching paths with no, or too much, moral guidance.

The local hegemony of Soviet ideology, an alternative to the global hegemony of neoliberal consumer capitalism, came to an end with the beginning of meaningful public discussions and political deliberations in Soviet society. This change started with Gorbachev's experiment with policies banning alcohol consumption in public and alcohol sales during the workday, which led to the alienation of the ruling group ("Soviet people's government") and the population, among whom the alcohol consumption culture was widespread, and to the accumulation of enormous social energy that could no longer find solace in alcoholic delirium (Hafso, 2019).[31] Government was becoming unpopular, and social contradictions were becoming visible to the sobered-up population. The change in the Communist Party's policy in favor of glasnost ("openness in discussions") and the weakening of party control over the press suddenly made the Soviet press the venue that provided access to increasingly uncensored information and public discussion.[32] At the same time, the free press was read and subscribed to by tens of millions of readers, some of whom turned, often involuntarily, into citizens (Gibbs, 1999, pp. 7–13). Thus perestroika became a time of emergence of a late Soviet, genuinely public sphere

---

31   Mikhail Gorbachev was the initiator of perestroika and the Soviet Union's liberalization in 1986–1991. Prohibition was one of Gorbachev's first perestroika policies and was aimed at a decrease in consumption of alcohol by the Soviet population. By the early 1980s, alcohol consumption had reached 10.5 liters per person per year. The policy prohibited the drinking of alcohol in public spaces, radically increased the price of vodka, and limited the sales of alcohol during the workday. The anti-alcohol campaign decreased the consumption twice over by 19987. However, during this campaign many vineyards and breweries were deliberately destroyed. Heavily alcoholized late Soviet society was split in the assessment of this policy: some perceived it as too harsh and illiberal, while others praised its positive impact on public health.

32   Glasnost is one of Gorbachev's perestroika policies that provided the Soviet press with more freedom in 1986. By 1990, the Soviet press had achieved full freedom and independence from the government and the CPSU.

and of Soviet societies learning about their multitudes in all their cultural, class, and ethnic diversity. And with this, the Soviet myth's hegemony — and Soviet identity   faded.

Soviet people's discovery of their own diversity was not a uniting experience but a divisive one. The chasms that started opening in the Soviet past and present were so out of sync with official ideology and utopian self-image that small cracks in the Soviet myth further widened over time into an unbearable fracture of Soviet collective identity. The collapse of a collective identity during caesura is normally followed by an encounter with one's self and one's own groundlessness, with Nothingness. The mass encounter with Nothing is at the core of caesura; and in this encounter human existences learn about the chaotic and random multitudes of what once was perceived as an order and truth. Soviet society was becoming multiple, and these smaller but still Soviet societies threw themselves into the post-communist transition, rethinking and reinventing themselves in three different ways: either as ethnonational (or else ethnolinguo-confessional) communities, or as sporadic groups of automized individuals, or in terms of political communities of citizens. The post-Soviet peoples usually combined these three types in some fashion in their nation-building efforts.

These self-discoveries were as destructive as they were creative. Perestroika, irrespective of its foremen's intentions, provided a path for the emergence of civic horizontals within which discussions about the highest common good began — something that had long been forgotten in Eastern Europe and northern Eurasia, something pre-Soviet, associated rather with the February Revolution of 1917 and the variety of republican projects that stemmed from it in Estonia, Finland, Latvia, Lithuania, and Poland (Minakov, 2017b).[33]

---

33 The events usually called the Russian revolution consist in fact of two revolutionary processes, referred to as the *February Revolution* and the *October Revolution*. The February Revolution was a revolutionary process that started in the Russian Empire in February 1917. The meaning of this revolutionary practice was connected with the establishment of a state in the form of a "bourgeois," national-democratic republic. This form was initially promoted by the revolutionaries in the Duma and temporary governments in St. Petersburg in the spring and summer of 1917. Later, after the victory of the Bolsheviks, this practice moved farther, to the western provinces of the empire, where nation-states

The emerging civic horizontal networks—journalists' associations, professional unions, debate clubs—quickly began to form along national and ethnolinguistic lines, triggering, with some exceptions, the nationalization of the Soviet republics and the politicization of certain local nonrepublican communities (either ethnic minorities, as in Abkhazia and Nagorno-Karabakh, or as Soviet communities that rejected the nationalization of the republics, as in Ukraine's Crimea or Moldova's Transnistria) (Brubaker, 2011 pp. 3–8; De Waal, 2018, pp. 8–9; Sasse, 2018, pp. 7–9). The Soviet Man thought not only in Marxist terms of class but also in terms of a Soviet concept of nationality. The closer the collapse of the USSR drew, the more this ethnonational imagination was encouraged, triggering processes that later led to the design of post-Soviet states and nationalities. In late Soviet society, ethnic thinking triumphed over class thinking.

At the same time, the values and practices of individualism were spreading wider and wider. In perestroika, the Soviet individual openly voiced a claim to the right to act in the private sphere in the domains of business, religion, intimacy, and sexuality. For more than four generations the Soviet totalitarian (Stalinist) and post-totalitarian system had attempted to control the private sphere by undermining the moral and economic autonomy of the family, by violent secularization (which effectively banned the autonomy of communication with the transcendent), by destroying the traditional village and suburb community, by inventing the Soviet city with its unemancipated citizens living mainly in shared communal apartments, by leaving individuals with almost no space for intimacy or diverse forms of sexual life, and by criminalizing

---

were created in Estonia, Finland, Latvia, Lithuania, and Poland in 1917–1920. Attempts to establish the same state forms were also undertaken in Armenia, Azerbaijan, Belarus, Georgia, Moldova, and Ukraine, as well as in Central Asia and Siberia, between 1917 and 1924. In contrast, the October—or the Great Socialist—Revolution was a revolutionary process connected with the Bolsheviks and a number of other competing Marxist/socialist revolutionary groups promoting a socialist state that would lead to a future classless society. By 1924 the Bolshevik political project had won against all the revolutionary and reactionary political alternatives, which allowed the USSR to start its seventy-year-long history.

entrepreneurship. The private sphere was hugely marginalized by the outsized Soviet public sphere.

During perestroika, however, the private domains and practices regained their legitimacy. But this new experience coincided with perceptions of one's neighbors as competitors and objects of suspicion rather than as fellow citizens. The result was an antisolidarity form of individualism that thrived in conflict. This would later culminate in a symptomatic post-Soviet devaluation of the social justice of the present and a focus on historical, collective justice. The first large-scale manifestations of antisolidarity and a collective justice (i.e., suspicion of one's neighbors) were the ethnic conflicts in the South Caucasus and Central Asia and a widespread — socially and geographically — criminal revolution.

In the end, perestroika led to the return of the pre-Soviet division between the public and private spheres, a division that had been eradicated by Stalinist totalitarianism and reproduced by post-Stalinist Soviet authoritarianism. In 1989–1991, the perestroika redivision of public and private spheres — and establishment of their structural equilibrium — gave impetus to the unique process of *private and public revolutions*. Thus a new world with opportunities for political and economic creativity was catastrophically emerging.

When writing about revolution, I am first and foremost adhering to the concept as articulated by Hannah Arendt (2006, pp. 18, 24). That is, I understand revolution as devolving from a weakening of old cultural, social, and political structures to such an extent that they can no longer contain the political creativity of citizens. Revolution is a brief (in terms of historical chronology) time and an unhindered (in terms of sociopolitical structures) space for the seeding of new beginnings in the world. In this time and space, individuals, small groups, and large societies are extraordinarily free to create, to seed new beginnings, and to use the newly opened perspectives for future development.[34] This is where the fragility of the passing world manifests itself and where the projects of the future are born,

---

34   For more on this concept of revolution, see chapter 1 and Minakov (2020a).

although only some of them will become reality thanks to the political creativity and imagination of the participants in the processes.

The 1991 Revolution is unique in that it saw the birth of new beginnings in both the public and private spheres simultaneously. In this regard, it makes sense to define post-Soviet societies as constructed through parallel movements: in the division of the Soviet universe into two spheres, public and private, new beginnings were assumed — as norms, practices, and institutions — simultaneously in both spheres. Such super-effort — on behalf of all individuals and communities living under those conditions — required a myth equal in power to that of the Marxist-Leninist utopia. It is from here that many national liberation movements' leaders of the 1990s developed the Promised Land prophecy. Many national democrats of the time applied the Moses myth and prophesied that when the last person born into "Soviet slavery" died, the liberated peoples would achieve true national sovereignty, democratic politics, and a functional market. The Post-Soviet Human was born hearing the lullaby of these prophecies even as the Soviet Man was perishing.

The creativity of the Post-Soviet Human manifested both in public revolutions and in the seeding of new beginnings in the private sphere. The latter included the entrepreneurial revolution, the sexual revolution, the criminal revolution, the religious revolution, and so on — the list could be much longer. For example, after half a century of prohibition, private business was allowed: the Soviet government gave permission for a small degree of entrepreneurship in a form of *khozraschet* and cooperative movements.[35] This step made the entrepreneurial underground legal, allowing active entrepreneurs to start cutting ties with the shadow economy and criminal underworld (Bandelin, 1998, pp. 24–26). In pursuing entrepreneurial activities, the Soviet Man was simultaneously reinventing capitalism and the value of money, which transformed him into Post-Soviet Human. By the end of the 1989–1991 caesura, the

---

35   *Khozraschet,* from the Russian *khoziaistvennyi raschet,* "economic calculation," is an early perestroika-era policy allowing government-owned industrial units — from factories to agricultural brigades — to function in a financially autonomous way and independently respond to economic demand. The activity of such a unit would be aimed at turning a profit without regard for the state's plan.

miracle of added value feeding into the first post-Soviet accumulation of wealth had started creating the foundations of a new entrepreneurial class and teaching the populace that money had a central role in the life of every person, family, community, and nation. The freedom to act economically in pursuit of one's own welfare, to undertake, and to earn quickly won out in Soviet societies, regardless of geography and proximity to the union center and regardless of whether many people were actually prepared to take advantage of this type of freedom or understood the risks it held for them.

The sexual revolution opened up space for the Soviet Man to rediscover his own and another person's body, to privately practice and publicly discuss the joys and dangers of sex, and to reevaluate the importance of marriage and family. Beauty contests broke Soviet puritanism. And hand in hand with the return of capitalist alienation, prostitution exposed the monetary dimension of a newly discovered corporeality. The emancipation of sexual behavior pushed back, if it did not abolish outright, the age of marriage and childbearing, as well as the dictates of tradition in acknowledging gender orientation. Planning childbirth was becoming a common practice. Homosexuality was coming out of the closet and escaping the criminal code. Services to prolong the sexual life sprang up, creating new market opportunities (Moghadam, 1990; Shlapentokh, 1992). All these beginnings would reach their peak in the 1990s–2000s, but they had their origins in the perestroika period.

The criminal revolution represented a radical change in the values and behavior of the broad masses, for whom a less repressive political order meant freedom to transgress legal norms and moral limits. Newly rich and entrepreneurial groups became the source of resources for a reorganized criminality. The informal rules of the Soviet criminal underworld were rapidly breaking down: the old "*vory v zakone*" were being disrespected and pushed aside by the "new lawless" generation of criminal lords.[36] The criminal revolution drew more and more young people into the growing ranks of organized crime networks, whose representatives

---

36   *Vory v zakone* (from Russian, "lawmen") were the men who embodied and ruled by *criminal laws*, the leading figures of criminal hierarchies.

preferred criminal entrepreneurship and ignored equally established traditions and officially sanctioned norms. The criminal revolution changed the speech practices and vocabulary not only of
the lower social classes but also of the emerging upper classes
(Kuzio, 2014; Waller & Yasmann, 1995). Even in 2022, the "*murchanie*" ("purring") intonations, gestures, and terms characteristic
of the criminal lingo were widely used by the majority of politicians, oligarchs, policemen, *petit* and *haute bourgeois*, and lumpen.[37]
Many specific terms were firmly embedded in the vocabularies of
self-description of the post-Soviet era, in the same way that the
criminal cadres became an important part of the post-Soviet power
elites in all countries.

The Soviet leadership's permission to celebrate the millen-
nium of the Baptism of Rus' in 1988 opened up a space of religious
freedom.[38] Soviet peoples started discovering Christianity and Islam and rereading atheist dictionaries with a new interest unexpected by the texts' authors.[39] The basic experience of Orthodox
Christianity, various Islamic professions, Catholicism, evangelical
denominations, and new, unprecedented religious groups was acquired before the collapse of the Soviet Union and became constituent of the post-Soviet experience. It's true that by the early years
of the twenty-first century, post-Soviet religious life had succumbed to obscurantism, clericalism, and confessional entrepreneurship. But the religious experience of the 1991 Revolution was
different: it was of a piece with the experience of personal freedom
and social progress, which opened up the possibility of communion
with human existence and the transcendent. This is how such

---

37 *Murchanie* (from Russian, "purring") refers to a linguistic practice based not
    only on a lexicon but also on special intonations and gestures that emphasize
    the speaker's belonging to criminal structures. In reality, this way of speaking
    and gesturing has spread far beyond the criminal groups themselves by way of
    social mimicry by many different social classes.
38 According to tradition, the Baptism of Rus' (in Kyiv and Novgorod) occurred
    in 988, shortly after Vladimir the Great was baptized. The Communist govern-
    ment allowed its celebration in 1988 despite a policy of atheism.
39 *Dictionary of the atheist* was a popular genre of Soviet nonfiction that spread the
    atheistic interpretation of major religious phenomena and concepts. In the ab-
    sence of religious texts in the libraries of Soviet families, these dictionaries were
    long the major source for learning the basics of religion in the late Soviet Union.

figures as Father Alexandr Men' and Teacher Khafiz Makhmutov came to prominence, who simultaneously symbolized the creeds of Christ and Mohammed, religious freedom, and the birth of the Post-Soviet Human (Forest, 1990; Sablin, 2022).[40]

Squeezed by the Procrustean bed of the Soviet legal order, the Soviet Man shrugged. The experiment with freedom and liberty in their most radical and nihilistic forms continued, and not only in the reopened private space.[41] The public sphere provided incalculable opportunities for the political creativity of Soviet communities.

Perestroika led to the 1989–1991 caesura, which made possible a situation comparable to Babylon's confusion of tongues. The Soviet "Tower of Babel" was coming to an end, and the tongues were tearing apart the fabric of Soviet society and beginning to build their own separate towers. The beginning of the post-Soviet era offered opportunities for nationalizing existing power structures and the founding of new nation-states (Brubaker, 2011). Since 1988, the lands on the periphery of the USSR, in the Caucasus and Central Asia, had been roiled by ethnic conflict (Tishkov, 1997). In the western republics of the USSR, national liberation movements took the form of secessionist movements with the clearly defined goal of achieving independence for Latvia, Lithuania, Moldova, and Estonia. The irredentist movements emerged in some regions of the Soviet republics, such as Azerbaijan's Nagorno-Karabakh, Moldova's Transnistria, and Ukraine's Crimea. By the end of 1990, most republics and a number of autonomous regions had declared their sovereignty in preparation for the bargaining for better conditions in the new treaty on rights and responsibilities of the Soviet regions. But the process of drafting the new Soviet Union Treaty did not result in reforming the USSR. The Soviet conservatives who organized the

---

40 Alexander Men' (1935–1990) was a Soviet dissident and Russian Orthodox priest and theologian who played an important role in bringing back the teaching of Christ to the Soviet Union. Khafiz Makhmutov (1937–2006) was a Soviet Tatar imam, dissident, and intellectual who was an important public figure in popularizing the teaching of Muhamad in the Soviet Union.

41 The failure of the legal transformation of post-Soviet nations was described in a special issue of *Ideology and Politics Journal*; see Antonov and Vovk (2021).

coup on the eve of the signing of the new Union Treaty in August 1991 failed to retain power and to strengthen the central government. On the contrary, they weakened the Kremlin and fortified the position of the republican power elites who advocated secession from the union. The leaders of this movement were Boris Yeltsin in Russia and some of the bigger elite groups in Georgia, Latvia, Lithuania, Moldova, and Estonia. In the fall of 1991, the same trend won out in Armenia, Azerbaijan, Belarus, Uzbekistan, and Ukraine. In December 1991 the Belavezha Accords and the Alma-Ata Protocol formally legalized the dissolution of the USSR into nation-states and the creation of the Commonwealth of Independent States (CIS), a mechanism in aid of the USSR's "peaceful divorce." Over the ensuing thirty years, the neighboring nations evolved from a commonwealth into a "commondearth," a nexus of hostilities, which contributed to the advent of a new caesura in the history of Eastern Europe and northern Eurasia in 2022.

The national statehood revolution of 1991 provided a path to the creation of fifteen independent states out of the former Soviet socialist republics, and to several unrecognized or partially recognized de facto states, such as the Republic of Abkhazia/Apsny (named after the Apsilae, early peoples in the area), in the South Caucasus; the Republic of Nagorno-Karabakh/Artsakh (a common Armenian name for the region, probably derived from early Greek sources labeling it *Orkhistene*), also in the South Caucasus; Transnistria/Pridnestrovie (Russian name), an unrecognized statelet lying between the Dnieper river and the Ukrainian-Moldovan border and legally part of Moldova; and the Republic of South Ossetia/State of Alania, a partially recognized state in the landlocked South Caucasus.[42] There were numerous other secessionist attempts—in the North Caucasus, Bashkiria, Kalmykia, Crimea,

---

42   The Georgian government, as well as most of nations worldwide, still considers Abkhazia a sovereign territory of Georgia. Nagorno-Karabakh is recognized by most countries as part of Azerbaijan, although until September 2023 it strived to govern itself as an independent republic closely affiliated with Armenia. South Ossetia (as well as Abkhazia) is recognized by only five UN members, Russia, Syria, Venezuela, Nicaragua, and Nauru, with the remaining UN members considering it a territory of Georgia occupied by Russia.

Tatarstan, and Central Asia – that from time to time, in moments of political crisis, made themselves known to the parent states. Although the new post-Soviet states were the products of the political imagination, where ethnonational and liberal-democratic elements were folded into legitimizing ideas, they mostly reproduced the power practices of the USSR. With the collapse of the Soviet Union, the Soviet societies did not disappear but multiplied and continued their historical path, slowly evolving into their post-Soviet forms. Some continuities survive caesuras, and elements of Sovietness were some of them. The replacement of Soviet class-related rhetoric with ethnonational and neoliberal vocabularies did not necessarily change the practices of the state-founding elites, at least at the beginning of the 1990s.[43]

In addition to a national statehood revolution, the 1991 Revolution included the reinvention of the practices of democracy and ideological pluralism. Already in the USSR, new parties of union and republican importance were emerging en masse. At first, these were the "democratic platform" in the Communist Party of the Soviet Union (CPSU) and in republican civic movements in support of perestroika. During the election campaigns for the Supreme Soviets of the USSR and the republics in 1988–1990, these movements transformed into national liberation movements and the first parties. This is how the all-union Social Democratic Party, the Lithuanian Communist Party (independent), the Ukrainian Republican Party, or the Armenian Dashnaktsutyun Party emerged.[44] The first parties formed along ideological lines, gathering into the newly formed networks Soviet citizens who considered themselves adherents of different ideologies and representatives of alternative political communities: Soviet, national (Georgian, Russian, Ukrainian), or subnational (Abkhazian, Chechen, Ruthenian). By 1991, ideological pluralism was the new beginning that made possible public

---

[43] A classic example of adapting Soviet vocabulary to ethnonational needs was the attempt by some Ukrainian specialists in "scientific communism" to replace their discipline's name with "scientific nationalism." However, already by the end of 1992, its authors had abandoned their initiative.

[44] For more on the late Soviet parties, see Gill (1994).

debate, political action by active citizens and counterelites, and the dramatic features of the first, still Soviet, election campaigns and referendums of 1988–1991.

Another new beginning seeded by the 1991 Revolution was the normalization—even idealization—of inequality, promoted by both the new power elites and the still Soviet intelligentsia. The Soviet population, especially in the period between the two world wars and until the late 1950s, existed under conditions on enormous inequality, which, however, was invisible in the context of the dominant totalitarian imagination.[45] Inequality had no place in the official Soviet vocabulary. Only the intellectuals of Khrushchev's Thaw era occasionally reminded the country that inequality existed.[46] But during the late Soviet "Era of Stagnation," the spread of ideological cynicism, Soviet consumerism, and alcoholic delirium repressed this topic in the collective subconscious of the 1960s–1980s.[47] Rare dissidents tried to give voice to this phenomenon, such as Vladimir Voinovich in his novel *The Life and Extraordinary Adventures of the Soldier Ivan Chonkin* (vol. 1, 1963).[48] But in the vacuum of Soviet publicity, and under the pressure of threats to be repressed, his voice was not heard.

In the late 1980s and early 1990s, however, under the influence of a new hegemonic ideological cocktail of neoliberal market

---

[45]   However, in the Soviet-banned literature of those years, inequality could still become a topic of discussion. For example, in Mikhail Bulgakov's *The Master and Margarita*, members of the writers association board discussed the "dacha issue."

[46]   The Thaw refers to the period from the late 1950s to 1964, during which time new CPSU Secretary General Nikita Khrushchev started de-Stalinization in the USSR. The term was coined by Ilya Ehrenburg to refer to the short-lived decrease in repression and censorship in the USSR.

[47]   The Stagnation was a time from the 1970s through the mid-1980s in USSR history. This period is associated with an ambivalent situation in which the Soviet Union's socioeconomic development and geopolitical influence reached its peak and stopped progressing further; when the party and the KGB attempted to return to repressive policies, while their leaders were swamped in growing corruption; and when society started losing faith in any officially promoted vision of the future.

[48]   Vladimir Voinovich (1932–2018) was a Soviet Russian writer and dissident who was forced into emigration in 1980. He was an author of many satirical novels and short stories; the saga of Ivan Chonkin is the best known among them.

fundamentalism, inequality came to be seen as the desired norm and as a driver of social progress. The most coveted inequality was of the socioeconomic kind, according to the new neoliberal imagination, which accepted it as monistically as Marxism had been accepted seventy years before. The entrepreneurial class was supposed to gain wealth and simultaneously to design innovations in production and create the service sector that was absent in the USSR. All this, in the neoliberal imagination, should have improved the quality of life for all, not just for the rich entrepreneurs.

In reality, inequality went both deeper and wider than the neoliberal worldview supposed. Related forms of inequality included, for example, the division into *locals* and *newcomers*. This could manifest in the form of historical inequalities, as when the Soviet population was divided into native citizens and noncitizens in Latvia and Estonia just a few years after perestroika. Or it could take the form of a "natural" inequality between an ethnic majority and diverse ethnic minorities; the latter, by definition, were newcomers. In radical cases, such inequality could lead to ethnic cleansing, as happened in the regions of the South Caucasus, or to civil conflicts, as in Moldovan Transnistria. The division between locals and newcomers might also manifest in requirements specific to some local groups but not others, such as the requirement to use special coupons in addition to Soviet rubles to buy certain products in certain localities.

These different forms and indicia of inequality, taken together, gave rise not only to a national but also to a neoliberal reinvention of the state. The state had to conform to an ethnonational majority's interests, but it also had to meet the demand for small government. In the first instance, government had to format the mass consciousness according to the political beliefs of the power elites, and therefore it would need to employ the apparatus of the state widely to control the spheres of culture, identity, language, and memory. In the second instance, under the rubric of neoliberal economics, the government was expected not to intervene in the spheres of economy, local governance, and social services. In particular, the state was to transfer the lion's share of state-owned enterprises to private owners and to move away from the rigid Soviet framework of labor rights and universal access to medical and educational services. After all, this combination was a compromise between the nationalist and neoliberal interpretations of the state's role.

The mixture of a nationalist and a neoliberal understanding of the state's role and functions was complicated by nostalgia for the Soviet era. Both during and after the collapse of the USSR, the population widely expected the government would continue being responsible for social assistance, job security, public health, and education.

The coexistence of these three conflicting views on the state's place in the post-Soviet political imagination had to be respected by the power elites in each nation-state since 1992. The construction of these states was largely determined by how successfully the elites could wield or suppress the ideological contradictions to preserve the post-Soviet specificity over the next thirty years.

The post-Soviet transition began with perestroika, with the ensuing caesura of 1989–1991, and with the complex of processes of the 1991 Revolution, all of which together created fresh opportunities for the creativity of the Post-Soviet Human to exert itself. The anthropocultural type of a Post-Soviet Human emerged as a short-lived, daring and tragic historical subject as societies were in the process of moving beyond the Soviet experience and releasing themselves from the tether of the past. The lives of late-Soviet peoples, who were in the process of reinstating the division between the public and private spheres, of reinventing freedom, citizenship, state, economy, sexuality, and religion, rested on a common Soviet foundation with all its beliefs, values, practices, and ideologemes. This provided a common framework and rhythm for starting the post-Soviet transition.

The Post-Soviet Diffusion, 1992–1994

In the three years following the collapse of the USSR, a new — if brave and brittle — political imagination confronted the harshness of social reality. There was so much freedom in the private and public spheres and so little order and security in society at large that the revolutionary impulse started fading and turning into its

opposite, passivity and a profound pessimism. Because of this pessimism, *chernukha*, which destroyed the remaining Soviet utopian
imagination of the 1980s, hampered the realization of neoliberal
economic and national statehood projects and undermined the legitimacy of the emerging political orders in the early 1990s. It also
gave rise to a symptomatic *Ostalgie*, a nostalgia for Soviet times.[49]

Despite the changing moods, the power elites who led the formation of the new states began to implement the program of a post-
Soviet transition that aimed at a deep and comprehensive transformation of all social, economic, and political institutions from the
Soviet autocratic condition to market democracies. Most of them
declared — and some of them even tried to fulfill — a commitment to
liberal democracy and pan-European unity. The logic of national
sovereignty demanded that the borders of the new political entities
be defined and that any alternatives to the authorities within them
be suppressed. The principle of translating Soviet administrative
borders into state borders was supported by the West. From December 1991 to December 1992, all fifteen Soviet republics were recognized as independent by the states of the world-system's core
and most of the periphery (Kolsto, 2018, pp. 11–15). This recognition was conditioned on the agreement to a nuclear-free status of
all post-Soviet states except Russia (which, as heir to the USSR, was
allowed to retain its nuclear capabilities and weapons). The CIS was
first and foremost an organization responsible for controlling the
Soviet nuclear legacy; only secondarily was it a platform for political cooperation among new nations in the process of separating
from each other and from their status as republics of the USSR. By
1994, Belarus, Kazakhstan, and Ukraine, on whose territories much
of the Soviet nuclear arsenal was housed, agreed to be "nuclear-
free" in exchange for recognition of their borders (Potter, 1994).
This consent was formalized in the Budapest Memorandum, which
defined both the formal agreement on the nuclear arsenal and the

---

49 The 1991 Revolution looked into the future and to the West and Europeanization with hope for fast development. Post-Soviet *Ostalgie* looked east, turning
its back on the West, while also sliding into nostalgia for the past.

informal deal on the Soviet administrative limits becoming state borders.

In the process of preparing this memorandum, the leaders of the new states agreed not to support each other's irredentist and secessionist movements. For example, by the end of 1994, the year when the Budapest Memorandum was signed, the Russian government had helped Ukraine regain control of Crimea, where the movement for secession from Ukraine and annexation to Russia, led by its self-proclaimed president, Yuriy Meshkov, had a chance of succeeding.[50] In fact, 1994 was the time when new secessionist movements — attempts by regional elites to disengage from already recognized post-Soviet states and create their own — lost Moscow's support. By this time, however, the unrecognized statelets of Nagorno-Karabakh, South Ossetia, Abkhazia, and the Transnistria had already formed. All these entities were put under strict international sanctions and developed under the constant threat of renewed conflict with their parent states (Minakov, 2021c, pp. 68–69). After the Budapest Memorandum went into effect in 1994 and until 2008, their status did not change. And since that same year, Russia has focused on solving the problems of its own federation and its own secessionist movements, primarily in the North Caucasus and the Volga region.

The elites of the new post-Soviet states faced an enormous challenge. They had to nationalize Soviet military structures, security and law enforcement agencies, administrative units and financial institutions. At the same time, decommunization, which began in the fall of 1991, was concluding: the structures of the CPSU, the KGB, Gosplan, the central bank, and the public symbolic space at large were being destroyed or reinterpreted.[51] The new states

---

50   Yuriy Meshkov (1945–2019) was a Ukrainian Crimean politician and leader of the pro-Russian irredentist movement in Crimea in 1993–1995. In 1994 he won in the illegal presidential elections in Crimea. In 1995, based on the informal agreement between Kyiv and Moscow, he was forced to leave Ukraine for Russia.

51   In the 2010s, the term *decommunization* acquired a new meaning: the establishment of an ideological monopoly of a patriotic government that asserted its hegemony by, among other tools, fighting the "Soviet vestiges." In the 1990s, decommunization was a set of policies that ended Soviet power practices and

needed to create their own national banks, bodies to manage the new economies and to collect taxes. At the same time, the post-Soviet governments were beginning to privatize state-owned enterprises, large and small. They also had to learn to manage the mass migration of people moving across the new countries from dangerous zones to less dangerous ones. Millions of refugees from the dangerous areas formed new, usually lower social strata in the areas of their immigration. In many ways, the Post-Soviet Human emerged from the experience of this historical diffusion, collective homelessness, and the need for a new home, personal and collective. The privatization of apartments that had previously belonged to the Soviet government and the nationalization of republics provided only a partial answer to this demand.

All post-Soviet countries when carrying out fundamental reforms in public and private sectors fell into categories of either fast or slow reformers (Åslund, 2013, pp. 11ff). The speed, depth, and efficacy of the reforms were interrelated, and their alignment could support or, if not aligned, undermine the success of the reform. Where political and economic reforms went hand in hand, the shock of radical reform was deep but short-lived and generally successful. Poland and Estonia, for example, established their political and economic systems quickly and reached a noticeable level of effectiveness in the second half of the 1990s, preventing rent-seeking groups from organizing into oligarchies and seizing political power. There were also the slow reformers, who managed to stop the economic crisis that began in 1991 by conserving remnants of the Soviet system and creating early post-Soviet dictatorships, as happened in Belarus and Turkmenistan. Yet other nation-states were relatively quick to reform the economy but slow to make political changes, or vice versa. In either case, the discrepancy in the

---

destroyed (or transformed) the most dangerous post-totalitarian institutions. However, it was also accompanied by a massive destruction of monuments to Lenin (and other Soviet leaders) and the changing of street and city names. Thus the decommunization of the 1990s increased the space of political freedom and ideological diversity, while the recent ideological processes have promoted the opposite. For a discussion of this topic, see Arel (2018), Berekashvili (2021), Kasianov (2008), Shparaga and Minakov (2019), and Trochev (2022).

timing of the changes provided rent-seekers with the opportunity to create effective tools for seizing both privatized and government-owned enterprises and for taking control of public institutions in all power branches. This is how the oligarchies of Georgia, Kazakhstan, Russia, and Ukraine emerged (Åslund, 2013; Hale, 2014; Slater & Wilson, 2004). In the case of Ukraine, the social shock was particularly deep and long lasting, which affected the stability and efficacy of the government up until 1996–1997 and also slowed the development of a language of national self-description, which would later be reduced to an image of "two Ukraines," Ukrainophone and Russophone, identifying with either the West or Russia.[52]

The post-Soviet political diversification was accompanied by the creation of national religious networks and units, which sometimes led to further fragmentation and to the state assuming administrative control over religious organizations. The Russian Christian Orthodox Church has experienced many divisions to date: in Estonia, Moldova, and Ukraine new Orthodox churches have emerged challenging the canonicity of the Moscow Patriarchy, same as Abkhazian Church did with the jurisdiction of the Georgian Orthodox Church. Churches and many religious groups banned in the USSR were revived, including the Ukrainian Greek Catholic Church, Jehovah's Witnesses, and a few evangelical currents. Islam at this time experienced its own renaissance and began to be practiced in very different currents, often quite radical. From a source of personal freedoms, religion became a font of fragmentations and divisions, a wellspring of new or revived identities — and of the related conflicts. To prevent these conflicts from deepening, the ruling groups of the new countries began to subordinate religious organizations either with the help of special services (in Central Asia) or by incorporating religious leaders into power structures (in Armenia, Belarus, Georgia, and Russia), or by making laws to prevent religious organizations from consolidating an extreme influence on

---

52 "Two Ukraines" is an ideological concept that promotes the view that Ukraine consists of two regions or sociocultural parts, Ukrainophone and Russophone, where the populations not only prefer to use one of the languages but also identify either with Europe or with Russia (occasionally both).

society and property in the hands of a single church organization (in Ukraine).

In one way or another, then, most post-Soviet states underwent a noticeable democratization in the first three years after the collapse of the USSR. Supreme power was fragmented vertically (along the axis of *center-local government*) and horizontally (into branches of government, with the emergence of a number of independent units not part of the branches of government, such as a central bank, a central electoral commission, an ombudsperson, or a constitutional court).[53] The early post-Soviet bureaucracies emerged, and formal and informal organizations of power elites began to take shape.

Simultaneously, the institution of the presidency, established by Mikhail Gorbachev as a power position outside the control of the Central Committee of the CPSU or the USSR Supreme Council, was adopted in most new political systems and developed into an institution constantly aiming to consolidate power despite constitutional provisions and a system of checks and balances designed to thwart such concentration (Minakov & Mylovanov, 2016). In post-Soviet times, the institution of the presidency was engaged in constant struggle with parliaments emerging from the Soviet Supreme Councils. This struggle quickly led to the first round of the post-Soviet political crises. For example, in 1993 the parliament building of the Russian Federation was literally shot at by tanks on the orders of President Yeltsin. That the same year, Ukraine was plunged into its first deep political crisis, which culminated in snap presidential and parliamentary elections and the rise to power of President Leonid Kuchma, who brought to Kyiv a group of reformers and Dnipropetrovsk oligarchic clans.[54]

---

53 This supreme power's fragmentation, however, did not last long. On that issue, see Pomeranz (2016, 2021).

54 Leonid Kuchma, the second Ukrainian president, served for two terms, 1994–2005. During his presidency Ukraine coped with the post-Soviet socioeconomic crisis, returned to growth, and evolved from a democratizing to an autocratizing country. Also during his presidency the Ukrainian oligarchy was established and institutionalized.

The post-Soviet transition was expected to change the Soviet socioeconomic system to a new one that would be neoliberal, free market-oriented, and globally open. This reconstruction led to a socioeconomic crisis expressed in the radical impoverishment of the populations of all the new countries — which was one major reason why the dreams of the 1991 Revolution were quickly forgotten. Instead of social and political progress, populations experienced declining livelihoods, galloping devaluation, and the refusal of governments to provide basic social services and curb crime. While the new power elites acted and saw their actions affecting the gradual emergence of new social and political institutions, the "ordinary people" were sinking deeper and deeper into hopelessness and de-modernization (Rabkin & Minakov, 2019, pp. 7–12).[55] The impulse toward social progress, so visible during perestroika and in the early years of independence, was replaced by fear of the challenges arising because of this progress and by a search for national salvation using the practices and models of the Soviet or pre-Soviet past.

The socioeconomic changes left hundreds of thousands of people without a place to live in the new states. The states were young, their governments were inexperienced, and their populations had to adjust to unfamiliar political systems and ideologies. And this adjustment went on in conjunction with the pushing of millions to the margins of progress or to seeking refuge in other countries. Between 1991 and 2001, over three million people changed their republic of residence in Eastern Europe and northern Eurasia (Korobkov & Zaionchkovskaia, 2004, p. 483). Some migrated because of the military clashes in their locality, others could not accept the change in ethnonational policy, and yet others were

---

55   The emergence of power elites, stable groups controlling centers of power and making decisions on which the lives of the population under their control depended, was uneven and asynchronous in the region. In the Baltic states and the South Caucasus, new power elites made themselves known as early as 1990. In Russia, these elites would go through a period of struggle and formation in 1990–1992. In Ukraine and Moldova, power elites took a long time to form, and their consensus has often been undermined by mass movements. In Central Asia, the power elites and their autocratic consensus were formed in the 1990s under the leadership of former young perestroika foremen on their way to becoming seasoned autocrats.

looking for better socioeconomic opportunities in work and life (Denisenko et al., 2020, pp. 6–8). Their pain and their voices went largely unheard in the emerging post-Soviet national worldviews. The social tensions of that time were partly smoothed over by a brand of post-Soviet stoicism that forced individuals to try to solve their own problems, to overcome the non-self-sufficiency of the Soviet Man in favor of the forced boldness of the Post-Soviet Human. Post-Soviet citizens, despite the temptations of *Ostalgie* and the cynicism of *chernukha*, became active voters who tried to personally influence the efficacy of their countries' and regions' leaders (Hutcheson & Korosteleva, 2006, pp. 24–26). Many became self-employed entrepreneurs and "shuttle traders" who earned a living by moving goods between the street markets of the post-Soviet countries, Poland, and Turkey (Radnitz, 2010). Many joined the criminal ranks, where "entrepreneurs of violence" could gain enough resources and power to provide security for themselves and to become major business figures and even politicians (Galeotti, 2017; Kupatadze, 2012). And for some, religion afforded a solution to problems and a path to success: in those years, traditional and new local cults, as well as doctrines whose origins lay outside the former Soviet borders (such as Moonism or Scientology), drew more and more people who only a few years earlier had been convinced atheists into communion with the transcendent. The leaders of many such religious trends acquired considerable capital (Gurchiani, 2017; Köllner, 2020; Men', 1997). Consequently, if the anthropocultural type of the Soviet Man who adhered to the Marxist vision of human existence and a human's role in the universe was rather solid, the Post-Soviet Human, who fleshed out during this stage, was a type with a great variety of faces.

By 1994–1995, the pace of change in social, cultural, and political domains was slowing, the momentum of the 1991 Revolution was weakening, and the demand for security and stability was becoming increasingly strident. The countries undergoing the post-communist transition were learning about the drawbacks of the freshly built political and socioeconomic systems and were starting to realize that the aims of the transition might not be so easily achieved.

Stabilization, 1995–2000

The second half of the 1990s was a time of social and political stabilization after the first two stages of the transition. From being a practice, freedom turned into a rhetorical exercise, approved by an ever-decreasing portion of the post-Soviet communities. Instead of progressive changes, this was the time of crystallization of order, the institutionalization of what had been achieved before. The time had come for consolidating what had been built, in the interests of both the power elites and the emerging middle class. Post-Soviet nations developed their constitutions, legal structures, public administrations, financial systems, and private corporations. And the Soviet experience was less and less relevant to peoples' lives.

During this period, the post-Soviet countries started diverging in terms of their foreign and domestic political orientations. The three Baltic republics opted for a development model directed toward EU and NATO integration, severing ties with other post-Soviet republics and establishing a relatively liberal democracy, which nonetheless institutionalized the division of their populations into citizens and noncitizens (as in Latvia and Estonia). Others, such as Kazakhstan and Ukraine, adopted a model of foreign policy multivectorism and ethnolinguocultural inclusivity: formally, civil rights were granted to the entire population, while in foreign relations the power elites tried to balance their own interests with those of the West and Russia. The peoples of Armenia, Azerbaijan, Georgia, and Moldova struggled to emerge from the trauma of wars and ethnic clashes; their states and nation-building endeavors were hugely influenced by these traumas. The peoples of Central Asia, Azerbaijan, and Belarus had already given over their freedom and rights into the hands of autocrats in the second stage of the transition and now saw an institutionalization of these unfree regimes.

In the second half of the 1990s, the first autocracies began to systematically take shape in the post-Soviet states. The young populist Aliaksandr Lukashenka, who was hurrying to build his authoritarian regime, was wrongly called "the last dictator of Europe" by Western observers. In fact, his regime was not in the rearguard of history: it was the pioneer of the European autocratic turn that we have witnessed in the past ten years (Lührmann & Lindberg, 2019). In the second half of the 1990s, autocracies were established in all five Central Asian countries, Azerbaijan, and Belarus. The rule of the military or ex-security cadres in Nagorno-Karabakh, South Ossetia, Abkhazia, and Transnistria offered a militant type of post-Soviet autocracy. Oligarchy with elements of polyarchy and democracy crystallized — and looked for supportive institutions — in Georgia, Moldova, Russia, and Ukraine (see Fisun, 2003; Hale, 2005; Shevtsova, 2001).

By the end of the twentieth century, all post-Soviet nations existed under a distinctive post-Soviet capitalism, whereby private entrepreneurship was associated both with economic activity proper and with the seizure, often by illegal means, of the Soviet industrial heritage, the takeover of oil and gas excavation sites, and even the privatization of government bodies. In Russia and Ukraine, stable oligarchic clans (in other words, the adopted political families) emerged and tried to organize the patronal pyramids — multilevel informal power structures based on personal, nonpublic relationships (Hale, 2014). They established informal control of the elements of the executive, legislative, and judicial branches of government; local authorities; police units and militant criminal groups; private and state corporations; and media holdings. It was the struggle among clans and the patronal pyramids that ensured the survival of the post-Soviet polyarchy, political competition, and even a space for civil liberties. But this liberty, poor in quality, contributed less and less to the development of new free states and economies.

During this period Russia was focused on overcoming the disintegration of its own federation. Two Chechen wars, a wave of terrorist attacks around Russia, criminal wars in the provinces, and media wars in Moscow were terrifying the citizenry and returned some legitimacy to the communists or representatives of the old-time security services.[56] In 1996, as a result of presidential elections,

---

56   The First Chechen War was started by President Yeltsin in December 1994 to suppress the Chechen separatist government. The military actions lasted until

Communist and opposition leader Gennady Zyuganov almost became president of Russia. At the same time, post-Soviet communism became a new ideological phenomenon, with party ideologues and supporters mixing elements of Leninism, Stalinism, national socialism, social conservatism, clericalism, imperialism, and ethnonationalism in their platforms (March, 2002). Both the Russian and the Ukrainian Communist Parties, as well as many other post-Soviet communist parties, were still radical, but they were no longer left-wing parties: thanks to their ideological cocktail, they were better categorized as right-left social-conservative radicals. However, the radicalism of the communists (and of other movements alike) was limited by the corruption of their leaders and the interests of their oligarchic sponsors in social stability. In general, most parties became just another type of enterprise that aimed at winning parliamentary mandates and ministerial seats to serve the interests of their sponsors. At this point, post-Soviet capitalism was still feeding the population poorly; it was fragile, and it was plunging into hitherto unknown—for the post-Soviet populations—economic crises (as in 1998). But this capitalism had already learned how to control social protest and even how to use the energy of protest to its own advantage.

The impulse toward social stability of this period nevertheless did not prevent a blossoming of the arts and sciences. The perestroika freedoms, the revolutionary creativity of 1991, and the experience and trauma of the radical changes and chaos of the

---

an armistice was signed in August 1996, followed by the humiliating peace treaty of Khasavyurt in 1997. During this war, up to 15,000 combatants and 100,000 civilians were killed, and many more were forced to seek refuge in other regions of Russia or in the West. The Second Chechen War lasted from August 1999 to April 2009. It started as a reaction to the Chechen guerrillas entering Dagestan and series of terrorist attacks in the inner Russian cities. By June 2000 the Russian government had established control over major settlements in Chechnya, but the Chechen resistance in the mountainous areas continued until 2009. The Chechen Wars were an important factor underpinning the Russian autocratic turn in the early twenty-first century.

A series of terrorist attacks took place in Beslan, Grozny, Kaspiisk, Moscow, Vladikavkaz, and many other cities between 2000 and 2004. In these explosions, thousands of people were killed in theaters, metro stations, trains, and in their homes. For more information, see Abdullaev and Saradzhayan (2006).

following decade bore fruit. At this time, for example, Russian and Ukrainian literatures exploded with daring experimentation, using wit and techniques foreshadowing modernism to comment on shifting social and political grounds. If in the early 1990s the postrevolutionary sobering was reflected in an anti-utopian critique, such as in Viktor Pelevin's *Omon Ra* or Yuri Andrukhovych's *The Moscoviad*, by the end of the last decade of the twentieth century these same writers were creating works focused on a new social reality, new social imagination, and a new hero of our times, the Post-Soviet Human.[57] In particular, this take on the rapidly changing times can be seen in Pelevin's novel *Generation P*, Andrukhovych's *Perverzion*, and Svetlana Alexievich's multivolume nonfiction saga, *Voices of Utopia*.[58] In these works the self-overcoming of the Soviet

---

57   Viktor Pelevin (b. 1962) is one of the most prominent Russian writers. His novels, plays, and short stories merge postmodernist irony, new sincerity, Eastern esotericism, and Western pop culture. His novels include *Chapayev and the Void* (1996), *Generation P* (1999), *Empire V* (2011), and *KGBT+* (2022). *Omon Ra* (1992) is a short novel in which Pelevin plays with Soviet absurd fatalism, fixation on self-victimization, ideological mysticism, and space exploration. Here, the protagonist breaks away from the tenets of ideology and inhuman authority in a wat that captures the spirit of the 1991 Revolution.
       Yurii Andrukhovych (b. 1960) is one of the best-known Ukrainian writers and public intellectuals and author of novels, essays, and short stories, including *Recreations* (1992), *The Moscoviad* (1993), *Perverzion* (1996), *Disorientation on Location* (1999), and *Radio Night* (2020). His novel *The Moscoviad* is a postmodernist, magic realist description of Moscow and the USSR in 1991 as seen through the eyes of a Ukrainian intellectual. The book explores a personal striving for freedom and moral autonomy, the trends that drove Soviet Man's self-overcoming and the birth of Post-Soviet Human.
58   The title of Pelevin's novel *Generation P* (1999) refers to the last Soviet generation that loved P(epsi cola) and caused a complete P(izdets, a Russian dirty word for a total fiasco) disaster that coincided with the fall of the USSR and establishment of a wild consumerist capitalism. The protagonist embodies the Post-Soviet Human who chooses money as a core value and joins in the grand mystical conspiracy network that rules Russia and humanity.
       Andrukhovych's novel *Perverzion* (1996) describes the metaphysical adventures of a Ukrainian poet in Venice. In the burlesque of events, parties, religious rites, and sexual adventures, the protagonist still tries to understand from the outside and explain what Ukraine is—the country's new humans, nationalized society, and postmodern culture—at the end of the 1990s.
       Svetlana Alexievich (b. 1948) is a Soviet and Belarusian writer, journalist, and historian who was awarded the 2015 Nobel Prize in Literature. Her nonfiction texts from the *Voices of Utopia* book series were recognized by the Noble Prize commission as "polyphonic writing" that best described "a monument to

Man and the deep dive into capitalist consumerism and marketing magic projected the face of the new cultural-ontological order created after the caesura of 1989–1991 and its new inhabitant, the Post-Soviet Human.

In the early 1990s, social science scholars were busy catching up on ideas and concepts that had been advanced in the West but gone unnoticed in the USSR because of the Soviet academic isolation of the 1930s–1980s. In 1988–1995, the still literature-oriented and reading post-Soviet societies absorbed writings in philosophy, the humanities, and social sciences that they had not had access to for seventy years. At the same time, the social sciences and humanities disciplines developed extensively, infiltrating old and new universities and academic communities and deploying Western theories, methods, and vocabularies. But in the second half of the nineties, two other processes left their mark on this sector: a curb on the study of natural and physical sciences (including those sciences used extensively by industry) and a qualitative change in the life of academic communities. The first process abruptly halted the teaching of natural sciences, undermining both the foundations of the scientific secular worldview and the pediments of modern industry itself in the newly formed post-Soviet societies.

The second process was less straightforward. On the one hand, social scientists and humanities scholars were freed to study societies, economies, and politics. But at the same time, the new power elites developed a taste for acquiring doctoral diplomas, and with this certification sought key positions in universities and research centers, marginalizing scholars and genuine research. As a result, classic, model studies conducted with academic rigor, such as *Ethnicity, Nationalism and Conflict in and after the Soviet Union, Social Madness,* and *Markets of Power,*[59] had to contend in the

---

suffering and courage in our time," in late and post-Soviet societies. The *Voices of Utopia* opus begins with *Zinky Boys* (1989), dedicated to the generation of the Soviet-Afghan War, continues with *Chernobyl Prayer: A Chronicle of the Future* (1997), and ends with *Secondhand Time: The Last of the Soviets,* which focuses on the experience of people reinventing themselves in the 1990s. The project began in the 1990s and was published in its entirety in 2013.

59   The book *Ethnicity, Nationalism and Conflict in and after the Soviet Union: The Mind Aflame* (1997), written by a leading Russian ethnologist, Valerii Tishkov

marketplace with a flood of the fake dissertations and related "academic publications" that the new generation of rectors and professors needed for their careers, not genuine research and advancement of scholarship. These processes in post-Soviet academies went hand in hand with the spread of fake or para-scientific popular literature produced by the "Gumilevians," the "Fomenkovians," and like groups.[60] Social sciences and the humanities flourished, but there were few true roses among them.

The post-Soviet artistic communities began to make themselves known — to their societies and the world. Post-Soviet contemporary art emerged from the underground to occupy the hitherto unfamiliar space of galleries, the platforms that structured both the creative process and its economic outcomes. Galleries such as BlankArt and Karas in Kyiv, Rigina and Vinzavod in Moscow, or the Soros galleries in Almaty, Odesa, Riga, and Vilnius provided new creative spaces for post-Soviet artists and publics (Muravska, 2002; Esanu, 2013). Individual artists and artistic groups were

---

(b. 1941), is a fundamental study of ethnonational developments in late Soviet and post-Soviet societies. The book *Social Madness: History, Theory and Practice* (1994) was written by Natalia Panina (1949–2006) and Yevhen Holovakha (b. 1946); these Ukrainian sociologists offered an early theory of post-Soviet sociopsychological transformation with some forecasts that were proved by later history. The book *Markets of Power: Administrative Markets in the USSR and Russia*, by the Russian sociologist Simon Kordonsky (b. 1944), offered a new politico-economic theory of power in Eastern Europe and northern Eurasia; even though this theory was connected with Kordonsky's studies of Russia, it was equally applicable to many other post-Soviet societies. All three books reflect genuine local scholarship and research, which was conducted indigenously, that is to say, apart from the Western academic hegemony but at the same level of scientific quality, which was an increasingly rare case in the post-Soviet era.

60   The Gumilevians are a generic name for the followers of Lev Gumilev (1912–1992), a Soviet ethnologist and historian whose works on the prehistory of Eurasia served to launch the para-scientific studies connected with biopolitics and the late Soviet and post-Soviet Eurasianism. For more on this movement, see Bassin (2016).
The Fomenkovians are a generic name for the followers of Anatolii Fomenko (b. 1945), a prominent Soviet and Russian mathematician and a founder of the New Chronology movement. The New Chronology is a conspiracy theory promoting the idea that events of ancient history attributed to the civilizations of Egypt, Greece, Rome, or Rus' actually occurred much later. This theory stipulates that ancient history has been falsified in the interests of the Vatican, the Habsburgs, or the Romanovs. For more on this, see Sheiko (2012).

finally able to wrest their attention away from the Soviet past and the traumatic experiences of the 1989–1991 caesura to focus on their contemporaries and the new social reality. At the same time, consumers began to develop a taste for actual art, which started slowly revitalizing the lifeworlds of the Post-Soviet Humans, hitherto limited to the products of Western mass culture in pirated copies.

During the same period, the mass media and the journalism community reached a certain maturity, moving away from the democratic romanticism of perestroika and adopting a monetary cynicism as the basis of their profession. The oligarchs' takeover of popular media outlets, the morals of *jeansa*, and media wars began to shape public opinion much more than the socially responsible journalism stemming from the idealism of the glasnost era.[61] At this stage, the mass media began their journey toward creating an alternative reality, a simulacrum of the actual state of affairs, in the post-Soviet societies.

The post-Soviet era began to recognize and express itself in the arts, mass media products, and social sciences. Thanks to these manifestations, the post-Soviet peoples were exposed to a revelation: by the end of the twentieth century they had settled on the world-system's periphery, poor but free, living in a high-risky society but with the opportunity to create small cozy worlds of consumption, unknown to the Western core but skilled in the cultural resistance to the West's hegemony in the form of copyright piracy and artists' squats. The mottos of the time were "Let there be no war again" and "Let's pray for economic growth." If the dashing 1990s began with the great dreams and tragedies of revolutionary acts, the decade ended with the humble joys of consumerism and the first signs of readiness to exchange freedom for financial and social security. And if the twentieth century began with great multidimensional revolutions in Eastern Europe and northern Eurasia, it ended with the philistines and bourgeoisie presiding over the ball.

---

61 "*Jeansa*" is a word from post-Soviet journalist slang that means paid content disguised as news or a media report. This phenomenon signified a critical step in the post-Soviet journalistic ethos from the values of the freedom of the media to cynical service to a paying client. For more, see Steblyna and Dvorak (2021).

New Century, New Conflicts, 2001–2008

The post-Soviet peoples entered the twenty-first century making the first attempts to evaluate their experience with the first decade of the transition. It was an inescapable fact that more than ten years after the post-Soviet migrations, many aspirations of the 1991 Revolution, including hopes for political freedom and improved well-being, had not been realized. The new societies entered the new century with the power elites opting for less free or openly nonfree regimes, with economies in which only a few families gained from the economic growth, and with poorly performing governments.

The post-Soviet power elites showed they were incapable either of serving the public interest or of efficiency in public administration. The Central Asian members of Gorbachev's team reclassified themselves as mature autocrats, establishing their dynasties. Former secretaries of the CPSU Central Committee still ruled in Azerbaijan, Georgia, and Russia, but they were rapidly aging, losing the vitality needed to govern in chaotic post-Soviet politics. So they began preparations to hand over power: some to their children, others to younger representatives of their adopted political families. In Ukraine, President Kuchma was acquiring a taste for ruling and started to create his own clan, trying to repeat the success of his Belarusian neighbor, the unchangeable President Lukashenka.[62] The post-Soviet political realities at the turn of the century did not suit either nationalists, or democrats, or communists, or oligarchs. Everyone was dissatisfied with the direction of their country's development.[63]

There were several responses to this discontent. One of them took the form of an authoritarian reinforcement of government to be better equipped to suppress the voices of discontent. However,

---

62   Aliaksandr Lukashenka (spelled also as Alexander Lukashenko, b. 1954) has been president of Belarus since 1994. His regime evolved from authoritarian in the late 1990s to autocratic in the 2000s, and to repressive after the mass protests of 2020. His takeover of the Belarusian republic signaled an authoritarian turn in Eastern Europe as early as the second half of the 1990s.

63   This dissatisfaction was widely shared also by populations, as can be seen in the results of the polls conducted by the Levada Center (Russia) or the Kyiv International Institute of Sociology (Ukraine) in 1999–2002.

strict control of the population does not equate with solving the causes of the problems that gave rise to the discontent. The Central Asian and Azerbaijani authoritarian authorities changed constitutions, political and legal norms, and electoral systems to suit their power interests. In each of these countries the social contract was denied in principle: the ruling group built a "power vertical" through a rigid system of domination with no room for civil liberties.[64] Despite the similarity of approach, each manifestation varied in specifics, from the totalitarian regime in Turkmenistan to the "father knows best" rule of Elbasy in Kazakhstan.[65]

In Moscow, the power elites invested in what looked like an enlightened autocrat — a Machiavellian "prince" — capable of folding rebellious provinces back into the federation, ending terrorism, making the country "governable," and beginning Russia's return to a core role in the world-system. By the end of his first term, in 2004, Vladimir Putin had managed to get the support of the vast majority of Russians for the first Putinist social contract, according to which they rejected political freedoms in favor of security and increased household income.[66] The oligarchs in Putin's circle subjugated the oligarchs in retiring President Yeltsin's circle, and together they entered into a single pyramid that drew the formal and informal institutions into one power network that stretched from the Kremlin to the outskirts of Russia. The Russians' autocratic choice was clear and, as it turned out later, not subject to revision.

Still, not all post-Soviet nations succumbed to that authoritarian turn. In Georgia, Ukraine, and Kyrgyzstan, for example,

---

64   The "power vertical" is a concept allegedly introduced by Vladimir Putin to describe his top-down governing system from the presidency and federal center to the federal lands' authorities, to the local communities' authorities. The founding principle of this governing system is opposed to democratic governance and citizens' equality. For more, see Monaghan (2012).

65   Elbasy (from Kazakh, "Father of the Nation") is an honorable title given to Nursultan Nazarbayev, president of Kazakhstan in 1991–2019. Starting as a supporter of Gorbachev's perestroika, Nazarbayev remained the head of Kazakhstan after the dissolution of the USSR and led the country for twenty-eight years. His regime was nonfree and corrupt, but Elbasy avoided open repressions and kept the civic interethnic peace for most of his rule.

66   The model of this social contract has become a standard for political elites in many other countries in the post-Soviet region.

attempts at a managed transfer of power within the ruling groups were thwarted by local civil societies in Western-backed mass protests. By 2003–2005, when a wave of color revolutions swept through the former republics of the USSR, the West had already integrated the three Baltic republics into its collective political and defense structures and was preparing to contain Russia by strengthening the Western presence in Eastern Europe and the South Caucasus. The new Russian elites' desire to regain major power status for the country was not welcomed in the West and in other post-Soviet states. Also by 2003–2005, civil society organizations in Ukraine and Georgia had gained considerable social and political weight. They were able to demand a return to the agenda of democratization and Europeanization and to reject the post-Soviet unexpected achievement of oligarchic rule. In Kyrgyzstan, tribal networks and civic movements were simultaneously growing in strength, while the government institutions (as, indeed, in Ukraine and Georgia) existed with minimal effectiveness. What emerged was a situation in which the demands of civil protest movements and Western governments' aims converged and increased pressure on the authorities of weak states, while corrupt post-Soviet elites were losing their nations' support, having failed to create effective government institutions (including institutions that might protect the rulers from the citizens' anger). This forced Presidents Eduard Shevardnadze of Georgia, Leonid Kuchma of Ukraine, and Askar Akaev of Kyrgizstan to acquiesce to the protesters' demands and hand over power to Mikhail Saakashvili, Viktor Yushchenko, and Kurmanbek Bakiyev, respectively.[67] The

---

67   Eduard Shevardnadze (1928–2014) was a Soviet diplomat and a Georgian politician. Among many other high posts in the USSR and post-Soviet Georgia, Shevarnadze served as the second president of Georgia, from 1995 through 2003. He lost power as a result of the Rose Revolution.
Askar Akaev (b. 1944) was a Soviet administrator and a Kyrgyzstani scholar and politician. He served as the first president of Kyrgyzstan in 1990 through 2005. In comparison with other autocratic regimes, his rule was rather mild. When his government was toppled by the protesters of the Tulip Revolution (2005), he emigrated to Russia, where he continued in an academic career.
Mikhail Saakashvili (b. 1967) is a Georgian and Ukrainian politician. He was a leader of the Rose Revolution in Georgia (2003) and became president of that country in 2004, serving until 2013. His regime started on the path of democratic

new leaders promised to implement a program of political reforms that largely repeated the 1991 Revolution's agenda: they pledged to establish effective liberal democracy, to move normatively and institutionally closer to the West, to carry out fair privatization, and to separate big business from government.

These promises were quickly forgotten. By 2007, Saakashvili's rule had lost its liberal-democratic features (Ditrych, 2010; Kavadze, 2018). Viktor Yushchenko respected civic freedoms until the end of his tenure, but under him, Ukrainian multipyramidal oligarchy — and the grand corruption associated with it — reached its peak (Huss, 2020; Kubicek, 2009). And Bakiyev's government quickly lost control of the situation in a country mired in interclan conflicts, leading to several subsequent though much less colored revolts. Only the Moldovan power elites managed to liberalize their political regime before the protests reached the level of a color revolution, ensuring greater stability for their republic.

While the situation with regard to civil rights and political freedoms in the countries that underwent color revolutions improved, if only briefly, in neighboring countries the loss of freedoms accelerated. Fearing that Ukraine and Georgia would become hotbeds of Western liberal influence, the ruling groups in Armenia, Azerbaijan, Belarus, Kazakhstan, Russia, Uzbekistan, and Tajikistan began to strengthen their autocracies by creating institutions capable of preventing and effectively suppressing both civil uprisings and the activities of civil organizations. In 2004–2007,

---

reforms, but later Saakashvili began concentrating power in his own hands. He left for Ukraine in 2014 after the Georgian police started an investigation into some crimes committed during his presidency. In 2018 the Tbilisi City Court sentenced him in absentia to six years in prison. The sentence was applied to Saakashvili when he returned to Georgia in 2021.

Viktor Yushchenko (b. 1954) is a Ukrainian politician who was elected president of Ukraine in the course of the Orange Revolution in 2004. He served as president from 2005 through 2010, a period of paramount political freedom in Ukraine. However, the democratic and anticorruption reforms that he started did not come to fruition and were curbed by the next president, Viktor Yanukovych.

Kurmanbek Bakiyev (b. 1949) is a Kyrgyz politician who served as the second Kyrgyzstani president from 2005 through 2010. He rose to power as one of the leaders of the Tulip Revolution.

counterrevolutionary reaction became mainstream in most post-Soviet countries and influenced the development of all political systems in the region without exception, including those of the revolutionary countries.

At the beginning of the twenty-first century, the political dynamics of revolutionary and counterrevolutionary countries in Eastern Europe and northern Eurasia were unmissable signs that the post-Soviet countries continued to be part of a single ecological system. Radical changes in some countries led inevitably to repressive reactions in others. The color revolutions and the reactions of neighboring governments to them sharply increased differences not only between the national elites of neighboring countries but also among the peoples of the region. While the early post-Soviet democratization was curtailed by the power elites and became less and less important to the development of post-Soviet peoples, nationalization and its corresponding identity politics were promoted by all power elites. In doing so the power elites increasingly controlled the social imagination of the populace. At the same time, in both revolutionary and reactionary countries, nationalization promoted a focus on collective memory, which usually took the form of highlighting past conflicts and grievances with neighbors and encouraging the development of a biased perspective. For this reason, parties that offered a conservative unity connected at least rhetorically to ethnonational traditions gained an advantage. Growing support for conservatives was accompanied by backing for their fundamental idea: conflicts with neighbors were historically justified. This conflictogenic idea would later define what a desirable future for these nations might look like.

The post-Soviet autocrats, democrats, and oligarchs alike learned an important lesson: it was much easier to rule if they could cajole the masses into adopting and internalizing a national-conservative imaginary as the basis of political identity. By 2008, interethnic antipathy in the post-Soviet space had reached a level that allowed the elites to start wars, first trade wars, then actual armed conflict. As part of the security strategies formulated during this period, each post-Soviet country began to prepare for conflicts with its neighbors.

Such conflicts allowed national elites to strengthen their control over the centers of power in each country. The rotation of power elites took place within the political class, a highly circumscribed group of actors who were good at preventing both counterelites and alternative civic groups from coming to govern. In some countries, the deeper the socioeconomic inequality, the more attention was paid to the criminal Soviet past and the complicity of non-native ethnic elements in it. In others, the 1991 Revolution's impulse was hastily criminalized, reduced to a negative outcome of the "dashing nineties." The idea of a dangerous past—the same idea that was once promoted by the Soviet rulers regarding their czarist predecessors—was once again on the political agenda of most post-Soviet leaders. Revolutionary and counterrevolutionary states alike created ideological institutions to manage the collective memory (and collective oblivion) and reinforced highly massaged "patriotic" content in the general educational system. Over time, these measures opened a path for the return of an ideological monopoly of governments and the transformation of internal social antagonisms into national and international conflicts.

The political and socioeconomic systems that came into existence by the beginning of the twenty-first century tended to produce conflicts not only between neighboring countries but also within their societies. These conflicts forced out new migrants, millions in number, who, unlike their predecessors in the early 1990s, considered the new states to be theirs. Despite being an integral part of the imagined communities, they just did not find a place in their national labor markets (Bartram, 2013). As post-Soviet nomadism became characterized by lack of opportunity to settle, the Eastern European nations lost between 10 and 20 percent of their populations to labor migration in the first two decades of the twenty-first century. In addition, the Central Asian states, which experienced a considerable growth in their populations, were unable to ensure "a workplace for everyone" and pushed out millions of their young men, who went to Russia, China, and the West (Dickey et al., 2018; Labanauskas, 2019; Laruelle, 2007; Libanova, 2018; Marat, 2009). The new Eastern European and northern Eurasian nations, like many other countries on the periphery of the world-system, did not create either efficient political systems or inclusive societies and economies.[68]

The Period of Conflicts, 2008 On

The final period of the post-Soviet era was characterized by increasing regional and interstate conflicts, an increasing tendency toward regional entropy, and a new historical caesura at the end of the period.

In 2008, the sum of the previous post-Soviet intranational conflicts erupted into an international conflict, the Russo-Georgian War. Georgian president Mikhail Saakashvili's attempt to regain popularity by conquering the breakaway South Ossetian region gave the Kremlin an excuse to activate its long-prepared plan, which culminated in the defeat of the Georgian armed forces, the establishment of new borders between Georgia, South Ossetia, and Abkhazia, and partial recognition of the independence of these two breakaway Georgian regions (Antonenko, 2008; Cornell & Nilsson, 2009; Sinkkonen, 2011). Through the war, Moscow regained control of its rebellious North Caucasus regions while establishing a foothold in the Caucasus; in addition, the war showed that Western governments were not prepared to engage directly on the side of post-Soviet countries in a direct military confrontation with Russia.

This war also proved to be acceptable, if not desirable, to all post-Soviet societies. A patriotic wave swept through Russia, in the foam of which Georgian migrants floated, humiliated and occasionally beaten. In Georgia, unwillingness to learn the culture and language of the country's northern neighbors was strengthened and

---

68   A world-system is an international socioeconomic system that relates to a large region or all of the world and to the outcome of the sum of the interactions between nations. In the past, world-systems were larger than single states, but were not global. Today's world-system refers to the global transnational system that divides nations according to their political, economic, and cultural influence into three categories: core countries, semiperiphery countries, and periphery countries. Core countries are most politically, economically, and culturally influential, while countries on the periphery are most influenced by the core, while semiperiphery countries attempt to join the core. Before the geopolitical divide of 2022–2023, the world-system's core included the developed countries that form the G7 group and China.

institutionalized in schooling and cultural policies. And both processes gained legitimacy through the support of the wartime leaders, regardless of the success of their military adventures. In addition, the Russo-Georgian War served to showcase the special emotional involvement of other post-Soviet peoples in the conflict, thus certifying their historical belonging to the common post-Soviet region.

The Russo-Georgian War marked the beginning of a new type of post-Soviet conflict. Focused military actions of low or medium intensity were only part of the active measures. For the conflict simultaneously accelerated the nation building of the de facto states on the internationally recognized territories of Georgia and Moldova and, since 2014, Ukraine. The mere existence of the de facto states undermined the political and economic development of the parent states and posed an obstacle to their joining the EU or NATO. The presence of out-of-control regional communities claiming statehood also distorted the logic of civil peace within the societies of the parent states: radical nationalists and politicians for whom liberal democracy was a foreign concept saw the weakened sovereignty of the parent state and seized the opportunity to reproduce and harden internal conflicts based on ethnicity, language, or religion. But when two de facto states, South Ossetia and Abkhazia, received recognition by Russia and its several allies, the damage to prospects for a stable peace among and within the post-Soviet nations grew considerably. In 2015, of the six countries in the Eastern Neighborhood region, only Belarus fully retained sovereignty over its internationally recognized territory.[69]

This model of warfare and its accompanying sociopolitical toolkit, tested in Georgia in 2008, was applied in Ukraine in 2014. With the victory of the Euromaidan protests in February 2014, the

---

69   The Eastern Neighborhood (or Eastern Partnership) policy is a joint initiative between the EU countries and the EU's Eastern European partner countries that since 2009 has aimed at enabling the partner countries to integrate closer politically, economically and culturally. Initially, the Eastern Neighborhood policy was envisaged as a way to strengthen commitment to international law and the EU's fundamental values among six nations on the eastern borders of the EU: Armenia, Azerbaijan, Belarus (with suspended status), Georgia, Moldova, and Ukraine.

Ukrainian government and the entire political system were plunged into a state of shock that endured for several weeks. That was sufficient time for the Kremlin to take advantage of Kyiv's temporary inability to control all its territories and communities: Russia illegally annexed Crimea and started backing the militarized secessionists and irredentists that sprang from the anti-Maidan movement. In April–June of 2014, the new Ukrainian government and pro-Maidan groups managed to overcome — in some cases peacefully, in others, as in Odesa, in bloody confrontations — four of the six secession attempts in the southeastern regions. But in Donetsk and Luhansk, two secession attempts have partially succeeded: two Russia-backed military-political statelets were proclaimed soon after. The war over the Donbas reached a peak in July 2014–March 2015, leading to a direct clash between the armies of Russia and Ukraine, with the involvement as well of pro-Russia combatants residing in the Donbas. By 2021, more than 14,000 persons from all sides of the conflict, both fighters and noncombatants, had died in the Donbas, and more than a million Ukrainians had sought refuge in Ukraine's interior and in Belarus, the EU, and Russia. In 2015–2021, Ukraine found itself in the same situation that Azerbaijan, Georgia, and Moldova had been in since the early 1990s: the military conflict took root on its territory, while the regions claiming statehood became long-term constraints on the parent country's political and economic development and participation in international alliances.

By 2022 the post-Soviet political ecology had become increasingly complex and given to conflict. The entire post-Soviet space had divided itself into several parts. The three Baltic republics had become members of the EU and NATO and were falling into ever deeper antagonism with Russia, while the latter was becoming less and less free and more isolated and militarized. The Central Asian states had adopted a "triple periphery" status, striving to balance the interests of Russia, China, and the West in their survival strategies while being careful not to align themselves too much with any one power. Azerbaijan and Georgia similarly tried their best to balance their national interests with those of Turkey, Russia, and the West. Armenia, which had returned to the democratization path in

2018 and had been defeated by Azerbaijan in the Second Nagorno-Karabakh War of 2020, struggled to ensure its own and the remnants of the Karabakh enclave's survival. Moldova developed under the strong influence of Romania, the EU, and Russia. And Ukraine, in a state of undeclared war with Russia between 2014 and 2022, was choosing its place in the deepening antagonism between Washington and Brussels, on one side, and Moscow and Minsk on the other.

Until the invasion of Ukraine in February 2022, Russia had partially succeeded in regaining its status as a regional superpower, straining its modest economic and demographic resources not for its own development but for whatever malevolent influence it might be able to exert on neighboring nations. Wars with its neighbors and the unending confrontation with the West have been costly to the citizens of the Russian Federation and have strengthened the ring of hostility around it.

The post-Soviet environment was further complicated by the presence of a growing network of unrecognized states. If in 2007, four unrecognized states—Nagorno-Karabakh, South Ossetia, Abkhazia, and Transnistria—were home to about one million people, by the end of 2021, even after the reduction of the territory and population of Nagorno-Karabakh, there were six such state entities, with the addition of the so-called people's republics in Ukraine's Luhansk and Donetsk oblasts, controlled by Russia. The population of these four statelets exceeded four million people, who lived in conditions of extreme periphery, that is, as outcasts from the global interstate system and under sanctions by the parent states and the West (Minakov, 2021c).

This growing foreign policy complexity in the post-Soviet region was counterposed by the simplification of domestic political processes. All recognized states and unrecognized political entities in the post-Soviet space (except for the People's Republics of Ukraine's Donetsk and Luhansk oblasts) can be seen as a product of the third wave of democratization on lands once controlled by the Soviet Union. By the beginning of the twenty-first century, this wave of democratization had subsided worldwide, and in the post-Soviet region its retreat had become evident already by the second

half of the 1990s. In its place the third wave of autocratization gradually picked up speed, and the Donbas's self-styled (by the in-
vaders) republics were shaped in that context.

The concept of waves of democratization or autocratization is
founded in a rather large generalization, which can be justified on
the basis that it reveals something crucial about the transnational
character of political development. The national imaginary affects
our analytical views and forces us to consider political and social
processes within nation-states. However, many political phenomena, including global "waves" of increasing or decreasing freedoms, point to the existence of transnational frameworks and networks that influence political action without respect to national differences and state boundaries. As a concept, the third wave of democratization highlights that between the mid-1970s and the early
2000s, the sum of actions by international, national, and local political actors led to an expansion of political, civil, and economic freedoms. These freedoms were supported by newly established political, social, and economic institutions, as well as by the value orientations of individuals and of small and large groups (Huntington,
1993; Inglehart & Welzel, 2005). The concept of a third wave of
autocratization describes and to some extent predicts that the sum
of the actions of very different political actors leads to the collapse
of the infrastructure of liberty and to the strengthening of autocratic
institutions. If previously humankind's political creativity was long
expressed by applying principles supporting civil liberties, human
rights, and a liberal cosmopolitanism, this same creativity now
works for subordination to superiors, for obtaining exclusive rights
by conservatively imagined groups, and for Schmittian state sovereignty and its absolute control of the legal-political order (Minakov,
2021a).[70] This understanding of the third wave of autocratization, it
seems to me, explains both the extremely humble democratic effect
of the victory of the Euromaidan in 2013–2014, the defeat of the

---

70   Carl Schmitt (1888–1985) was a German conservative legal and political thinker.
      He defined sovereignty as a quality of the sovereign, that is, the one who has
      absolute control over the legal-political order and who decides who should be
      included or excluded from such an order. His concept was directed against lib-
      eral, universal, and cosmopolitan theories of sovereignty.

mass protests in Belarus in 2020–2021, and the victory of authoritarian Azerbaijan over democratizing Armenia since 2020.

The growing autocratic trend in Russia, Belarus, Azerbaijan, and some other countries of the region began to destroy not only the post-Soviet democratic achievements but also the foundations of post-Soviet statehood as such. By taking the war with Ukraine to a new level of aggression in February 2022, Putin's Russia brought the transnational and intranational warmongering behavior in the post-Soviet region to the point that there is a real chance that the entire political ecosystem in Eastern Europe and northern Eurasia could disappear. The attack on Ukraine triggered a new caesura, in the depths of which the post-Soviet era, the Post-Soviet Human, and post-Soviet societies found their completion. The new era has not yet begun, but it is already structuring political and social processes beyond the post-Soviet tetrad of democratization, marketization, nationalization, and Europeanization.

The literature and cinema of the period between 2008 and 2022 went along with the sociopolitical current and exhibited two trends. Art for the masses tended to reinforce ethnonational stereotypes and discord and to support the state's ideological indoctrination of the subordinated populations and the definition of yet another generation of "enemies of the people" (or "national traitors," or "foreign agents") within and outside the borders of the country.[71] Governments distributed solid funds for the production of films, books, and TV series promoting "correct" worldviews and sanctioned forms of patriotism.

Critical artists, on the other hand, resisted the approved, art-for-the-masses trend by working through anti-utopian or dystopian themes. Here, perhaps the most visible were such movies as *Hard to Be a God* (directed by Aleksei German, Moscow, 2013), *Atlantis* (directed by Valentyn Vasyanovych, Kyiv, 2019), and *The Petrovs in Flu* (directed by Kirill Serebrennikov, Moscow, 2021); all of them channeled the popular dissatisfaction with the results of the post-

---

71   On such a turn in post-Soviet cinematography, see, for example, Isaev (2020) and Shlikhtar (2020).

Soviet development.[72] The same stance can be seen in novels, such as Pelevin's *S.N.U.F.F.* (2011), Sergiy Zhadan's *The Internat* (2017), and Vladimir Sorokin's *Dr. Garin* (2021). By the end of the post-Soviet era, the social and political imagination had entered a two-stroke phase, oscillating between official, mediocre patriotism and the hopelessness of defeated liberalism.

Contemporary visual art offered an even better opportunity to grasp post-Soviet social reality. In the most recent post-Soviet decade, the revolution in visual art made it possible to translate into artifacts the experience of victims of war, internal conflicts, inequality, and suppression by both authoritarian and polyarchic authorities and to defend the last frontiers of civil freedom and human dignity.[73] However, this sphere could remain immune neither to the art market nor to official patriotism, which led to the emasculation of the artistic resistance and of freedom.

The period of conflicts that began in 2008 deepened and accelerated social entropy until it triggered a new caesura with unpredictable consequences for both post-Soviet peoples and their neighbors in Europe and Asia. And this period ended the post-Soviet era, the habitat of the Post-Soviet Human.

Concluding the Era

The Eastern European and northern Eurasian countries reached the end of the post-Soviet era in a very different form from what many observers had expected in 1991. Most of the region's populations

---

72   *Hard to Be a God* is a 2013 Russian epic science fiction film directed by Aleksei German (1938–2013), a prominent Soviet and Russian director. The film is based on the 1964 novel of the same name by Arkadii and Boris Strugatskys and is highly critical of the direction of Russian sociopolitical development. *Atlantis* is a 2019 Ukrainian post-apocalyptic film directed by the notable Ukrainian director Valentyn Vasyanovych (b. 1971). The film tells the story of a veteran struggling with postwar life in a near-future Ukraine following a war with Russia. *The Petrovs in Flu* is a 2021 metaphysically ironic dark comedy written and directed by Kirill Serebrennikov (b. 1969) based on Alexey Salnikov's novel, *The Petrovs in and around the Flu*. The film is a hallucinatory story about life in the Russian periphery of our times.

73   On such aspects of Ukrainian and Russian contemporary art, see Barshynova and Martynyuk (2021) and Jonson (2015).

live under the rule of autocrats. Even though the space of economic freedoms today is larger than in perestroika USSR, political freedom, socioeconomic equality, and access to basic social security are arguably worse. Those countries that preserved a certain level of political liberty are in systemic and existential conflict with their autocratic neighbors and in need of external protection.

The post-Soviet countries developed in a certain common rhythm. The post-Soviet tetrad with all its dialectical forces nonetheless kept the differing trajectories of the new nations loosely within the same framework. But the closer the region drew to 2022, the greater the dissonance became. National and subregional — Baltic, South Caucasian, Central Asian, and so forth — trends diverged more and more. With the launch of the Russian invasion of Ukraine in February 2022, the post-Soviet era and region ceased to exist.

The ideals of liberal democracy and the rule of law had lost whatever influence they had on political and legal practices almost everywhere in the region by 2022. These ideals still influence the democracies of Latvia, Lithuania, and Estonia. But they have limited influence on the hybrid political systems of Armenia, Georgia, Kyrgyzstan, and Moldova and almost no impact on the autocracies of Azerbaijan, Belarus, Kazakhstan, Russia, Tajikistan, Turkmenistan, and Uzbekistan (as well as on the surviving unrecognized statelets). And Ukraine, on whose lands the Russian Federation launched an unjust and unprovoked war, is experiencing one of its worst moments since 2014.

The European part of the post-Soviet countries has seen a decline in population in 1991–2021, with the demographic losses over the three decades in some cases reaching a quarter of the population. In Central Asian post-Soviet states, by contrast, the population has grown between 10 and 60 percent, but neither the societies nor the economies of the region need their young people, who are less easily controlled than older cohorts and more open to novel perspectives. The uprising in Kazakhstan in January and the protests in Uzbek Karakalpakstan in February 2022 showed that Central Asia has a huge revolutionary potential whose creative and destructive power autocrats are increasingly unable to contain.

The shrunken post-Soviet populations had great opportunities for action and consumption as long as they did not interfere
with the ruling groups' interests or go against official ideology. The
Russian-Ukrainian war of 2022, however, set in motion the kind of
destructive mechanisms that can erode the economic foundations
of consumer capitalism in the region. From a two-century historical
perspective, the Eastern European and northern Eurasian nations
appear to have already experienced their best days: they reached
their peak of progress in the first decade of the twenty-first century,
and the near future holds no promise of plenty and stability.

Remarkably, and in contrast to most other sectors, the arts
flourished in the three decades of creative freedom. If the post-Soviet era has justified itself in anything, it is in the breakthroughs in
the arts and a revival of hope as expressed in literature. The era that
was snuffed out when Russia launched its war against Ukraine had
its own voices and imageries, and in the future, the memory of that
era will be vivid and poignant only because of the arts and literature.

The post-Soviet leap toward individual and collective democratic emancipation was real but short-lived. Several years of democratic creativity were followed by decades of authoritarian creativity. In their search for a unique national path by all fifteen-plus
nations, the impulse toward civic political rationality was constantly countered by ethnic emotions, the impulse toward entrepreneurship was tethered by the instincts of monopolism, the magic of
capital was in contradiction to the archaic of wealth, and the ideals
of the republic were undermined by the logic of oligarchy. This is
how the initial post-Soviet modernization was reversed and turned
into a demodernization.

In chapter 4 I evaluate the outcomes of both processes, the leap
toward democratic emancipation in the modernizing post-Soviet
states and the subsequent halting of that leap and demodernization.
First, however, I propose looking at the political imagination of the
post-Soviet era. How were Post-Soviet Humans and their habitat
understood, and how did this understanding change over the past
three decades? These questions I take up in the next chapter, which
focuses on how perceptions of the post-Soviet development
evolved.

3.   The Evolution of Perceptions of Post-Soviet Development

History moves not only continuously in the intervals from one caesura to another one but also in two interconnected dimensions —
one of events, the other of narratives about those events. In the previous chapter I described how the events of the post-Soviet era un-
folded and the stages of that unfolding. Here I turn to the evolution
of the ideas, concepts, and visions through which scholars and politicians made sense of their times. In a way, this chapter is a short
conceptual history of studies of the post-Soviet transition and related narratives.[74]

Ever since the discovery of the historicity of the human condition — that is, that we live not only in the present moment but also
between the past and the future, in a history that unfolds according
to its own laws or patterns — temporal imagery has turned out to be
a crucial element of collective life. For example, the idea of progress
invokes imagery that has been extremely influential in constructing
the social reality of the past three centuries. This progress has been
seen in many ways: as moral advancement, secularization, the
spread of nation-states, the scientific-technological revolution, civic
emancipation, and even as the emergence of a classless yet harmo-
nious society. This last vision sparked the global communist movement, which resulted in the creation of the "socialist camp" or "second world," comprising the communist-led Soviet Union and sat-
ellite states in Europe, Asia, Africa, and Latin America. Between
1917 and 1991, the imagery of communist-led progress ran the
gamut from a "wayfinder toward the happy future of humanity" to
a "gulag eternity." Progress and socialism were long seen as inseparable, and their nexus still remains a powerful image.

---

74   This chapter is based on a previously published chapter by Mikhail Minakov,
"The Transition of 'Transition': Assessing the Post-Communist Experience and
Its Research," in *Meandering in Transition: Thirty Years of Identity Building in ost-
Communist Europe*, edited by Ostap Kushnir and Oleksandr Pankieiev (Lanham,
MD: Rowman & Littlefield, 2021), pp. 25–41. All rights reserved.

It's paradoxical but true: the dissolution of the Eastern Bloc and the USSR was also seen as progress. This was progress characterized as a *transition* (or *transit*) from an unfree society, politics, and economy to a civil society, democracy, and free markets. This progressive transition, as it was viewed then, was a positive and profound cultural transformation that was welcomed by many inside and outside Central and Eastern Europe (CEE), Russia, the South Caucasus, and Central Asia. The new opportunities for capitalist modernization inspired the new CEE elites to get involved in the post-communist transition. The cost of the initial phase of this transition, however, would be the dissolution of the Eastern Bloc and the socialist camp, which had provided humanity with an alternative to Western capitalism; the second world committed suicide in order to merge with the West's first world (Arrighi et al., 2003, pp. 4ff.). However, this merger did not go according to plan, and the second world joined the world-system's periphery, not its core.

Together, the launch of this new progress and the rejection of the old one in post-communist (and more narrowly post-Soviet) societies created a void in political, social, economic, and ethnocultural imagery from 1989 to 1991. The territory, populations, cities, and villages were still in place in the large area bordered by Western Europe, Turkey, Iran, and China, but the familiar temporal concepts and spatial representations once inseparable from this region were no longer applicable to their new reality. Scholars, journalists, politicians, diplomats, and experts from inside and outside the region had to create new signifiers for the fast-changing chaos of the post-communist and post-Soviet space and time. The creation of such new imagery together with the new reality entailed the crafting of a new prophecy expected to answer three questions of relevance to the uncertain times:[75]

- What is the future?
- What is to be desired in this future?

---

75   In the social sciences, a prophecy is a claim about reality that has predictive force for the future. A transition prophecy implies a vision for the future, a way to get there, and the epistemological argument for why this is correct.

- What is to be feared on the way to realizing the desired future?

The production of a transition prophecy immediately became a field of contestation between and within different academic, political, and ideological camps. The intellectual centers of the West have, as expected, won, although, as the events from 2014 on have shown, a defeated Moscow (as well as Baku or Minsk) did not give up and was eager for revenge. The chase after hegemony in the formulation of the aims, emotions, and means of the post-Soviet transition has been unceasing over the past thirty years. Social reality has forced all the parties in the pursuit to review their initial forecasts as this reality has deviated relentlessly from the expected direction of the transition—away from democratization and Europeanization, for example.

Such contestation between and among reality, scholarly concepts, and the popular, mass-mediated imagination reflects a process that is simultaneously creative and destructive. There is nothing specifically Eastern European or northern Eurasian about this creative destruction. It was Joseph Schumpeter who came up with the phrase, now permanently linked to his name, that transformed Marx's idea of a specific development of capitalism and Werner Sombart's concept of *schöpferische Zerstörung* ("creative destruction") into an understanding that the constant struggle between old, new, and newer economic forms and processes, with each superseding what came before it, is a precondition of capitalism's existence: it requires "the perennial gale of creative destruction" (Schumpeter, 2013, p. 83). Even though Schumpeter defined this concept in a totally different historical context, the general idea was proven by developmental patterns in Eastern Europe and northern Eurasia. The reemergence of nonstate capitalism in the post-Soviet void has turned the region into a space of ever-growing struggles between and among productive forces, productive relations, economic structures, and sociopolitical superstructure.

Since the caesura of 1989–1991, through the process of postcommunist creative destruction, the political imagery of peoples living in Eastern Europe and northern Eurasia has changed

dramatically. Tony Judt has called this alteration of spatial perception in post-communist Europe a "rediscovery" that provided a
new map to the new reality (Judt, 1990, p. 24). Alexander Etkind
and I have described this rediscovery in terms of a transition from
a collective imagination controlled by a monopolistic Soviet Marxism to a period of multiple clashing imaginations that spread "individualism, neoliberalism, democratic liberalism, libertarian anar-
chism, ethno-nationalism, religious conservatism, and anti-pro-
gressivism, all of which combined frivolously or even merged in a
public sphere that had been long deprived of critical discourse"
(Etkind & Minakov, 2020, p. 10). Afterward, during the first years
of transition, the redundant symbolic diversity caused fatigue; the
need arose for the crystallization of some overarching imagery,
which ended up in the all-encompassing post-communist transition
combining democratization, marketization, and Europeanization.

The peripheralization of post-Soviet (and, more broadly, post-
communist) societies that had previously been part of the "alternative core" led to their political imagination becoming dependent on
the perceptions and concepts formed in the societies of the Western
core in the new unipolar world-system that emerged in the early
1990s as a result of the collapse of the socialist camp and the unfet-
tered domination of the West. In this regard, the need for a clear
understanding of one's place in history and the world was anticipated in the concept of the post-Soviet (or wider post-communist)
transition and its four tendencies — democratization, marketization,
nationalization, and Europeanization. In the ensuing three decades,
it was this conceptual four-trends vision that the post-Soviet peoples tested in their lives.

This test of the correlation between political events and our
vague perceptions of and structured narratives about them led to
different results at three different stages:

1. During and soon after the caesura of 1989–1991 and the beginning of the transition.
2. Then approximately ten to fifteen years after the dissolution of the USSR and the Eastern Bloc.

3.   Finally, in the last fifteen years of the post-Soviet era (which coincides with the last stage of event-driven post-Soviet history described in chapter 2).

In this chapter, I show how the concept of transition lost its prophetic character and narrative energies took on a more realist account of democratization and Europeanization.

Stage 1:
Living through the Caesura and Revolutionary Change, 1989–1994

The public statements of intellectuals and political leaders from 1989 to 1991 highlight a mixture of concepts that the people living through the caesura and revolutionary changes—or witnessing them from outside—used to describe the surrounding social chaos. They were surprised by the speed and depth of the transformation. Yet that surprise was manifested in the criticism of "real socialism" and through attacking loopholes in the Soviet system.[76]

The participants in and observers of revolutionary events in the Eastern Bloc (1989–1990) and the USSR (1989–1991) configured their experiences and observations through two interconnected images. First, the 1991 Revolution was seen as the end of the division between the West and the East. The Cold War had ended and a new era of peace in One Big Europe was about to start. The economic, political, and symbolic "Berlin Wall" had to crumble, and the norms, institutions, and practices of Western Europe were to be extended to all parts of the continent, "from Dublin to Vladivostok"

---

76   Perhaps most telling in this regard are the articles and remarks printed in the journal *East European Politics* from no. 4 (1988) to no. 10 (1994); in the 1990 issue 119 (1) of *Daedalus* journal; and in the first three issues of *Demokratizatsiya: The Journal of Post-Soviet Democratization*, published between 1992 and 1994. The archive of research and polemical texts by leading Soviet, Central and Western European, and American historians, philosophers, and political scientists allows us today to look at the events of the 1989–1991 caesura and the beginning of the transition through the eyes of the people who were experiencing a dramatic period in their history, and to compare their experience of the caesura with outsiders' contemporaneous observations and with our observations decades later.

(Coppieters et al., 2004, p. 12; Schmahl & Breuer, 2017, p. 7). This prophecy was also expressed as a "return to Europe," with many national and subnational meanings coined within this ideologeme (Maier, 1999, p. 20). The creative destruction in the East involved dismantling norms and institutions built between 1922, 1945, and 1988, thus returning post-communist societies to the idealized interwar past. Or else such societies were pushed toward embracing some version of a neoliberal political-economic universal model, without attention to the local — national or even subnational — specificities. The image of a continental unity initially concealed emerging and deepening socioeconomic and ethnocultural traumas, with far-reaching later consequences, but it also gave legitimacy to the political will to implement neoliberal reforms.

Second, the creative destruction of the Soviet Marxist vision of the future was substituted by a vision of moving from authoritarian politics, state censorship, political police, and the administrative economy of state capitalism toward civil freedoms, liberal democracy, pluralist politics, and a free market. This was characterized as an "all-encompassing transition" in 1989–1991. As Charles Fairbanks expressed it in the debates in the pages of the *Journal of Democracy*,

> As communism collapses, democracy and a market economy are emerging as the next political formula to be tried. (Fairbanks, 1990, p. 23)

The trial of this formula, as Oleh Havrylyshyn later demonstrated, required a multitude of political considerations. First of all, how fast should the reform be conducted — as "shock therapy" or as a "slow, well-thought-out reform"? Second, how should privatization, which would lead to the creation of a proprietary class and a new enterprise sector, be carried out? Third, what were the limits with respect to the social costs of the transition? Finally, should market institutions, democracy, and the rule of law be created simultaneously or in a specific sequence during the transition (Havrylyshyn, 2006, pp. 21–22)? The answers to these almost metaphysical questions were an integral part of the imagination, theory, and practice of the all-encompassing post-Soviet transition.

The four elements — democratization, marketization, nationalization, and Europeanization — were definitive for understanding
and explaining the post-communist developments in the early
1990s. How were they evaluated in this period?

For intellectuals on the left (predominantly noncommunist
and post-Marxist), the fall of the Eastern Bloc and the USSR was an
existential issue. A profound anxiety for the Soviet-led "second
world" was expressed by Immanuel Wallerstein and scholars from
his circle.[77] The leftist intellectuals who disagreed with "real socialism" and undermined its legitimacy — Daniel A. Bell, Ralf Darendorf, Jürgen Habermas, Václav Havel, Tony Judt, and Leszek Kolakowski, among others — welcomed European reunification and,
though somewhat less enthusiastically, saluted the transition to
democratic capitalism as an opportunity for the rectification of
communist crimes and distortions of socialism.[78] From their perspective, Europe's East and West were to establish a *common*, not
Westernized, space where the best of the two would create a region
of peace, shared values, and political cooperation — an agenda institutionalized by the Council of Europe. However, the left also
sensed a danger in the idea of progress through transition: the an-
ticommunist revolution of 1989–1991 was hostile to noncommunist
socialism, promoted a conservative orientation toward the past,
and lacked any positive objectives that could guide post-Soviet social development (Habermas, 1991, p. 26).

At the same time, the caesura of 1989–1991 provided the left
with an opportunity for building a Europe of social equity and justice. The left saw the dissolution of the Eastern Bloc as a chance for
reformed social democracy, for "the continuing process of political
communication that prevents the institutional framework of a constitutional democracy from becoming desiccated" (ibid., p. 45). For
the left's vision of a socially just Europe to win in the competition
of the future, Bell and Darendorf called on their colleagues to rectify

---

77 See, e. g., Wallerstein (1984, pp. 90–94).
78 A few highly visible texts of the time are Habermas (1991), Judt (1988), and Ko-
    lakowski (1990).

the misdeeds of communism, to think as "revisionists" (i.e., outside of Marxist dogmas; see Bell & Dahrendorf, 1989).

If the leftist intellectuals watched the events in the East with hope and fear, the liberals and neoliberals saw huge prospects for their cause there.[79] For them, European integration was less important and too abstract as an objective. Instead, they sought inspiration from Hernando de Soto, Francis Fukuyama, or Samuel Huntington, whose ideas — in spite of their disciplinary context and academic hypotheticality — were perceived by neoliberal politicians and experts as providing practical guidance for the shift toward free economies, open societies, and pluralist democracies.[80] Liberal ideas of that time were hastily translated into neoliberal practices owing to the growing hegemony of the Washington Consensus.[81]

From the outset, the neoliberal economists looked at post-Soviet development through the lens of a transition toward a capitalist, free market economy. One of the most important documents that cemented the intuitions of this group was the Deutsche Bank's report assessing the prospects of the Soviet republics' economic development in 1990 (Corbet & Gummich, 1990). The report's authors expressed a mixture of truly prophetic vision and blindness to what was coming in the post-communist future. On the one hand, these economists were right in foreseeing the USSR's imminent dissolution (something that many political scholars did not expect to happen). On the other hand, their long-term forecast for the outcome of the economic transition — "to draw level with the economic and cultural standards of Western Europe" — was a remarkable cocktail of ambiguous deductions (p. 7). The report states that "six of the republics have a high economic potential, five a moderate potential, and four a weak one" (p. 7). Among the Soviet republics with the best prospects, the neoliberal analysts identified Ukraine. Today,

---

79   Since in the context of this chapter they are not relevant, I do not address the differences between the liberals and neoliberals in the times after the Washington Consensus, and hereafter I refer to them by the common name of neoliberals.

80   On neoliberal ideas providing guidance, see Bromley (1990), Fukuyama (1989), and Huntington (1991). Compare Vachudova and Snyder (1996, pp. 1–35).

81   For details of its amalgamation in U.S. foreign policy, Latin American social experience, and Eastern European early transition plans, see Williamson (1993).

thirty years later, this seems to be tragically incorrect: Ukraine (along with Georgia and Moldova) has one of the smallest GDP and purchasing power parity (PPP) growth rates since 1990, even though it enjoys a rather high ranking in terms of democracy among the post-Soviet countries.[82]

Thus, in 1989–1991, predictions for the future of the post-Soviet nations and the broader post-communist region confected the conceptual elements of transition as such (internally oriented economic and political processes of democratization, marketization, and nationalization) and Europeanization (a multilateral, externally oriented process).[83] These predictions, or prophecy, came into being in a rather paradoxical manner: the neoliberals connected the post-communist transition to political economy, once the domain of Marxists, while the left intellectuals looked at the East in relation to values and culture, a stance generally associated with a conservative inclination. The "Marxist way" of the neoliberals pushed them to upgrade the economic basis of emerging post-Soviet societies in the hope of promoting change in the super-structure, in politics and ideology. In turn, the left initiated a common European dialogue within the legal frameworks of the Council of Europe and, later, the EU, which was constantly undermined by new emerging actors: conservatives, nationalists, neoimperialists, and sovereigntists.

Despite ideological differences, however, representatives of both camps were convinced that after the caesura, a new era had dawned — an era of progress and great prospects for all new societies, post-Soviet (from Belarusian to Turkmenistani) and post-communist (from Bulgarian to East German).

Stage 2:
Humbled Conceptualization, 1995–2003

The great expectations of the 1991 Revolution and the post-Soviet transition soon came up against the brute reality of poverty,

---

82   The socioeconomic dynamics and comparison of Ukraine with other Eastern European countries can be seen in Minakov (2020b).

83   Yegor Gaidar and the economists of his team wrote about this revolutionary connection in *The Economy of the Transition* (Gaidar et al., 1998).

interethnic conflicts, disorganization, and other negative experiences, which did not quite fit the initial splendor envisioned by the transition prophecy. The expectations were still alive, though their ambitions were humbled.

The humbling of the transition imagery and narratives started well before 1995, especially among the leftist intellectuals. Their vision's encounter with reality is well described in Havel's thoughtful commentary, published already in 1992:

> The return of freedom to a place that became morally unhinged has produced something that it clearly had to produce, and therefore something we might have expected. But it has turned out to be far more serious than anyone could have predicted: an enormous and blindingly visible explosion of every imaginable human vice. A wide range of questionable or at least ambivalent human tendencies, quietly encouraged over the years and, at the same time, quietly pressed to serve the daily operation of the totalitarian system, has suddenly been liberated, as it were, from its straitjacket and given free rein at last. The authoritarian regime imposed a certain order on these vices. . . . This order has now been broken down, but a new order that would limit rather than exploit these vices . . . has not yet been built. (Havel, 1992, p. 4)

Post-Soviet intellectuals also drew attention to a disturbing reality. For example, as early as 1994, Natalia Panina and Yevhen Golovakha pointed out that liberation from Soviet totalitarianism did not mean rejection of totalitarianism as such:[84]

> The path of a society from totalitarian ideology to democracy turned out to be associated with the necessity to pass through an extremely painful stage of a peculiar neo-totalitarian state—total normlessness and devaluation of values, which in the media and in the public opinion received the name derived from their prison type of relations: "bespredel"—economic, political, legal, national and egoistic lawlessness, etc. And after that, politicians, social scholars and journalists enriched their political lexicon with the terms more familiar to psychiatrists: political hysteria and apathy, mania of national exclusivity and xenophobia, social schizophrenia and general depression, mass psychosis and madness of the people, etc. (Golovakha & Panina, 1994, p. 4)

---

84   In the following, *bespredel* ("limitless") is a Russian word whose sense here originated in prison slang. It denotes the behavior of a person without regard for the fundamental rules of a criminal community.

Somewhat later, Bell described the result of the clash between the initial vision and the ensuing reality of societies in transition as leading to an unexpected crisis:

> The collapse of communism was not initially seen as a crisis for social democracy. (Bell, 1996, p. 247)

Yet the latter arrived with the disappearance of the second world and even infected political orders in the West. In other words, in the course of the post-communist transition, hegemony was achieved by neoliberalism in the economy and nationalism in politics, while the social democratic alternative lessened its influence in all parts of Europe.

However, the decline of the alternative proposed by the left was much more visible in the third world. Immanuel Wallerstein and Giovanni Arrighi have analyzed how the disruption of the Eastern Bloc and the following post-communist transition redivided the world-system to the benefit of the West, which turned into the global north; simultaneously, the periphery adopted the form of the global south and accommodated some of the post-communist countries (Arrighi et al., 2003, p. 4).

By 2001 the idea of One Big Europe had been implemented in the form of membership for all European states in the Council of Europe. The EU was also enlarging to include countries in Central and even Eastern Europe (namely, the Baltic states, which are now imagined as part of the Nordic country group; see Coppieters et al., 2004, pp. 17–18). From the formal point of view, the ongoing Europeanization was a success. Yet with the humbling of expectations, transition studies became much more empirical, and thus started registering problems. Ten to fifteen years after the caesura of 1989–1991, the post-Soviet and post-communist states developed into a variety of regimes, from autocracies to liberal democracies. The Balkans endured painful ethnic wars and NATO military operations. The global dichotomy between northern and southern actors redivided Europe. The post-Soviet core — Russia — started its own reintegration process, which would soon collide with the EU's and NATO's centripetal attraction of states (Minakov, 2017a, pp. 47–49).

The role of ideological stances decreased not only on the left but also among neoliberals: by 2003, academic studies of the post-communist transition were seeing their partisan affiliations dwindling. The researchers of the post-Soviet transition processes went through their own disciplinary transition. As Richard Sakwa has rightly pointed out,

> The actual course of transformation proved more complex than was assumed in the early post-communist days. The reform process itself generated new phenomena that raise questions about the received wisdom of the political sciences and economics. (Sakwa, 1999, p. 7)

This self-critical turn can be described as a gradual dropping of the concept of an all-encompassing transition and a move toward paying more critical attention to the post-Soviet social reality, in which increased civil liberties and political rights often did not ensure the democratic quality of either the political system or the political regime.

This trend is especially evident in the change of tone, vocabulary, and subject of publications in the three pivotal journals in transition studies during that period — the *East European Politics Journal,* the *Journal of Democracy,* and *Demokratizatsiya.* Analysis of these journals' contents shows a decrease in use of the term "transition" with every year from 1995 to 2003, while "democratization" was often substituted by "political pluralism" or "electoral democracy." More and more publications were looking into nationalism and Euroskepticism, as well as "systemic corruption." By 2003, the subject of systemic corruption and "shadow economy" had become the center of everyone's attention. Moreover, the tone of the publications was drastically different from that in the 1989–1994 period.

While working with the content of these journals, I noticed that post-communist transition studies appeared to have been conducted in several stages. In 1989–1994, the journals were open for debates among (1) the older generation of Kremlinologists and communism scholars, inclined to use concepts from the times of the Cold War, (2) former dissidents and ascendant political leaders in Central and Eastern Europe, the Southern Caucasus, and Central Asia, (3) a younger generation of post-communism scholars, and

(4) development experts and practicing economists. At that time, the pieces published ranged from standard academic papers to intellectual thought pieces. One of the most significant outcomes of this period in transition studies was the creation of a common language and visions, often ideologically biased, which scholars and practitioners of politics and economy used to describe the new social reality in Eastern Europe and northern Eurasia.

After 1994, and especially after 1997–1998, the publications lost their open partisanship and became more reality-oriented. The dialogue between scholars, experts, and politicians dropped to a minimum. The papers were more descriptive and less analytical in character. By the time of the tenth anniversary of the 1989–1991 caesura and the Eastern Bloc's collapse, the contributors appeared to have developed reservations about the victorious speeches of political leaders from the start of the decade.[85] Finally, by the time of the color revolutions and Russia's authoritarian turn, that is, in roughly 2003–2005, the academic community had turned from its initial post-Soviet enthusiasm to data collection, critical analysis, and reflection on its own conceptual apparatus.

This final stage of the humbling of transition studies — let us call it the ultimate sobering — was critical to both political agents directing the reforms and post-communist scholarship itself. For example, Shale Horowitz and several other contributors started expressing doubts about whether the drive for democratization and a free economy was key to understanding the events of the 1990s. For them, the depth and character of the conflict during the dissolution of the Eastern Bloc were more important than ideological or economic factors (Horowitz, 2003, p. 120). Simultaneously, John Dryzek and Leslie Holmes admitted their concerns with regard to the moral issue: post-communism studies envisaged not only the scrutiny of communism and its overthrow but also the establishment of an "ungenerous and unforgiving" capitalism, superimposed on "severe environmental pollution, and inherited creaking state bureaucracies" (Dryzek & Holmes, 2002, pp. 3–4). The social reality was constantly becoming richer and more volatile, while the

---

85   See, e.g., Jeffries (2004).

academic theories were losing their ability to keep pace. Therefore, the post-communist and post-Soviet studies were to become more finely focused on specific instances as a way to keep scholars from taking political sides.

These points were capably summarized by John Pickles and Adrian Smith as two issues of the post-Soviet and wider post-communist political economy. First, there was a marked lack of empirically grounded theories in the post-Soviet studies that would support the "neoliberal view of transition wielded by Western multilateral agencies and advisers to governments in ECE [East Central Europe]." And second, the concept of transition was too simplified in 1990s so that it looked like "a one-way process of change from one hegemonic system to another" (Pickles & Smith, 2005, pp. 1–2). These conclusions stemmed from a discussion that began back in 2002–2003 on whether the notion of a post-Soviet and post-communist transition had any scientific value at all.

The harshest critique of the transition concept and paradigm came from Thomas Carothers, who dared calling for the review of the five core beliefs of the transition theory. The scholar called for (1) not equating the abandonment of Soviet authoritarianism with a movement toward democracy and (2) recognizing that democratization can take place in several stages and at different speeds and in different directions. Also, he suggested that (3) elections are indeed an important factor in the establishment of democracy, but (4) "the level of economic development or ethnic composition as well as the historical experience of a society" are also decisive for both the pace of the transition and the quality of democratization. Finally, he called for the recognition that (5) the third wave of democratization achieves sustainable results only in a functionally strong state (Carothers, 2002, 5–12). Even though this call was not widely supported right away, it helped pull post-communist transition studies "out of the box" of the tetrad.[86]

The 1995–2003 period of understanding and assessing the post-Soviet transition concluded not only with Carothers repeating

---

[86]   A critical reaction to Carothers's article can be seen, for example, in Gans-Morse (2004).

Bell's call for revisionism (this time the revision of transition theory biases) but also with more attention paid to the role of ethnonationalism in Eastern Europe, the contradictions in post-communist state building (also in de facto state building), the political culture and its place in democratic or authoritarian consolidation, the contribution of Western international agencies (e.g., the International Monetary Fund, the World Bank, the U.S. Agency for International Development, and the Technical Assistance to the Commonwealth of Independent States) to the developmental agenda in the East, and finally the growing dissatisfaction with expansion for democracy and a market economy among regional elites and societies.

Ten to fifteen years after the caesura, the transition of transition studies happened once again—not only for the reason discussed above but also because of the wave of color revolutions and the emotional response to them, in particular the response of post-Soviet authoritarian leaders. In turn, the accession of some post-communist and post-Soviet states to the EU challenged transition observers to grasp the region not only in a more sober way but also by revising and redefining the meaning of the transition in different geopolitical contexts.

Stage 3:
Questioning Post-Soviet Progress, 2003–2022

The wave of color revolutions, from the Rose Revolution in Tbilisi (2003) to the Orange Revolution in Kyiv (2004) and the Tulip Revolution in Bishkek (2005), sparked events that were probably decisive for the evolution of assessments of the post-Soviet transition. These mainly peaceful, civic protests that resulted in the change of ruling elites in the countries of protest, a new wave of democratic reforms, and new prospects for European integration awoke the forgotten enthusiasm of the transitologists, liberal politicians, and civil rights activists. The revolutionary momentum offered the chance to rectify the failures of the previous post-Soviet developments; it showed that the post-Soviet transition itself, with the lessons learned from the previous decade, might be restarted in a more cautious and effective way (Cheterian, 2009, pp. 157–158).

However, this enthusiasm did not last nearly as long as in the early 1990s: revolutionary promises sank in the political struggle among the winners, in endemic corruption, and in the authoritarian reaction in Russia and other nonrevolutionary countries (Beacháin & Polese, 2010, pp. 10–12). Such a short cycle from hope to disenchantment was nonetheless therapeutic for the transition scholars: the numerous publications on the color revolutions demonstrate how fast, within a couple of years, enthusiasm was supplanted by balanced analysis.

Simultaneously, post-Soviet studies of societies have begun to take into account processes in post-communist societies as well. For example, the crystallization of Euroskepticism, growing evidence of informal links between corruption in Central European states and Russia, and the vibrancy of right-wing ideologies became the center of attention for the new transition studies.[87] In 2009, Vladimir Tismaneanu had to bitterly acknowledge that, despite the wealth differences, belonging to different geopolitical networks, and depth of reforms, the Central European region remains united, from the Visegrád Four to Russia and "other once-Soviet republics" (Tismaneanu, 2009, ix).[88]

The new understanding of transition emerged in the West and East simultaneously. This was a transitology of disenchantment: the post-Soviet and wider post-communist societies, after breaking with communism, were seen as sliding into new political regimes founded partly on new, partly on old political-economic elements. Socialism and capitalism were no longer seen as mutually exclusive: they overlapped, amalgamated, and gave birth to the political economy of the new Eastern Europe and northern Eurasia with their own conflict dynamics (including the 2008 Russo-Georgian War and, since 2014, in Ukraine) and collaboration of regimes.

---

87   Some of the most exemplary publications are Bugaric (2008), Neumayer (2008), and Szczerbiak and Taggart (2008).

88   The Visegrád Four (also Visegrád Group or V4) is a political alliance of four Central European countries—the Czech Republic, Hungary, Poland, and Slovakia—that aims to strengthen its members' cooperation in security, political, and economic affairs. The V4 was created in 1991 to further these countries' integration with the EU and continued to function even after all its member states joined the EU in 2004.

The new transition studies started evaluating political and economic processes in terms of noncompliance either with the values of the Council of Europe, or with those of the EU, or with the key indicators of liberal democracy and rule of law. The new trend in transition studies focused on the effectiveness of political regimes, the results of socioeconomic development, and informal power networks. Thus the concepts and language of competitive authoritarianism, patronalism, neopatrimonialism, and a mafia state began appearing regularly in the description, analysis, and forecasting of political and international security processes. Based on the study of political transition in all parts of the global south, including the CEE states, Steven Levitsky and Lucan A. Way argued that in transitional societies, a strong democracy is too often precluded by a weak state that is unable to ensure legal order and rule of law, while successful state building increases the chances for authoritarian consolidation, which in turn is toxic for civil rights and good governance (Levitsky & Way, 2010, pp. 355–357). Oleksandr Fisun and Henry Hale showed the critical importance of informal, personalist (patronal, patrimonial) networks to the development of post-Soviet regimes; and based on this perspective, Hale offered a systematization of post-Soviet political systems into single-pyramids and competing pyramids (Fisun, 2012, pp. 88–89; Hale, 2014, pp. 64–67). Bállint Magyar applied the same principle of coordination between formal and informal power institutions in Hungary; his study demonstrated that the country, formerly a champion in European integration and post-communist transition, had nonetheless developed into a "mafia-state," a political system based on patronage and corruption comparable to those appearing in the post-Soviet region (Magyar, 2016, pp. 22–24). Subsequently his system was successfully applied to the analysis of other CEE and northern Eurasian countries, including Belarus, Romania, Russia, and Ukraine (see Magyari, 2019; Minakov, 2019a; Petrov, 2019; Rouda, 2019).

Second, the concept of Europeanization, which for so long had evaded critical debate, is also being revised by contemporary transitologists. For example, Richard Youngs has shown how the concept and practice of European integration have changed after thirty years—the period coinciding with the post-Soviet development (Youngs, 2019). Based on an analysis of today's political and administrative practices of Europeanization, Youngs identifies five forms, some of which do not fit into transition modes or correlate with democratization. The first form is a "residual Europeanization" that still preserves the transitional and democratic gravity toward the EU, but less and less so as the 2010s wore on. The second form is a "politically neutral Europeanization," which was quite an influential practice as regards real political processes but was "detached from macro-level political trends, either in a democratic or anti-democratic way" (ibid.). The third form—an antidemocratic Europeanization—is discernible in those "illiberal trends within the EU [that were] giving oxygen to illiberal actors in the wider European space" (ibid.). The fourth form, a reverse Europeanization, was practiced in wider Europe, whereby the EU and its policies exhibited an openly decreasing relevance. Finally, the fifth form embodies a mixture of the above forms in a "two-directional Europeanization," which "can work either to democracy's advantage or disadvantage" (ibid.). Youngs's critical and realistic examination of the practices of Europeanization once associated with the concept of a democratic transition opened up a whole new field of inquiry into both the types of Europeanization and the widening gap between how Europeanization is actually practiced and the original conceptualization of Europeanization.

A new development in perspectives on and assessments of the post-Soviet transition is the increasingly greater role played by leftist intellectuals of the global south. One of the most influential critiques, for example, comes from Dayan Jayatilleka, a leading representative of the contemporary decolonial movement, whose revision of the older transition concept—namely, the one that anticipated the movement from socialism to democratic capitalism—is framed as the dismantling of the global north's hegemony in assessing the post-communist and post-Soviet development. Jayatilleka argues that the Western control over the memory of the Soviet Union and over evaluations of post-communist countries' transitions is part of the global north's power strategy, which undermines the progressive movements in the south (Jayatilleka,

2014, pp. 2–3). Jayatilleka and African and Latin American scholars alike offer counterhegemonic explanations, arguing that the origins and driving forces of the crisis of communism were not in the global north but in the Eastern Bloc itself. In this view the Eastern Bloc was not beaten but rather collapsed for internal reasons. Thus the belief promoted by the global north that socialism crumbled because of capitalism's economic superiority is not necessarily true since the post-Soviet and Central European countries remain poorer than the core Western nations despite their three decades' experience with capitalism's hegemony. Jayatilleka's conclusion is that socialism was not doomed, it could have been reformed, and that the lessons of the post-Soviet development need to be studied with no less care than neoliberal theories of development (ibid., pp. 3–4).

In addition to the rising important of new perspectives on transition from the global south, the voice of the Chinese academic community with its research perspective on post-Soviet transition issues is gaining more prominence. I can judge these studies only from sporadic English-language publications, which nonetheless show contemporary China's continuing interest in the dissolution of the USSR and Eastern Bloc, as well as in the post-communist transition. An example of such interest is the series of research programs on the Soviet Union's crisis and post-Soviet development initiated by the Chinese Academy of Social Sciences and conducted from 1993 to 2006 (Guihai, 2010, p. 506). According to Guan Guihai, those studies were directed at the historical causes of the USSR's collapse and the lessons of the post-communist transition in CEE and Russia (p. 507).

During the same period, doctrines—and the corresponding social imaginations and vocabularies—were in active development that radically contradicted the perspectives of more traditional transitologists. The doctrines were conceptualized and promoted by researchers and intellectuals from the neotraditionalist spectrum, which includes ethnonationalist, Panslavist, neoimperialist, social-nationalist, neo-Eurasianist, national-Bolshevik, sovereigntist, and many other ideological persuasions. What unites them is their conceptual optics: they look at the period from 1991 to 2022 from the various perspectives of the "pluralist ontology" of the people, ethnogenetics, the *longue durée* history of the "primordial nation," "sovereign democracy," and popular geopolitics.[89] Recycling separate elements of Martin Heidegger's philosophy, Carl Schmitt's theory of sovereignty and political theology, and ideas garnered from a number of local national-conservative ideologues of the late nineteenth and early twentieth centuries, these thinkers, ideologues, and politicians were for a long time on the margins of mainstream theorization about the post-Soviet period.[90] But the stronger the third wave of autocratization became and the closer the epoch neared the 2022 caesura, the stronger was their influence on politicians, scholars, educators, and the media. Eventually the Russian-Ukrainian war of 2022 and the radical changes in international relations that ended the post-Soviet era, among other things, led to the imagery and vocabulary of the neotraditionalists being adopted by many political leaders, military chiefs, and diplomats. In this imagery, the period after the caesura of 1989–1991 was the historical crisis of the East (i.e., the USSR and Eastern Bloc), which was to be followed by a "great awakening" of the Eurasian peoples and was projected to lead either to the establishment of an "ontologically just geopolitical pluralism" or to a world crisis and the long "loneliness" of countries like Russia (Dugin, 2021; Surkov, 2018, pp. 1–2). The new system of governing populations that had adopted national-conservative orientations, with the authorities managing collective memory, also began to play an increasingly important role.[91] By the end of the era, the post-Soviet public debate was largely being carried on between different camps of national

---

89 For example, these concepts are articulated and justified in the works of Alexander Dugin (2010, 2015), Yurii Mykhalchychyn (see, e.g., his 2011–2019 series of articles in the national-revolutionary journal *Varta*), or Vladislav Surkov (2008, 2018, 2019). For analytical works on this type of imaginary, see Gelashvili (2017), Shekhovtsov (2017), Shekhovtsov and Umland (2014), and Umland (2023).

90 On the specificity of the reading of Heideggerian philosophy by the neotraditionalists, see, for example: Apollonov (2015), Lavrukhin (2016), and Love (2017).

91 On the collective memory wars, see Kasianov (2022), Langenbacher and Shain (2010), and Mälksoo (2009).

conservatives, with the scant participation of marginalized — often repressed — liberal and leftist thinkers.

At the same time, it is striking how reliably and irrevocably the post-Soviet imagination did not accept either Marxist or non-Marxist left critiques. Part of the common post-Soviet social reality was not only the savage Eastern European sort of capitalism and blatant inequality on a multitude of dimensions but also the rejection of socialist or social democratic ideologies for party building or protest movements. Already in 1998 Myroslav Popovych bitterly pointed out that leftist ideas in the post-Soviet context seemed regressive and reactionary to the majority of the population, whereas nationalist ideas promoted "conservative Renaissance," "the construction of a New Society," and "the creation of the State . . . and the Nation out of an amorphous mass" (Popovych, 1998, pp. 65–66).[92] This nationalized imagery was effective in many ways also because the demand for social justice was constantly channeled by populists like Aliaksandr Lukashenka in Belarus, Vladimir Zhirinovsky in Russia, or Yulia Tymoshenko in Ukraine. And although leftist and left-liberal ideas — and even some groups driven by these ideas — were always present in the post-Soviet countries, they failed to turn into reality the idealistic aims of the Bolotnaya protests in Russia (2011–2013), the Euromaidan in Ukraine (2013–2014), Belarus's mass protests in 2020, or the antiwar movements in Belarus and Russia since 2022.[93] The post-Soviet leftist intellectual

---

92 Myroslav Popovych (1930–2018; also spelled Miroslav Popovich in English-language publications) is a Soviet and Ukrainian philosopher who in the 1990s was an active social democratic intellectual. His legacy includes the books *Logical Ideas in the Cultural-Historical Context* (1979), *Ukraine and Europe: The Right and the Left* (1996), and *The Red Century* (2005).

93 Here I list the major protests in Eastern Europe and northern Eurasia since 2011. Mass protests on Bolotnaya Square in Moscow lasted for about two years and were motivated by the suspicions of journalists and political activists the elections of 2011–2012 were fraudulent. The Euromaidan was a mass protest against autocratic tendencies in Ukraine and triggered by government's decision to delay signing the Association Agreement with the EU in 2013. Belarus's mass protests followed rigged presidential elections and police violence in 2020. The antiwar movements in Belarus and Russia followed Putin's decision to attack Ukraine on February 24, 2022; these movements were not mass, but they had arguably potential for it.

movements did not become a counterweight to either neotraditionalists, or neoliberals, or technocrats, and their influence on narratives of transition was even smaller than that of the conservatives.

War and the Interrupted Transition

The post-Soviet era, its transition, and the narratives that sought to
make sense of this period came to an end in 2022. It is now possible
to continue research in this field on new grounds: with the completion of this era, the post-Soviet transition and various analytical perspectives on it are available as a completed subject of study, permit-
ting researchers to maintain a necessary distance. Despite various
drawbacks, as detailed in the preceding stages, transitology in the
three decades of the post-Soviet era turned out to have made important contributions as a transdisciplinary academic discipline,
yielding a set of images and narratives that has long been at the
center of the political imagination in post-Soviet societies. Researchers in this field have faced several changing but interrelated
circumstances, including the progress and regress of post-Soviet societies and the plurality of methods and positions within the discipline itself. Now the societies of Eastern Europe and northern Eurasia have emerged from the post-Soviet state and have plunged into
a new historical caesura, preparing to enter a new era that will have
different characteristics, largely unrelated to the Soviet legacy
proper.

It is particularly noteworthy that the understanding of processes in the post-Soviet countries in recent years has depended less
and less on the vocabulary and optics of various Western schools of
transitology. At the same time, the national and sovereigntist perspectives in the social and political sciences, which found themselves under the ideological control of European and Eurasian governments, became increasingly strong. Although Eastern Europe
and northern Eurasia remained on the global periphery, the hegemony of concepts born in Western universities and research centers
was significantly shaken in the last decade of the post-Soviet era
and remains so today, during the caesura. Its influence on the vocabularies of self-description of the societies, peoples, and power

elites of Eastern Europe has been and is being undermined by the academic centers and ideological groups that have described socio-opolitical and cultural processes in societies after the collapse of the USSR in terms of national or even subnational history.

The post-Soviet transition was hostage to a political belief in liberal progress, always referencing a desired, better future. This belief answered the demands of both late Soviet communities and the emerging post-Soviet national worldviews. The struggle for control over a vision of the future was won by the intellectuals promoting nationalization, who set the tone for interpreting this future in terms of "correcting" — or, more likely, repeating — the mistakes of the past. Myroslav Popovych was right to point out the dialectic of national-conservative hegemony, which derived from "national renaissance" a progress oriented toward the past. This is why institutions of collective memory management became so important, and why the conflicts of the last period of the post-Soviet era weaponized collective memory and memory studies.

In the transformations of the post-Soviet imagination, the meaning of transition lost its point of reference: the future not only began to resemble the past, it also lost its own life-directing value. Post-Soviet development was a nomad that began its exodus as the Soviet Union was collapsing, but on its way to the promised land of freedom and prosperity the prophecy that guided it was forgotten. The Post-Soviet Human became disoriented, just as Yuri Andrukhovych had dreamed. But this disorientation does not mean that Post-Soviet Humans have lost their *orientality* (i.e., both *Eastern-ness* and *ability to orient* in the fast-changing world) and have become the inhabitants of the European center. Instead, they have simply lost their way in the vast spaces of Eurasia.

4. The Achievements of Post-Soviet Political Creativity

Even though the post-Soviet era, that time between the dissolution of the Soviet Union and Russia's full-scale invasion of Ukraine in 2022, was rather short, it was a time of dramatic change and daring attempts by the peoples inhabiting Eastern Europe and northern Eurasia to carve out a larger space for freedoms and reimagine their future. An evaluation of the results of their actions is crucial both for understanding the reasons for the fragility of the democratic outcomes and of the infrastructure of peace among the peoples of the region and for predicting future processes in this part of the world. During this second interwar interval (the first interwar interval being that between the two world wars), Eastern European and northern Eurasian societies reinvented statehood, ideological pluralism, competitive politics, citizenship, nationality, social inclusion, wealth, poverty, and many other political and sociopolitical phenomena, institutions, and practices. And in these creative processes, freedom and subjugation, democratic creativity and authoritarian innovation coexisted and struggled for dominance in each society and in the region as a whole.

In this final chapter I attempt to put together a kind of balance sheet for the period under review: what exactly the Post-Soviet Human achieved in terms of meaningful democratic and autocratic institutional outcomes. In doing so, I use empirical data and develop generalizations based on these data to elucidate the results achieved through different political and socioeconomic processes in the post-Soviet countries.[94] In this way I hope to show plainly the

---

94   I used the Varieties of Democracy database (V-Dem) as the major source of data and generalizations. According to its website, V-Dem provides a multidimensional data set that "reflects the complexity of the concept of democracy as a system of rule that goes beyond the simple presence of elections." Its researchers "distinguish between five high-level principles of democracy: electoral, liberal, participatory, deliberative, and egalitarian, and collect data to measure these principles" across all nations, including the post-Soviet ones. For more on the V-Dem database, please see the website for Varieties of Democracy at https://www.v-dem.net/.

democratic and autocratic outcomes of Post-Soviet Humans' creativity.

The Democratic Outcomes of Post-Soviet Political Creativity

Perhaps the most significant achievement of democratic creativity among post-Soviet peoples was the founding of new states. Because states had existed in Eastern Europe and northern Eurasia since long before the post-Soviet period, state building in the past thirty years or so can be seen as a refounding of statehood oriented at democratic form of governance. This refounding was primarily related to overcoming the Soviet political experience: the new states had to ensure political freedom (in individual and collective terms), the possibility of entrepreneurship, and guarantees of a nonreturn to Soviet power practice.

New political institutions were rebuilt in the course of adjusting the public-private balance, highly weighted toward the public side, that had existed in the Soviet Union. The Bolshevik sociopolitical experiment, Stalinist totalitarianism, and post-Stalinist Soviet authoritarianism had largely manifested in an expansion of the public sphere, which absorbed most of the private sphere. Here it is important to stress that the Soviet system colonized the lifeworlds of Eastern European and northern Eurasian communities with an alternative program of modernization in which a scientific-secular industrial worldview and a Marxist universalist ethic coexisted with the subjected, unemancipated individual and a specific collectivity, the communist "classless society," that was blind to inequalities in the Soviet social structure (Minakov, 2020a, pp. 18–20). In this structural imbalance between the two spheres, the public sphere lost its emancipatory power, and the private sphere was unable to protect the cultural rhizome responsible for giving meaning to the lives of individuals and communities. Party ideological divisions created ideological surrogates that supplanted the lost value and meaning structures of the previous lifeworld. This worked for some time, but by the end of the 1980s, these substitutes were no longer effective and were leading Soviet society into a profound existential crisis.

The sprawl of the public sphere stemmed from the fact that the super-organization of a single party, the Communist Party of the Soviet Union, controlled all public, state, economic, financial, and cultural spheres and institutions, along with many other aspects of life. The CPSU was a kind of reimagined and restructured civic super-organization. Western CSOs are usually small organizations, at least in comparison with the governmental structures such as the army or bureaucracy. The Communist Party was organized not as a classic political party but as an unusually large organization that wielded control over state and private institutions, including family, community, business, and religious institutions, even intimate relations. In the setting of a sprawling public sphere, the CPSU merged with and absorbed the centers of power, becoming itself the new and sole vertical of power.

Since the Communist Party was so important, the energy of post-Soviet political creativity in 1989–1991 was directed toward destroying the party's monopoly of the union's center and the Soviet republics. As early as the electoral campaign of 1989, when the first almost-free elections were held in the USSR, the fight against the privileged position of the Communist Party, established by Article 6 of the USSR Constitution of 1977, became a priority for opposition deputies. This article of the Soviet Constitution stated:

> The leading and guiding force of Soviet society, the nucleus of its political system, state and public organizations is the Communist Party of the Soviet Union. The CPSU exists for the people and serves the people.

With the beginning of decommunization in all of the Soviet republics in 1991, the CPSU, the KGB, and their substructures were in line to be targeted by prohibitions. Thus, for example, the Communist Party was banned by decisions made either by the Supreme Soviets of the union republics (in Ukraine on August 30, 1991, and in Latvia on September 10, 1991) or by republican presidents (in Uzbekistan on August 29, 1991, and in Russia on November 6, 1991). As a rule, these decisions were later affirmed and reinforced by court decisions. The CPSU's assets were transferred to republican governments. The enormous party superstructure was quickly destroyed, and as it collapsed, the dam that had held back the energy of political creativity in Eastern European and northern Eurasian communities also collapsed.[95]

Post-Soviet state building was based on the inception of real multiparty systems in the new societies, liberating governmental institutions from the (or any) super-party's control while at the same time placing the emerging institutions and distributed branches of power under democratic control. In this way the new societies started overcoming their Soviet experience.

The citizens of the late Soviet Union had two types of personal experience with the public sphere, politics, and the state: their participation in a late Soviet authoritarian society and their imagining what the "freedom of the West" might look like in their own society. This imagining was instrumental in resisting Soviet propaganda and in absorbing information about politics from "Western sources," and contributed to the growing awareness of diverse political beliefs during the perestroika era. If the Soviet political experience was an experience to be overcome, political and economic freedom constituted an indefinite object of political imagining and a guiding principle for implementation. In practice, few actors in the post-Soviet transformation knew from their own personal experience what freedom was, what a political party was, how ideological diversity functioned, how to structure a system of checks and balances, and where the line demarcating the public from the private sphere lay. Post-Soviet Humans and their histories began with the audacity to create new states, political regimes, and legal systems without the necessary experience or knowledge of liberty and rule of law—which only emphasizes both the boldness and the courage of the revolutionary endeavors of the time.

The post-Soviet states were built as if from scratch, during the caesura of 1989–1991 and within the public and private dimensions of the 1991 Revolution, as described in chapter 2. (Here I would just stress that people with no personal experience of political,

---

95   For more on the decommunization of the early 1990s, see Kasianov (2008, pp. 22ff.) and Muhametov (2018, pp. 204–209).

economic, social, or religious freedom seed the beginnings of new states at their own risk.) A wave of revolutions in the private sphere led to the emergence of new enterprises, the privatization of Soviet enterprises, and the launching of new services and financial institutions previously unknown to the Soviet Man. Family, sexuality, gender, and intimacy proved to be spaces for new experiences of self and of close ones. At the same time, a wave of revolutions in the public led sphere to the seeding of new states, constitutions, political systems, competitive politics, ideological pluralism, and legal systems and the creation of space for civil movements and organizations.

The irony is that the post-Soviet states grew out of the soviets: it was the central Supreme Soviet and the Supreme Soviets of the republics, those councils elected in 1989–1990, that became platforms for the creation of new — post-"soviet" — political spaces. The USSR Supreme Soviet began to lose importance rapidly in August 1991 with the attempted coup and the interruption of the process of preparing a new Union Treaty. Although Soviet citizens supported the idea of a "renewed Soviet Union" in a March 1991 referendum, neither President Gorbachev nor the USSR Supreme Soviet were able to implement the expressed will of the citizens. With President Yeltsin's victory over the putschists in Moscow, the Supreme Soviets (or Supreme Councils) of the republics were able to create independent states on the territory they individually controlled. Within the framework of the Soviet political system, the Supreme Soviet was formally the highest body of state power, in the structure of which the executive and legislative branches were merged. Formally, only the judicial branch in the USSR existed separately. Republican and union state structures also existed separately (with the exception of the Russian Soviet Federal Socialist Republic, which was mainly governed by the USSR's official institutions). But all these formal differences had little real weight, thanks to the overarching control of the CPSU.

Elections to the Supreme Soviets of the republics in 1990 brought to power a new generation of politicians who had done away with communist control. Formally, many of them were still members of the Communist Party, although noncommunist candidates were allowed to run. Thus in the Supreme Soviet of the RSFSR, 86 percent were communists, while 11 percent were deputies from the Democratic Russia party; in the Supreme Soviet of the Lithuanian republic, 32 percent were communists, while 68 percent were deputies from the Solidarity movement; in the Supreme Soviet of the Ukrainian republic, 53 percent were communists, while the rest were independents or representatives of four other blocs; and in the Supreme Soviet of the Georgian SSR, communists held about 30 percent of the seats, the rest being held by representatives of ten blocs, with the Round Table–Free Georgia bloc winning 54 percent of the mandate (Olson & Norton, 2007; Turovsky, 2011). Whether the CPSU members held a majority or not, it was these Supreme Soviet councils that decided on the independence of their republics and the new distribution of power after the collapse of the USSR.[96]

Since 1992, two branches of power have grown out of the Supreme Soviets: the executive branch and the legislature, which in the early 1990s were fighting each other for institutional supremacy within each political system. This struggle could assume radical, even violent form, such as the shelling of the parliament building in Moscow in 1993 on the orders of President Yeltsin or the "shakeup of deputies"—Belarusian president Aliaksandr Lukashenka's personal repression of independent MPs—in Minsk at the end of the 1990s. By the beginning of the twenty-first century, the contest between the executive branch and the legislature had led to the emergence of six parliamentary republics (Georgia, Armenia, Latvia, Lithuania, Moldova, and Estonia), two formally semipresidential republics (Azerbaijan and Ukraine), and seven presidential republics (Belarus, Kazakhstan, Kyrgyzstan, Russia, Tajikistan, Turkmenistan, and Uzbekistan). Presidentialism had also been established in four unrecognized post-Soviet statelets: Abkhazia (territory of Georgia), Nagorno-Karabakh (territory of Azerbaijan),

---

96   This usually took the form of the creation of constitutional commissions and the adoption of new constitutions (Hale, 2011, pp. 600ff). In some cases, however, it may have taken place in the form of temporary "constitutional treaties" between the president and the parliament, as in Ukraine (Sharlet, 2019).

Transnistria (territory of Moldova), and South Ossetia (territory of Georgia).[97] In the parliamentary republics, parliaments remained the leading political institution, approving laws, effectively controlling the cabinet of ministers, and limiting presidential power. In the presidential republics, presidents led the executive branch and controlled parliaments by formal and informal means. In the case of Ukraine, which had a mixed presidential-parliamentary system, the president and the parliament fought for control of the cabinet of ministers from 1992 through 2019, when President Zelensky created a single-party ruling majority in the Verkhovna Rada (Minakov, 2023, pp. 141–143). In all these cases, in one way or another, the acceptance by both elites and the population of the idea of the division of power into branches and between central and local governments, along with the implementation of this separation of powers in practice, was critical to the construction of a post-Soviet democratic state.

Division of Supreme Power into Branches and Levels

How this separation has become part of post-Soviet political practice can be seen in the Division of Power Index (figure 1).[98] This index answers the question to what extent elected local and regional governments can operate without interference from unelected bodies (V-Dem 2023a). Accordingly, the lowest score is given to a country where elected offices are subordinate to nonelected offices and

---

97 The same form of government was formally established in the state formations of the so-called Donetsk and Luhansk People's Republics in 2014–2022.

98 Here and below, all values of indices and other indicators (unless otherwise noted) are taken from the V-Dem database (https://v-dem.net/data_analysis/VariableGraph/). In all cases the post-Soviet processes are compared across four countries: Estonia, Russia, Ukraine, and Uzbekistan. Estonia exemplifies a country with consistently high indicators of democratic development and exhibiting the strong influence of the Council of Europe (CoE), the EU, and NATO institutions. Russia exemplifies a country with a high level of autocratization after a short period of democratization, with some influence from CoE institutions. Ukraine exemplifies a country that weathered several transitions from growing to declining democracy, with short periods of autocratization and exhibiting some influence of CoE and EU institutions on its political and legal systems. Uzbekistan exemplifies a country with a long period of autocratization following a short and insignificant period of democratization, with minimal outside influence on its political structures.

the highest score is assigned to a country where elected authorities can operate without interference from nonelected entities (ibid.).

Figure 1.   Division of Power Index: Estonia, Russia, Ukraine, and Uzbekistan, 1989–2022

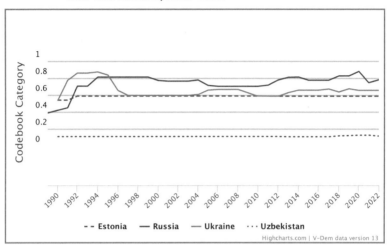

As figure 1 shows, in three of the four illustrative cases, a separation of local and central bodies occurs clearly and unambiguously between 1990 and 1992. In Estonia, this division had already taken hold before 1994 and has remained stable up to the time of this writing. In Ukraine, separation of the two branches of government also occurred between 1990 and 1992 but remained the subject of a struggle over the autonomy of local and regional administrations in a mixed semipresidential republic (although formally, in 2006–2010 Ukraine established a parliamentary-presidential model of government, which resumed in 2014). The situation in Russia resembles that in Ukraine, despite Russia being formally a federation. The case of Uzbekistan presents a model of those post-Soviet states that moved very quickly after the collapse of the USSR to a one-person executive branch.

Figure 2. Legislative Constraints on the Executive Branch Index: Estonia, Russia, Ukraine, and Uzbekistan, 1989–2022

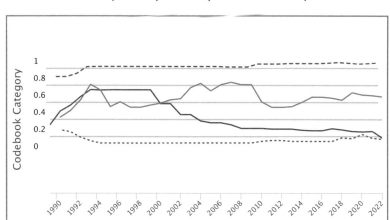

This picture is complemented by data from the Legislative Constraints on the Executive Index. The data in figure 2 describe the ability of the legislature, together with the attorney general and/or ombudsman (institutions introduced from external democratic models but reinterpreted in post-Soviet states), to oversee the executive branch (V-Dem, 2023a). In this chart, the Estonian and Uzbek cases illustrate opposite poles, with the dominance in Estonia of the legislature over the executive in a parliamentary republic contrasting with the dominance in Uzbekistan of the executive over the legislature in a presidential republic with a strong authoritarian regime. The cases of Russia and Ukraine show how the struggle between the two branches of power, conducted throughout the 1990s, ended with the domination of the executive branch in the Russian Federation in the twenty-first century, while in Ukraine, confrontation between the two branches continued, at least up to 2019.

Refounding the State and the Nation

No less important was the idea of the source of the sovereignty and legitimacy of each reestablished state. For some post-Soviet states (Turkmenistan, Uzbekistan, Ukraine), this source was found in the will of the citizens as expressed in a referendum. For other new states (Azerbaijan, Georgia, Latvia, Lithuania, Moldova, Estonia), the source of sovereignty was located in the historical tradition of statehood, which had been suppressed by the USSR and was restored with the collapse of the union. In still other cases, decisions were made by the Supreme Soviets as representative bodies of the republics and their populations. But in all cases, the common thread included not only the will of the population or historical precedent but also an embrace of the values of democracy and the rule of law. If we consider the texts of post-Soviet declarations of sovereignty and independence, along with early post-Soviet constitutions, as documents that capture the political imagination of new political communities, we find them all linked to the idea of these communities as the founders of democratic political systems:

> The Supreme Council of the Ukrainian SSR, expressing the will of the people of Ukraine, striving to create a democratic society, proceeding from the needs to ensure human rights and freedoms, respecting the rights of all ethnic groups, caring for the complete political, economic, social and spiritual development of the people of Ukraine, recognizing the need to build a state based on the rule of law, aiming to establish the sovereignty and self-government of the Ukrainian people, proclaims the State sovereignty of Ukraine. (*Declaration on the State Sovereignty of Ukraine*, July 16, 1990)

> The Supreme Council of the Armenian SSR, expressing the united will of the people of Armenia, realizing its responsibility for the fate of the Armenian people in realization of the aspirations of all Armenians and restoration of historical justice, proceeding from the principles of the Universal Declaration of Human Rights and generally recognized norms of international law, realizing the right of nations for free self-determination, based on the joint decision of the Supreme Council of the Armenian SSR and Nagorno-Karabakh National Council of December 1, 1989 "On reunification of the Armenian SSR and Nagorno-Karabakh Republic," developing the democratic traditions of the independent Republic of Armenia established on May 28, 1918, with the purpose of creating a democratic society based on the rule of law, proclaims the commencement of the process of establishment of independent statehood. (*Declaration of Independence of Armenia*, August 23, 1990)

> As an expression of the will of the people, the Supreme Council of the Republic of Lithuania . . . solemnly declares that the exercise of the sovereign rights of the State of Lithuania, violated by alien force in 1940, is restored and that from now on Lithuania is once again an independent State. The Act of the Lithuanian Council on Independence of February 16, 1918, and the Resolution of the Constituent Seimas of May 15, 1920, on the Restoration of

the Democratic State of Lithuania have never lost their legal force and con-
stitute the constitutional basis of the Lithuanian State. . . . The State of Lithuania emphasizes its commitment to the universally recognized principles
of international law, recognizes the inviolability of borders as set forth in the
Final Act of the Helsinki Conference on Security and Cooperation in Europe
of 1975, and guarantees human, civil, and minority rights. (*Act on the Restoration of the Independence of the State of Lithuania*, March 11, 1990)

Along with their respective assertions of democratic legitimacy,
these documents each contain a civic and/or ethnic nationalist argument: emerging democracies were founded as states rooted in
ethnonational communities. In the early 1990s, as republics were
being founded, the democratization and the nationalization of political systems went hand in hand. Throughout the post-Soviet period, these two trends both supported and undermined each other,
creating a dynamic of political regimes that differentially exploited
the possibilities of the newly emerged political systems and managing the diversity of populations in the territories under their control.

As conceived by the republican leaders who managed the collapse of the USSR, new states would emerge within the administrative boundaries of the Soviet republics. But democratization involved citizens in decision-making, which made them active participants in decision processes concerning borders. Meanwhile, the
nationalization of the political imagination linked borders to ethnic,
linguistic, confessional, and other identity groups. This intercon-
nection led to a "parade of sovereignties" not only among the former union republics, the fifteen constituents of the former USSR,
but also within the republics themselves. In Azerbaijan, Georgia,
Kazakhstan, Moldova, the Russian Federation, Ukraine, and Uzbekistan, this internal conflict led to irredentist, separatist, and often secessionist movements (Minakov et al., 2021c). Thus the
bloody conflicts in the South Caucasus led to ethnic cleansing and
the formation of three unrecognized states, two of which, Abkhazia
and South Ossetia, were supported by Moscow and one, Nagorno-
Karabakh, by Yerevan, in 1990–1993. The Moldovan government
lost control of Russia-backed Transnistria in the fight over sovereignty. Ukraine's territorial integrity was also threatened by the

separatist movement in Crimea in 1992–1994. Indeed, the Russian Federation itself was in danger of disintegration, at risk of losing territory either to military force, in the North Caucasus, or to political struggle, such as in Tatarstan and Bashkortostan.

On the one hand, irredentism and secessionism were a continuation of the same processes of social fragmentation that had led to the emergence of new states from the former Soviet socialist republics. Post-Soviet political creativity and mass movements were not necessarily limited to the administrative boundaries of the former union. On the other hand, the wars and ethnic conflicts that emerged in the process of this fragmentation had the most negative impact on the democratic quality of post-Soviet political creativity. Some of the problems associated with these processes were resolved by the signing of the Budapest Memorandum on Security Assurances in 1994. As was described in chapter 2, formally, the memorandum provided Belarus, Kazakhstan, and Ukraine with security guarantees within their administrative borders in exchange for a partial handover of nuclear weapons to Russia and the partial destruction of the Soviet nuclear arsenal on their territories (Grant, 2014). Informally, however, the memorandum secured the borders of the newly formed states and stopped Russian support for secessionist and irredentist movements in the post-Soviet republics (Minakov, 2020b). This informal influence was realized in the return of Crimea to Kyiv's full control with the support of the Kremlin, as well as in the preparation of bilateral treaties of friendship and cooperation between Russia and the republics in 1994–1997. The recognition of sovereignty and borders allowed relations to normalize between the emerging post-Soviet political entities and facilitated the entry of these entities into various integration projects, especially with Europe.

The Liberal-Democratic Potential of European Integration

The most important integration project for the democratic creativity of the post-Soviet nations was accession to the Council of Europe. The Council of Europe is a regional international organization, membership in which is possible after a country's adoption of its political and legal systems of norms and rules basic to a functional democracy and the rule of law. Lithuania and Estonia were accepted into the Council of Europe in 1993; Latvia, Moldova, and Ukraine joined it in 1995; Russia followed in 1996, Georgia in 1999, and Azerbaijan and Armenia in 2001. This type of European integration supported democratization and the democratic harmonization of the political and legal systems of most post-Soviet countries. However, in only three cases — Estonia, Latvia, and Lithuania — did this type of European integration actually intensify within the framework of the EU and NATO, providing these member states with more support for the institutionalization of democracy, the rule of law, and security without threatening political freedoms. At the same time, European integration was only a supporting factor: it was the citizens and nations at large that took the creative initiative, although Western models of democratization allowed these impulses to translate into less fragile practices than in other post-Soviet states. From that perspective, the Council of Europe and the EU can be seen as the model-promoting institutions.

Rule of Law

The fusion of internal creativity and external factors is particularly noticeable in the formation of post-Soviet constitutional and legal systems, which developed under simultaneous internal and external demands for the rule of law. The first legal reforms in post-Soviet countries were connected with the introduction of normative approaches to the formation, approval, and execution of laws, based on a normative way of imagining the rule of law, while the imagination and practice of positive law were marginalized, at least in the 1990s (Antonov, 2021; Antonov & Vovk, 2021; Rabinovych, 2021; Varlamova, 2021). The first wave of writing, discussing, and approving the constitutions of the new states in 1990–1994 was a crucial part of state and nation building. The new legislation was an important component of post-Soviet democratization, supporting political and economic freedoms, incorporating human rights and Council of Europe norms into national legal systems, and supporting the autonomy of the judicial branch.

The general outcome of these political and legal processes can be assessed by the Rule of Law Index. This index is a generalized assessment of the extent to which laws are transparently, independently, and equally enforced and the level of compliance they receive from government officials (V-Dem, 2023a). In figure 3, the Estonian case represents the greatest success on the part of a post-Soviet political system in applying the rule of law, owing in part to support by local constituencies and in part to the country's membership in the Council of Europe, the EU, and NATO. The cases of Russia and Ukraine show how the impulse to establish the rule of law was an important moment for the emergence of new independent states in the 1990s and how this impulse later came under pressure from autocratic tendencies. The Uzbekistan case illustrates how, as early as the mid-1990s, the initial post-Soviet legal achievements were being defied as power became concentrated in the presidency.

Figure 3.   Rule of Law Index: Estonia, Russia, Ukraine, and Uzbekistan, 1989–2022

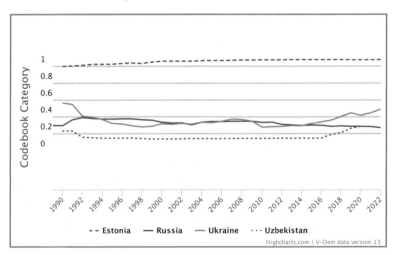

All four cases show that the rule of law began to be practiced by politicians and statesmen in the early 1990s and either strengthened democratic tendencies or became the object of targeted destruction by actors supporting the autocratic program.

Autonomy of the Judicial Branch

Another important achievement was the relegation of the judiciary to a separate, autonomous branch of government. While the executive and legislative branches came out of the Soviet Supreme Soviets, the judiciary was formed in the process of the Soviet judiciary's leaving party control and coming under the control of republican governments. Although all post-Soviet constitutions establish judicial autonomy and some empower constitutional courts or Supreme Courts as "guarantors of constitutional rights and freedoms," in reality, executive officials and legislators fought a long battle for the right to appoint judges and influence the judicial branch by other means (see Barrett, 2021, p. 261).

The Judicial Constraints on the Executive Index affords a comparative perspective on the extent to which the executive branch respected the constitution and complied with court decisions, as well as the extent to which the judicial branch was able to act independently (V-Dem, 2023a). As with the previous indices, Estonia and Uzbek offer radically contrasting examples of, respectively, successful democratization and rapid autocratization in the post-Soviet period (figure 4). The cases of the Russian Federation and Ukraine illustrate the gradual divergence of political and legal systems: in Russia, the courts were increasingly influenced by the executive branch, while in Ukraine the autonomy of the courts fluctuated, increasing during periods of democratization (in the early 1990s, between 2004 and 2010, and after 2019) and decreasing during periods of autocracy (from the late 1990s to 2004 and from 2010 to 2018).

Figure 4.   Judicial Constraints on the Executive Index: Estonia, Russia, Ukraine, and Uzbekistan, 1989–2022

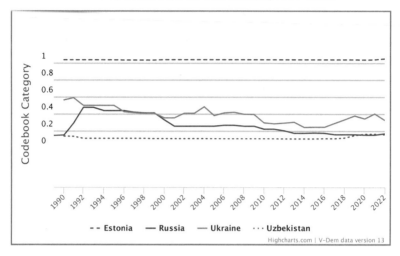

Elections as a Right and a Practice

A further important product of post-Soviet democratic creativity was the institution of elections. Elections in the Soviet political system had an important ritual significance: Soviet subjects demonstrated their loyalty to the government and imitated participation in the change of elites by filling out ballots lacking alternative choices. Participation in Soviet elections was an important disciplinary practice precisely because of its imitative nature. With the beginning of democratization, elections became perhaps the most important sign of political freedom. The first experience of free elections for people living in the Soviet Union came in 1989, when a new USSR Supreme Soviet was elected. Although 750 mandates were distributed by the leadership of the Communist Party and Soviet "civic organizations," a much larger proportion of the council seats, 1,500, went through open and competitive elections. The enthusiasm characteristic of revolutionary moments was such that 89.8 percent of the eligible Soviet population participated in the elections. In these elections, the late Soviet population learned how to elect representatives and publicly debate with fellow citizens the merits of this or that candidate. In fact, it was a matter of simultaneously reinventing elections to a representative parliament, active responsible citizenship, and open public debate leading to a redistribution of power. All this was new to the Soviet population.

The experience of free political participation was repeated and crystallized in 1990, when elections to the republican Supreme Councils were held. Despite the continuing legislative obstacles to pluripartyism in the USSR, parties, blocs, and movements participated in these elections, offering the population not only a diversity of opinions and candidates, as in 1989, but also party programs with different ideological orientations. Elections went from electing a representative to electing a political force with which a voter shared ideological positions. It was these republican Supreme Soviets that led to the establishment of the independence of their republics, the separation of the executive and legislative branches, and the beginning of a transformation within the framework of the post-Soviet tetrad.

Subsequently, the electoral element of democracy became the strongest practice influencing the noncontrolled rotation of elites, even in countries governed by authoritarian regimes. As can be seen in figure 5, in our sample of four post-Soviet countries, the populace's recognition of the importance of elections is demonstrated by the constant and significant (50 percent or more) participation of voters in the election of presidents and parliaments. It is worth noting that presidential elections tend to attract more voters than parliamentary elections, as evidenced by the turnout patterns in the Russian, Ukrainian, and Uzbek cases. In the Estonian case, participation in national legislature elections is consistently higher than in European parliamentary elections.

Figure 5.   Voter Turnout by Election Type: Estonia, Russia, Ukraine, and Uzbekistan, 1989–2022

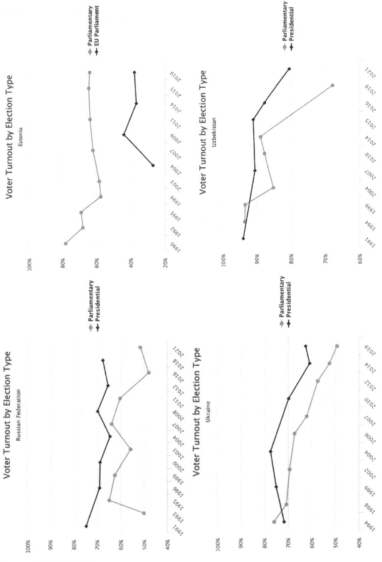

Elections have become the most important democratic institution in post-Soviet political systems. Using summarized data from the

Electoral Democracy Index, we can see the institutional development of elections in the post-Soviet period (figure 6). The electoral
principle of democracy aims at "making rulers responsive to citizens," a goal achieved through (1) competition for the approval of
the electorate, (2) the free operation of political and civil society organizations, (3) elections free of fraud or systematic irregularities,
(4) changing the elected chiefs of the executive, and (5) the freedom
of independent media to present alternative views on matters of
political relevance (V-Dem, 2023a). As figure 6 shows, since 1993–
1995, electoral democracy in Estonia has reached consistently max-
imum values, while in Uzbekistan the values are consistently at a
minimum. In the case of Russia, before the beginning of Vladimir
Putin's rule, the level of electoral democracy was high, but since the
start of the twenty-first century the index has been steadily decreasing, approaching a minimum over the last nine years. In the Ukrainian case, electoral democracy experienced a heyday in the first half
of the 1990s, from 2004 to 2010, and again after 2019, with short,
scattered periods of decline in political freedom.

Figure 6. **Electoral Democracy Index: Estonia, Russia, Ukraine,
and Uzbekistan, 1989–2022**

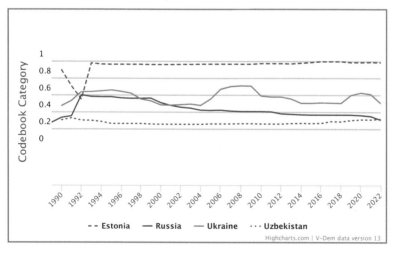

Democracy as a Unity of Electoral, Liberal, and Deliberative Practices

It is also possible to compare the electoral component with the two other components of democracy, liberal and deliberative practices (figure 7).[99] In all four country cases, whatever the level of freedom and however stable the form of government, the electoral component was more significant than the liberal and deliberative components.

---

99   The liberal principle of democracy emphasizes the importance of protecting individual and minority rights from the tyrannies of the state and the majority. This principle judges the democratic quality of a government by the limitations imposed on it through constitutionally protected civil liberties, a strong rule of law, an independent judiciary, and effective mechanisms of checks and balances (V-Dem, 2023a).
The Deliberative Democracy Index focuses on the process by which decisions are made in a state. A deliberative process (deliberation) is one in which public debate about the common good motivates political decisions and is distinct from emotional appeals, identity-based solidarity, or other modes of coercion by citizens or minorities. According to this principle, democracy requires respectful dialogue between informed and competent participants who are open to each other's arguments (V-Dem, 2023a).

Figure 7.   Comparison of Electoral, Liberal, and Deliberative Democracy Indices by Country: Estonia, Russia, Ukraine, and Uzbekistan, 1989–2022

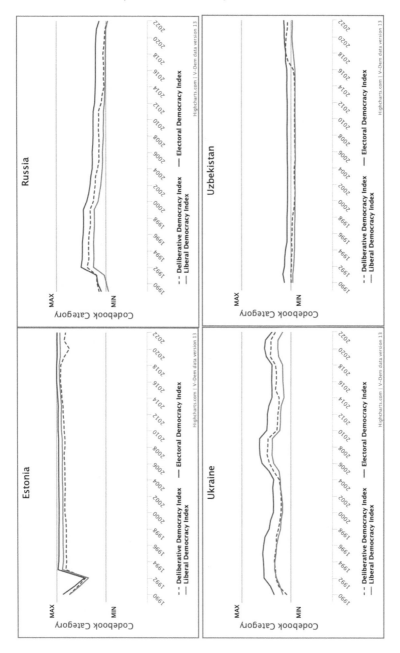

It is worth noting that the significance of elections for citizens of post-Soviet countries extends beyond the politically pragmatic to the moral. That is, not only do elections effect a rotation or change of elites in representative bodies of power and central and local councils in a way that is not controlled by the ruling groups, they are also imagined as a process for the "moral renewal of authorities." The entire electoral process, from the nomination of candidates to the counting of votes, has carried the meaning, often contrary to the experience of its participants, of a moral choice between good and evil – or, more often, between a greater and a lesser evil. The undermining of trust in election results throughout the post-Soviet period has had the capacity to provoke mass protests and sometimes regime change. It is this moral-political aspect that can be found among the main factors leading to the color revolutions not only in Georgia, Ukraine, and Kyrgyzstan in 2003–2005 but also in Armenia in 2018. It is also noticeable in the protest movements of Moldova in 2008, Russia in 2011, and Belarus in 2015 and 2020.[100]

Post-Soviet democratic creativity linked elections, the rotation of elites, and the legitimacy of regimes to the possibility of free discussion of significant issues. The rejection of the Soviet experience was associated with the emergence of political debates out of kitchens and into public spaces, a move that was structured around the availability of free media and platforms for academic and cultural self-expression. A summary of the experience of creating such institutions and platforms is captured in the Freedom of Expression and Alternative Sources of Information Index. This index assesses the extent to which a government respects press and media freedom, the freedom of individual citizens to discuss political issues in the public sphere, and freedom of academic and cultural expression (V-Dem, 2023a). As shown in figure 8, institutions and platforms in Estonia and Ukraine have advanced significant levels of government respect for press freedom and debate throughout the post-Soviet period. In Russia, the Putin regime gradually curtailed opportunities for free and reasoned public dialogue. The same opportunities were curtailed in Uzbekistan in the early 1990s, but in

---

100   On that, see Minakov (2022c), Mitchell (2012), and Tucker (2007).

2016–2017 the regime eased some of the political restrictions, though not to the point of meeting the basic requirements for democracy.

Figure 8. Freedom of Expression and Alternative Sources of Information Index: Estonia, Russia, Ukraine, and Uzbekistan, 1989–2022

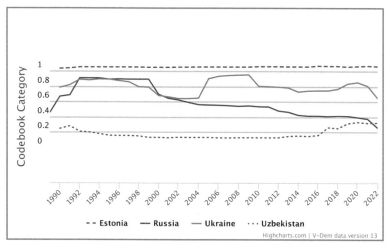

Figure 9. Mobilization for Democracy Index: Estonia, Russia, Ukraine, and Uzbekistan, 1989–2022

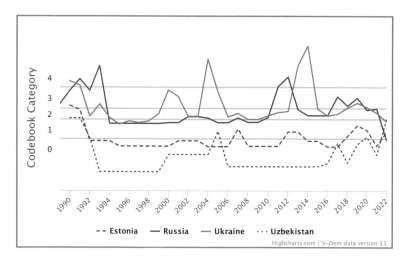

Once the populace was afforded competitive elections, divided branches of government, and freedom of discussion, ideological diversity and citizenship developed through the involvement of citizens in decision-making. It is even possible to speak of a kind of excess of diversity in the 1990s, which at times provoked political escapism or support for reactionary measures by the authorities. However, throughout most of the post-Soviet period, political freedoms remained important for the populations of all the new states and led from time to time to mass movements in support of democracy. For example, the Mobilization for Democracy Index (figure 9) demonstrates that mass movements in support of civil liberties occasionally emerged in all four country cases. Furthermore, pro-democracy mobilizations in support of free and fair elections, independent courts and parliaments, and freedom of association and speech had a common regional rhythm. Regional pro-democratic mobilization peaks are evident in the years 1989–1993, 2004–2008, 2011–2005, and 2018–2020.

Mobilization in support of political freedoms in countries with high levels of democracy (e.g., Estonia) has generally been moderate, as the energy of such movements has been channeled by political institutions into productive decision-making that does not threaten the political order. However, mass pro-democracy movements in the Russian and Uzbekistan autocracies posed a direct threat to their regimes and, to some extent, to their political systems. Ukraine is a case of a hybrid political system (as are Georgia and Moldova, as well as Armenia since 2018) that has experienced periods of improving freedom and periods of democratic decline. Here, pro-democratic mobilizations have engaged citizens in creative political processes, leading to an increase in freedom and a return to the exercise of basic constitutional rights.

In many ways, post-Soviet democratic creativity has been linked to the gradual growth of the role of civil society. The sphere of civil society lies in the public space between the private and public spheres, or, as Cohen and Arato (1994) have conceptualized it, in cooperation with and opposition to both "political society," driven by the struggle for power, and "economic society," structured by competition for profit. In this framework, civil society is a set of associations of citizens (interest groups, activist groups, trade unions, religious organizations engaged in social or political activities, social movements, professional associations, charities, etc.) formed to pursue collective interests and ideals related to both power and economic goals.

Civil society organizations can be divided into two broad categories, traditional and modern. Traditional organizations include territorial and religious communities and small ethnic communities associated with sociopolitical interests, while modern organizations include nongovernmental and nonprofit organizations (NGOs, NPOs), trade unions, and charitable foundations. In the post-Soviet period, CSOs from both categories experienced a renaissance, contributing to the building of horizontal social structures and creating a public demand for freedom of conscience and religion, as well as for the systemic participation of active citizens in control over state authorities. Specifically, citizens sought oversight of the implementation of laws and procedures by parliaments and governments, as well as oversight of electoral committees and bodies responsible for the use of budgetary funds, the penitentiary system, and media licensing. In most cases it was NGOs or NPOs that were engaged in such oversight. However, charitable foundations, trade unions, and informal activist groups also pursued many socially relevant public interests, such as support for the poor, workers' rights, wildlife protection, and the fight against alcoholism and drug abuse.

The Core Civil Society Index demonstrates the path of post-Soviet democratization through the lens of the sustainability of civil society and its influence on the public and private spheres (V-Dem, 2023a).

Figure 10. Core Civil Society Index: Estonia, Russia, Ukraine, and Uzbekistan, 1989–2022

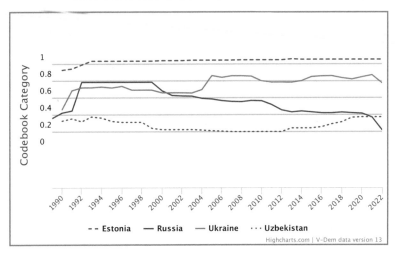

According to figure 10, in all four countries considered, the influence of CSOs has been growing since 1989, but as early as 1991–1993 some differences were evident among these societies. In the Estonian case of a stable democracy strongly influenced by European institutions, the influence of civil society has been high and stable. In Uzbekistan, with a stable autocracy, civil society has been under constant pressure from the government but has found some openings to exert influence during moments when one autocrat is replaced by another. The cases of the Russian Federation and Ukraine show democratization to be accompanied by an increase in the influence of CSOs, with these organizations losing their significance in periods of democratic decline.

The importance of civic organizations in post-Soviet societies is associated with a peculiar dialogue between the political creativity of local communities, the Soviet experience, and Western models. For example, local communities and trade unions in the post-Soviet period often tried to apply the Soviet experience to the new political and socioeconomic realities and therefore remained only minor actors in the post-Soviet democratization. At the same time, NGOs and NPOs as a specific organizational and cultural form were not connected with the Soviet experience: they were the result of applying a Western model of civic organizations that included a division between governing and administrative functions, funding through grants, and public accountability. Successful NGOs and NPOs could develop their sources of funding, as well as increase their degree of influence on governments, from either inside or outside the country of origin.[101] In some cases, NGOs could develop to the point of becoming "NGO-crats," exclusive influential groups able to operate beyond the boundary of their legitimate sphere in civil society (Lutsevych, 2013, pp. 3ff.). Oligarchic clans often used this device, actively developing groups that imitated CSOs, such as charitable foundations, analytical centers, and other NPOs (Minakov, 2019b; Puglisi, 2003). In periods of democratic decline or autocratic turns, as in Uzbekistan since the mid-1990s or Russia since 2011, respectively, NGOs and NPOs have been systematically suppressed (Gilbert & Mohseni, 2018; Heiss, 2019).

In sum, with respect to democratic political creativity, the post-Soviet period was a time for all the societies in the region to experience

---

101   In the last thirty years, an entire infrastructure has been created to support post-Soviet CSOs in the west, and then in the east, of the region. International and state organizations such as the United Nations Development Program, the World Bank, USAID, the Canadian Development Agency (CIDA), the British Council, the Swedish Development Agency (SIDA), the Turkish Cooperation and Coordination Agency (TIKA), and many others have shared project and organizational culture and provided rich funding for NGOs and NPOs in Belarus, Russia, Uzbekistan, Ukraine, and other post-Soviet countries since the 1990s. Also active in the region were private foundations (e.g., the network of foundations of the Open Society Institute founded by George Soros) and special intermediary organizations (e.g., the Eurasia Foundation, Chemonics) between Western governments and local organizations. Such cooperation was legitimized by a number of intergovernmental cooperation and development treaties in the early 1990s, but later it went far beyond these agreements. In periods of democratization, this cooperation was not opposed by governments, but in moments of autocratization, the ruling elites of post-Soviet regimes imposed restrictions on external funding for CSOs. Examples of the latter are the banning policies in Tajikistan and Uzbekistan in 1998–2001 or the crackdown on "foreign agents" in Russia, which began in 2012–2013 and peaked in 2019–2023. In post-Soviet countries, political beliefs have also spread the view that many NGOs and NPOs serve the interests of their donors rather than of the recipient societies. On this, see Atlani-Duault (2008), Hemment (2012), Kudlenko (2015), Silitski (2010), Sundstrom (2006), and Uhlin (2006).

freedom, even though for some of them it was not a lasting experience. Several generations of people living in the Eastern European and northern Eurasian countries were able to realize their potential for building institutions of political freedom. The outcomes of post-Soviet democratic creativity included (1) new states with separate branches of government, (2) political and legal systems based on or aiming at the rule of law, (3) strong parliaments elected in competitive elections, with more than half of the voters routinely participating in voting, (4) courts much more autonomous than in the Soviet era, (5) multiparty systems with reasonably robust ideological pluralism, (6) free media, and (7) a powerful civil society. For most of the post-Soviet period, political freedom and democracy have inspired individuals, small groups, and entire societies of the region to actively engage in entrenching institutions and practices of political freedom that draw on local and Western experience.

All of these outcomes are of a democratic nature, and they attest that the post-Soviet period was a time of democratization that enriched the political experience of Eastern European and northern Eurasian societies. Still, the depth of this democratic experience has varied from nation to nation. In some cases (Azerbaijan, Armenia before 2018, the Central Asian states apart from Kyrgyzstan), democratization was a short-lived trend with few lasting outcomes. Kyrgyzstan represents the case of a country where democratic and autocratic elements are in constant conflict, not allowing the political system to institutionalize enough to produce a stable regime. In Belarus and Russia, democratization proved to be a somewhat longer-lived process, but it was still ultimately overcome by authoritarian leaders. Nevertheless, the democratic experience of these nations has left an important trace in their political cultures that may be used for new democracy-building efforts in the future. Georgia, Moldova, and Ukraine are unstable polyarchies with a rich experience in both democratic and oligarchic events, along with some autocratic ones, and with a strong interest in European integration, which may ultimately improve the democratic quality of their political and legal systems. After a radical regime change in 2018, Armenia seems to have joined the group of unstable polyarchies. Finally, Estonia, Latvia, and Lithuania are stable democracies whose membership in the EU and NATO adds to their internal and external stability.

The Autocratic Outcomes of Post-Soviet Political Creativity

The post-Soviet period was a heyday of flourishing political creativity, only partly represented by the impulse toward democracy. It was also a period when many individuals and communities directed their creative capacity toward institutions and practices that were distant from or openly hostile to democracy and political liberty.

In the previous section I demonstrated the politically creative post-Soviet process of transforming the political structures of the late Soviet Union into democratic institutions and elements of political systems. The task of this section, in contrast, is to demonstrate how that same political creativity was invested in outcomes of an autocratic nature. Achievements of this kind were linked to collective action shaped by priorities very different from attaining political freedom, the rule of law, or civic emancipation. As a rule, these priorities were related to the survival strategies of individuals, families, and communities under the worst conditions of the deep socioeconomic crisis of the 1990s, which drove post-Soviet societies exactly into a state of what Panina and Golovakha rightly called "social madness" (1994, p. 8). The founders of post-Soviet states were acting under conditions of complete unpredictability and institutional chaos in 1991–1994. Their political will and imagination, when linked to the ideas, models, and practices of the post-Soviet tetrad, led to democratic transformations, as discussed earlier. However, the founders of today's Estonia and Russia, Ukraine, and Uzbekistan witnessed not only democratic enthusiasm in the capitals but also depression on the peripheries, the spread of ideas of national exclusivity and xenophobia among both elites and masses, the rapid and severe impoverishment of those who had but recently been considered Soviet middle class, waves of criminal revolution, and the war of all against all in times of primary capital accumulation (Kupatadze, 2012; Pain, 2007; Round & Williams, 2010;

Shnirelman, 2023). Under these conditions, all the prerequisites for creativity hostile to freedom and to those who promoted it were in place.

Figure 11. GDP Per Capita (Purchasing Power Parity): Estonia, Russia, Ukraine, and Uzbekistan, 1990–2022

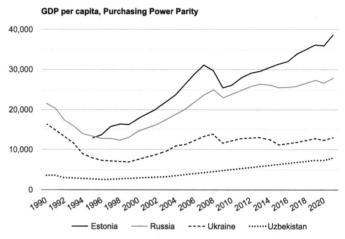

GDP per capita, Purchasing Power Parity

—— Estonia   —— Russia   - - - - Ukraine   ·······Uzbekistan

Measure: U.S. dollars
Source: The World Bank

At the end of the twentieth century, many regions of the world found themselves living under conditions of a "risk society," that is, a society increasingly preoccupied with the future as a source of risks, threats, hazards, and insecurities "induced and introduced by modernization itself" (Beck, 1992, p. 21). But the post-Soviet societies, whose economies had survived years of hyperinflation and annual degrowth of up to 20 percent between 1990 and 1996, experienced the trauma of living in "super-risk societies" (Adam et al., 2000; Beck, 1992).[102] A dramatic drop in the quality of life and a lack of social and even existential security forced a huge portion of the new societies to invest their creative potential in survival and the quest for security at any price (see figures 11 and 12 for 1990–2000).

---

102 On hyperinflation and degrowth, see figure 11; compare with data on the socioeconomic crisis in Åslund (2013, pp. 22ff).

Figure 12. Homicides per 100,000 Population: Estonia, Russia, Ukraine, and Uzbekistan, 1990–2022

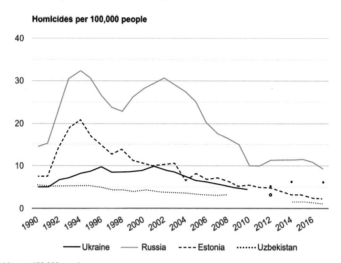

Measure: homicides per 100,000 people
Source: The UN office on drugs and crime

The rapid transition from Soviet predictability to post-Soviet revolutionary chaos was both an opportunity and a challenge for the more than 285 million people whose destiny was defined by the post-Soviet transition. The 1989–1991 caesura broke with Soviet continuity and opened up possibilities for seeding new social worlds. These opportunities and challenges allowed an exit from the traumatic Soviet state, but this exit was no less traumatic in itself. Post-Soviet political creativity was defined not only by the contradictory and painful set of Soviet ruptures that had been spelled out in the perestroika discussions and found their way to realization in the national and democratic movements of that caesura; it was also defined by a new, post-Soviet trauma. The horror of the world that opened up after the end of Alexei Yurchak's "Soviet eternity" created a peculiar demand not only for democracy but also for dictatorship (Yurchak, 2013). The anthropocultural type of the Soviet Man was not ready for the test of freedom and risk, turning rather quickly into a sort of post-Soviet consumer of dictatorship services designed to protect people from their own sins and from crime while enabling participation in ethnic conflicts, religious radicalism, and social atomization (Gudkov, 2022; Levada, 2000). Significant social groups demanded paternalistic tutelage and paternal care from post-Soviet governments and were willing to give up their unexpected freedom in exchange.

Unified Supreme Power and Neopatrimonial Rule

Perhaps the most notable act of authoritarian creativity was the invisible adjustment of state building in those countries where democrats and nationalists were still powerful in the mid-1990s. The division of the branches of power, along with the gradual separation of authority between central and local governments, was an important element of democratic creativity. But its counterpart was autocratic creativity, which invested enormous social energy in informal institutions and practices. The nexus of democratization and marketization gave birth to so-called "small government." This neoliberal model took on its own twist in the post-Soviet context. Indeed, post-Soviet states not only lost the unity of supreme statal power but also radically reduced their own role in the economy, culture, society, and other spheres (Collier, 2011). The state remained an important player in the public sphere, but even there it was not the only one. And in the private sphere the state disappeared, which totally changed the familiar political and cultural landscape of Eastern Europe and northern Eurasia in the twentieth century.

The early post-Soviet small government resulted in a power vacuum, which was filled by informal structures, which later came to be referred to in the academic literature as oligarchic clans, neopatrimonial networks, patronal pyramids, or mafia state organizations.[103] These structures returned some stability and efficiency to the post-Soviet political order amid the social chaos—the by-product of democratic creativity—of the time. The emerging post-Soviet governmental political institutions needed a social anchor, which often took the form of clanlike groups whose solidarity was based on informal personal relationships, connections that had more

---

103 Once again, for more on this, see Fisun (2012), Hale (2014), Ledeneva (1998), and Magyar (2016).

power and weight than formal authority. Relationships between formal and informal institutions can be divided into two types: those that are and those that are not effective in fulfilling the formal institutions' functions and goals. When formal and informal institutions interact, they can increase the effectiveness of the formal institutions—or they can oppose each other, undermining each other's effectiveness and leading to mutual destruction. There is also a third possibility: if the informal institutions are more effective than the formal ones, the informal institutions can subordinate the formal structures to their own interests.[104] Nations where this happens end up in a situation of "grand" or "systemic" corruption.[105] These structures returned some stability and efficiency to the post-Soviet political order in the face of social chaos.

A dominance of informal structures over formal public institutions, however, undermines the effectiveness of democracy and the rule of law. In countries where informal structures have established such dominance, they have turned the state into a hybrid combining a democratic façade with a "deep" or "shadow" state. The institutions and organizations making up this deep or shadow state are like clans in that they exhibit a personalistic logic of relationships and trust based on the experience of joint illegal actions. Clans are informal, stable organizations that cross the boundaries of the branches of power with respect to their responsibilities, creating parallel worlds of power, the power verticals, that include representatives of presidential administrations, cabinets, parliaments, courts, regional and local self-governments, media, criminal groups, and CSOs.[106] In the post-Soviet context, clans united strong, creative individuals, who used the chaos of the 1990s not only for survival but also for personal enrichment, which stemmed from the subordination of streams from the state budget, privatization of the Soviet industrial heritage, and privatization of post-Soviet formal institutions.

---

104 For more on this matrix of interactions between formal and informal institutions, see Helmke and Levitsky (2004, pp. 728–729).
105 For more on these terms, see ECA (2021) and Lough (2021).
106 For more on this, see Minakov (2019b).

In some cases, post-Soviet autocratization went the way not of open dictatorship but of oligarchy. As figures 6 and 7 show, in the Ukrainian and Russian cases, oligarchization, that is, the establishment of clan control over key public institutions for the benefit of several individuals (oligarchs), peaked in influence at the end of the 1990s and triggered the decline of democracy and the start of an autocratic trend. Once state structures had fallen under the influence of several clans, these groups, organized as patronal pyramids, began to struggle for dominance in the country, that is, for the establishment of one-pyramid rule, leading to full-fledged autocracy. For post-Soviet societies that had made real progress toward democratization but had not received the kind of strong external support from European and Euro-Atlantic structures that characterized the Estonian case, autocratization via oligarchization had become a common trend by the early twenty-first century.

The mass protests of the color revolutions, however, brought to a halt some of the region's autocratization. In 2003–2005, differences crystallized in the region of Eastern Europe and northern Eurasia between stable liberal democracies (Estonia, Latvia, and Lithuania); unstable polyarchies, in which periods of democratization were succeeded by periods of democratic decline and autocracy and vice versa (Ukraine, Georgia, and Moldova); and stable autocracies (Russia, Azerbaijan, Belarus, and four Central Asian countries).[107]

Azerbaijan and the Central Asian countries had already established autocracies by 1995, instituting tight control over any political creativity in their populations. Here the democratic, ethnonationalist, and Islamist impulses yielded to dictatorships of varying severity, from the enlightened authoritarianism of Nursultan Nazarbayev and Heydar Aliyev to the totalitarian rule of Saparmurat Niyazov.[108] The personalist regimes of these countries drew the

---

107 Armenia and Kyrgyzstan fall outside this classification. Armenia moved from the camp of autocracies to that of unstable polyarchies in 2018. Kyrgyzstan is an unstable autocracy where mass protests have led to several regime changes but have not affected the political system or form of governance.

108 Heydar Aliyev (1923–2003) was a Soviet and Azerbaijani politician who served as president of Azerbaijan from 1993 through 2003. During this time he ended

energies of the post-Soviet peoples into the rapid adaptation of Soviet authoritarian institutions to new national institutions. They used the logic of a "vertical social contract" that offered the population real stability in the political order in exchange for ephemeral rights and freedoms.

The authoritarian regimes of Aliaksandr Lukashenka and Vladimir Putin were established somewhat later, when Belarusians and Russians had already had their experience of democracy and the market economy, at least in the form that those took in the 1990s. As early as 2001–2003, Lukashenka used the Belarusian population's reaction to democratization, marketization, and nationalization to reshape democratizing Belarus into an autocratic political system, which prevented the emergence of oligarchic clans there. In Belarus, state building proceeded quickly and efficiently within the framework of the personalistic authoritarian regime, significantly overtaking nation building and preventing the formation of informal power structures — except for Lukashenka's own family clan.

At the same time, the Putin regime emerged as an authoritarian reaction to both democratization and oligarchization. Putin's social contract of the early 2000s offered Russians a socially conservative world based on significant restrictions on the political freedoms of citizens and oligarchs in exchange for significant household income and the physical protection of citizens from crime and war (see figures 11 and 12 for Russia in 2000–2008). Putin's patronal pyramid either absorbed or destroyed the oligarchic clans. After the demonstrative anti-oligarchy crackdown of 2003–2006, the Russian oligarchs lost their political status.[109]

---

the civil war in the country and established a dynastic rule that was continued by his son, Ilham Aliyev (b. 1961), president since 2003. Saparmurat Niyazov (1940–2006) was a Soviet and Turkmen politician who ruled from 1990 through 2006 and established the harshest dictatorial, arguably totalitarian, regime among all post-Soviet autocracies.

109 With the outbreak of the war against Ukraine, Putin's regime lost the ability to provide income and physical security for its citizens. The "Crimean syndrome," the rise of imperial patriotism among Russians after the annexation of Crimea, briefly legitimized Putin's regime in 2014, but economic hardships since 2015 and military failures in 2022 have dried up this source of legitimacy for the Russian government as well.

Autocratic creativity thus aimed either at preventing the division of supreme state power or at undermining the institutions that provided the system of checks and balances for such a division. The ideal institution for the fulfillment of this trend was presidentialism. The post-Soviet presidency that was invented by Gorbachev in his struggle with the CPSU Central Committee was perfected in the early 1990s by the presidents of the Soviet republics and became a source of constant threat to political freedoms and of growing hope for a return to a state with a single supreme power (Minakov & Mylovanov, 2016; Partlett, 2018). In reinventing the effective state, the political creativity of the Eastern European and northern Eurasian peoples often reproduced the old model of the one, indivisible supreme power as the common political heritage of post-Soviet societies (Pomeranz, 2016, pp. 1ff).

It is hard to deny the fact that our research tools are imperfect, since they come from an interest in democracy and are mainly aimed at determining its quality. But the success of authoritarian creativity can also be measured, for example, by the way in which it developed as a neopatrimonial rule (figure 13) and influences the autonomy of other branches of government, especially the judiciary (figures 2 and 4).

The Index of Neopatrimonialism Rule indicates the extent to which governance in a given country is based on the personal authority of the ruler. Neopatrimonialism rule reflects the idea that personalistic forms of authority pervade formal institutions in a regime that combines patronal political relations, unrestricted presidentialism, and the use of state resources for its political legitimation (V-Dem, 2023a; compare Clapham, 1985, and Fisun, 2012). The index is constructed by summarizing sixteen indicators assessing patronalism/clientelism, presidentialism, and regime corruption. Low scores in figure 13 indicate a more democratic situation, while higher scores indicate a less democratic one.

Figure 13. Neopatrimonialism Rule Index: Estonia, Russia, Ukraine, and Uzbekistan, 1989–2022

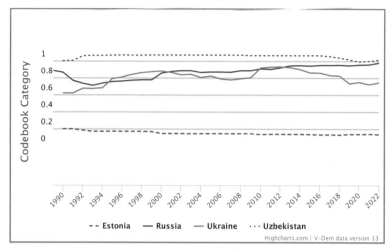

Figure 13 shows that neopatrimonialism rule caused rapid autocratization in Uzbekistan and gradual autocratization in Russia. The democratic outbursts in Ukraine in 2004 and 2014 coincide with the decline of neopatrimonialism, while in the Estonian case this factor is minimal.

Accordingly, figures 2 and 4 show how the legislature and the judiciary maintained their independence from the executive branch. Whereas during periods of democratization, these two branches of government limited the power of the executive branch and the opportunities for corruption of its chiefs and representatives, during periods of autocratization the system of checks and balances disappeared or became dysfunctional. Figure 4 shows that the autonomy of the judiciary in particular has been in crisis since 1992 in Uzbekistan case and since the beginning of the twenty-first century in Russian and Ukraine. According to figure 2, the subordination of the parliament in Uzbekistan also occurred between 1991 and 1994; in Russia, it occurred partly in 1993, and then much more significantly from 2000 on. In Ukraine the Verkhovna Rada experienced a decline in autonomy between 1993 and 2002 and from 2010 to 2014. Only in the Estonian case did the independence

of the legislature and the judiciary remain uninterrupted and un-
challenged from 1992 on.

These data, it seems to me, indicate that after the first successes
of democracy, the political creativity of post-Soviet peoples belonging to the developmental types represented by the Uzbek and Russian cases was redirected in an autocratic direction. In the Ukrainian case, there were also periods marked by the prevalence of autocratic creativity. In other words, the political creativity of many
post-Soviet societies was often redirected toward autocracy. Both
representatives of the power elites and civic activists increasingly
took non- or antidemocratic priorities as the basis for their actions.
This is how a new generation of post-Soviet subjects grew up, sharing the ideals of nationalism, imperialism, and all sorts of conservative reactionary, revolutionary, and neo-Sovietist views. Similarly,
new generations of bureaucrats, politicians, and judges grew up for
whom serving the unlawful state was more important than serving
the public interest, the electorate, or the law.

Post-Soviet Sovereigntism

The legitimation of this type of political creativity was associated
with a conservative turn in post-Soviet societies in the late 1990s.
This turn was fueled by post-Soviet nationalization, which was no
stranger to authoritarian experiments and the *Ostalgie* that was evident in, for example, social choices, when candidates from the KGB
participated in presidential elections and received a considerable
percentage of the votes.[110] Furthermore, even if the number of
NGOs and NPOs was on the rise, these organizations were often
driven by antidemocratic, militaristic, and authoritarian ideas.
While religious freedoms were important for post-Soviet democratization, the development of faith-based organizations and communities gave rise to support for clericalism and the specific

---

110 In 1993, 98 percent of Azerbaijani voters voted for Heydar Aliyev, who was
among the key figures of the late Soviet KGB; in 1999, 8 percent of Ukrainian
voters voted for Yevhen Marchuk, a Ukrainian KGB general; and in 2000, 53
percent of Russian voters voted for Vladimir Putin, who started his career in
the KGB, in Russia. In all three cases, the electoral campaigners drew competitive advantage from their candidate's history of service in the KGB.

ethnonationalization of Christianity (or Islam, or Buddhism). Taken together, these different trends have led to a sovereigntist turn that over the past decade has fused them into a single ideological system in a number of countries (Minakov, 2021a). This kind of sovereigntism has become dominant, for example, in Azerbaijan, Russia, and Uzbekistan. Sovereigntism pitted citizenship and the rule of law against nationality and tradition, offering to overcome liberal-democratic individualism by means of collective allegiance to the state's supreme power.

The influence of sovereigntism extends far beyond post-Soviet autocracies. Over the past ten years, even in the freest post-Soviet societies, there has been an increasing trend away from ideological pluralism and toward the restoration of an ideological monopoly.[111] Countries throughout the region seem to have succumbed to freedom and diversity fatigue, surrendering instead to the temptation of ideological and cultural homogeneity.

This can be seen, for example, in the Ideology Index (figure 14). This index answers the question of the extent to which the government of a given country promotes a certain ideology in order to justify the existing regime (V-Dem, 2023a). The data in figure 14 show that after the deideologization of post-Soviet nations, the resumption of ideological monopoly occurred as early as 1992 in Uzbekistan. In Russian, reideologization began with the rule of Vladimir Putin and reached a significant level by 2012. In the Ukrainian case, attempts to establish an ideological monopoly coincided with the postrevolutionary rule of 2005–2009 and 2014–2018. An ideological monopoly was absent in Estonia throughout the post-Soviet period but seems to have returned after 2014 as a reaction to the Russian invasion of Ukraine.

---

111 See the cases described in Minakov (2022c).

**Figure 14.   Ideology Index: Estonia, Russia, Ukraine, and Uzbek-
istan, 1989–2022**

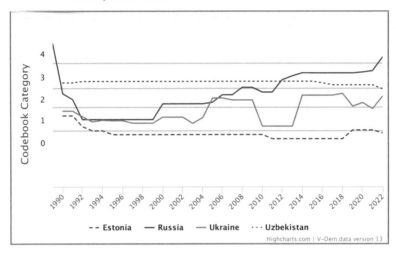

The emerging homogeneity was largely understood through the
logic of historical tradition and rootedness. The ideological doctrines of Saparmurat Niyazov's *Rukhnama*, Islam Karimov's secular
national conservatism, and Vladimir Putin's recent constitutional
reforms are examples of such neotraditionalism.[112] The less accessi-
ble a fair trial in a reasonable time became, the more societies focused on historical justice as its surrogate. The more depressed the
prospects for socioeconomic development became, the more often
there was talk of national memory (Kasianov & Minakov, 2020). In
post-Soviet societies over the last decade, conflict between emerging majorities and internal and external "others" matured, more
and more noticeably seeded and managed by ruling groups

---

112 *Rukhnama* (Book of the Soul) is a two-volume book authored by Saparmurat
Niyazov. The book, it was officially declared, was inspired by Turkmen ancestors urging Niyazov to his compatriots to the "golden path of life." *Rukhnama*
served as a tool of state propaganda and was mandatory reading in schools,
universities, and public organizations during the life of the ruler. Islam Karimov (1938–2016) was a Soviet and Uzbek politician who served as a president
of Uzbekistan from 1990 through 2016. For more on neotradionalism, see Abdullaev (2023), Kiryukhin and Shcherbak (2022), and Zabortseva (2018). See
also the article by Sergei Grigorishin in the same issue of the *Ideology and Politics
Journal* (Grigorishin, 2023).

through the media and mass education. External others were presented as probable (and, with the outbreak of wars, real) enemies, while internal others from the legitimate opposition became potential henchmen of external enemies. Hence the growth of systemic repressions of individuals and groups declared "foreign agents" and "national traitors."

Such acts by autocratic — or autocratizing — authorities were in constant opposition to the norms that remained in constitutions and national legislations from the early 1990s. In 2012–2022, seven of the twelve constitutions and national legislations of the recognized states of Eastern Europe and northern Eurasia (the three Baltic countries excluded) underwent a series of amendments that either repealed the liberal-democratic norms of the early post-Soviet period or diluted them with neotraditionalist and geopolitical language, introducing discord and contradictions into the norms of their legal systems.[113] Only a relatively small proportion of these amendments relied on referendums, while a larger proportion relied on the decisions of governments. However, even the referendum decisions demonstrated that post-Soviet autocracies had learned to use the will of the people and the instruments of direct democracy for their own purposes (Blackburn & Petersson, 2022; Schmäing, 2021).

In addition, the political parties that had blossomed since 1990 around the Eastern European and Northern Eurasian countries were partially transforming from political organizations of active citizens that had coalesced around ideological programs and whose competition was important for democratic politics, the rotation of elites, and ideological diversity into organizations assisting autocrats or oligarchs with managing their countries' counterelites and general populations. By 2022, most post-Soviet societies had witnessed the rise of parties of power or one-leader parties. The parties of power were political organizations of bureaucrats created to ensure executives' control of central parliaments and local councils

---

113 In 2022, the constitution of Kazakhstan underwent the reverse process. But this process was already a sign of the politics characteristic of the caesura of 2022 rather than of the post-Soviet period.

154 THE POST-SOVIET HUMAN

(Ambrosio, 2015, p. 52; Gel'man, 2006, p. 546; Way, 2021, p. 485). Parties like Turkmenistan's Democratic Party, Russia's United Russia, and Ukraine's Our Ukraine and Party of Regions served as additional instruments representing the interests of the president or a small ruling group in parliaments and local councils. They also provided a pool of cadres for autocratic or oligarchic governments, supplying potential functionaries whose loyalty was proved by allegiance to the party in power.

Another non- or antidemocratic transformation of post-Soviet parties was connected with the political organizations created around some popular politicians. These parties would create a team of people who served a popular front-person—Vladimir Zhirinovsky in Russia, Yulia Tymoshenko or Arseniy Yatseniuk in Ukraine, Mikhail Saakashvili in Georgia—in the expectation of being granted high positions in the government upon achieving electoral victory. A party like this would specifically promote elections in order to leverage the leader's popularity for success while using oligarchic support to further increase the leader's popularity. In the postelectoral phase, such parties would serve their sponsors rather than their constituencies. Nevertheless, their constituencies could and did vote for these popular leaders many times over decades despite the usual nonfulfillment of promises. The long-term populist success of Tymoshenko or Zhirinovsky exemplifies this pattern (Minakov, 2019c, pp. 92ff.; Reuter, 2017, pp. 33ff.). The non- or antidemocratic transformation of post-Soviet political regimes and systems abused the diversity of parties to bring politically active citizens under greater control and channel their creativity toward autocratic outcomes.

The Autocratic Effects of War

But the strongest influence on autocratic creativity stemmed from war—or the threat thereof. Civil wars (as, for example, in Georgia and Azerbaijan from 1991–1993, in Tajikistan from 1992–1997, and in the North Caucasus from 1994 to 2002) channeled human creativity in an autocratic direction. As a result, the civil conflict in Azerbaijan led to the establishment of the dynastic rule of the

Aliyevs (Sultanova, 2014). The war between different groups of citizens in Georgia, with significant Russian intervention, led to a long delay in Georgia's democratization and economic development, while the legitimate government lost control over part of the country to the Abkhaz and Ossetian separatists (Wheatley, 2017). The Chechen wars halted the democratization of Russia as a whole, led to an accelerated demodernization of communities in the North Caucasus, and established some of the conditions for Putin's rise to power (Tishkov, 2004; Treisman, 2011). Internal military conflicts have been highly influential factors limiting democratization and supporting autocratic creativity.

International warfare in the post-Soviet period, such as that between Georgia and Russia in 2008 or that between Russia and Ukraine beginning in 2014, was no less influential for the depth and speed of autocratization. Losing the war with Russia reinforced authoritarian tendencies in Georgia during the tenure of Mikhail Saakashvili from 2003 to 2013 (Way, 2016). Winning the war with minimal deterrence from the West led Moscow to believe that military operations in the post-Soviet space were quite legitimate, or at least would not be opposed, paving the way for the illegal annexation of Crimea, support in 2014 for pro-Russian secessionism and irredentism in Ukraine, and the start of a full-scale invasion in 2022 (Kuzio, 2022). The post-Soviet region entered the stage of military conflict in 2008, after the Russo-Georgian War, which led to the creation of an entire authoritarian belt in the region (Minakov, 2019a). The presence of hostile ethnic or ideological groups, peoples, and geopolitical blocs created the preconditions for the formation of images of the enemy that could be used to direct the political creativity of post-Soviet societies toward autocratic outcomes.

To summarize, the post-Soviet period can only partially be associated with democratic creativity; autocratic creativity was no less significant during this time. This is confirmed by the Mobilization for Autocracy Index (figure 15). This index assesses the frequency and size at a given time of events of mass mobilization for pro-autocratic aims. Events are considered to be pro-autocracy if they are clearly organized in support of undemocratic forms of government or in support of leaders who question the basic principles of democracy, or if they generally aim to undermine democratic ideas and institutions, such as the rule of law, free and fair elections, or freedom of the press (V-Dem, 2023a).

Figure 15. Mobilization for Autocracy Index: Estonia, Russia, Ukraine, and Uzbekistan, 1989–2022

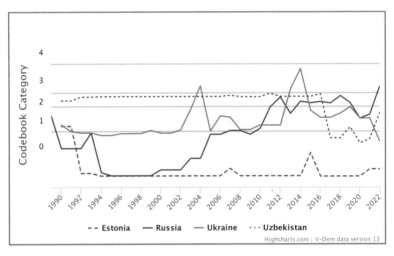

Figure 15 allows us to see in comparative perspective how, when, and with what regularity the waves of mass movements in support of autocracy have swept through the post-Soviet countries. Accordingly, the Uzbekistan case shows a long-standing high level of pro-autocratic mobilization, which decreased in 2016 with the change in regime and the growth of some civic freedoms. The Estonian case shows three sporadic bursts of pro-autocratic mobilization linked to the socioeconomic crisis of 2007–2008, the annexation of Crimea and the start of the Donbas war in 2014–2016, and Russia's attack on Ukraine in 2022. Even in a stable democracy, war provokes pro-autocratic mobilization. The Russian case shows a small surge in mobilization at the beginning of the First Chechen War, then again with the beginning of the Second Chechen War and Putin's regime, and ultimately a significant, permanent increase in the index with the reaction to the color revolutions, peaking with the annexation of Crimea. Finally, in Ukraine, pro-autocratic mobilization was associated with the camp opposing the 2004 Orange Revolution, reactions to the Euromaidan and the annexation of Crimea, and finally the 2017–2018 shift of the Poroshenko regime into a national-conservative stage. As a rule, in this type of states, pro-autocratic waves were replaced by pro-democratic waves, and the fruits of autocratic creativity were undermined by the achievements of democratic creativity, and vice versa. In such shifts, any formal institutions became particularly fragile, open to the influence of informal groups from both inside and outside.

Thus, post-Soviet autocratic creativity and its outcomes were comparable to the region's democratic creativity in the same period. The lives of several generations of people living in Eastern Europe and northern Eurasia between 1989 and 2022 have been invested in autocratic outcomes as well as in democratic ones. These autocratic outcomes include, first of all, the subordination of formal state institutions to the interests of stable, informal groups (clans, neopatrimonial networks, and mafia state structures). Another autocratic achievement is the post-Soviet presidentialism, able to transform the civil liberties achieved in the early 1990s into structures of systemic subjection. Also, the fact that parliaments and courts were able to combine formal autonomy with full or partial subordination of their decision-making processes to presidents or oligarchic clan signifies the autocratic impact on how power is distributed to different branches of government. Among the autocratic achievements, there were the ideological monopolies that ascribed a positive meaning to restricting civil liberties and involving citizens in military conflicts. Finally, the transformation of the post-Soviet region into a region of wars supported the demand for military-style leadership and a disciplined society with loyal citizenry.

From the autocratic perspective, the post-Soviet nations can be divided into the following groups. The stable autocracies of Azerbaijan, Belarus, Kazakhstan, Russia, Tajikistan, Turkmenistan, and Uzbekistan based their rule on all five autocratic outcomes, which has allowed them to undermine the democratic achievements of the early 1990s. The polyarchies of Armenia, Georgia, Kyrgyzstan, Moldova, and Ukraine might have gone through periods of autocratization or democratization but have been able to preserve a formal or informal system of checks and balances and to increase cooperation with the EU (with the exception of Kyrgyzstan, whose geographic position does not allow for strong Western influence). The three Baltic countries have political and legal systems that do not allow strong pro-autocracy mobilization. However, ideological monopolies or war-related illiberal practices may yet come to influence their political and legal systems.

Conclusion

The post-Soviet period was in its own way an unprecedented era in human history. Its uniqueness lies not only in the fact that the caesura of 1989–1991 and the 1991 Revolution opened up opportunities for the peoples of Eastern Europe and northern Eurasia to experience freedom and test their creative powers but also in the fact that these opportunities did not extract a price in life or death comparable to the cost in human lives of the Russian revolution and the Civil War of 1917–1924. Attempts at building national republics and just social systems subsequent to those conflicts were paid for in the coin of millions of lives lost in the continued violence of World War I and the "class struggle," and in the establishment of a long-lived Soviet totalitarian system. The post-Soviet attempts at establishing free politics and economy have led to the sacrifice of tens of thousands killed in interethnic clashes and the criminal revolution of the early 1990s, as well as in the upended lives of several million forced migrants. But we must not forget that those who survived the Soviet system were given opportunities that their ancestors were deprived of in the early 1920s, for Post-Soviet Humans gained collective emancipation and personal freedom, a minimally invasive state (at least in the 1990s to early 2000s), and the real possibility of taking charge of their lives.

Post-Soviet Humans have lived through this era without meeting expectations — of their own, their parents', or those of their contemporaries in other parts of the world. It is hard not to agree with Vladimir Sorokin that the Post-Soviet Human has disappointed even more than the Soviet Man (Sorokin, 2015). *Homo sovieticus* was horrifying in its selflessness and cruelty to others as it strived to fulfill the Communist utopian project. Post-Soviet Humans, on the other hand, disappointed much more by failing to fulfill their historic mission of a titanic self-overcoming — overcoming the Soviet legacy. Although the dashing — as well as free and daring — 1990s offered every opportunity for Promethean achievements, the Post-Soviet Human too often succumbed to the simple pleasures of opportunism, the terror of the possibilities of freedom, the instincts of conflictual individualism, the temptations of consumer capitalism, and the lures of postmodern decadence. Political creativity under such conditions was increasingly fitful, inconsistent, and unsophisticated, and the results were a fragile freedom and sturdy subjugation. The authoritarian tendency seems to have prevailed in the political creativity of Post-Soviet Humans.

Looking back from the 2022 caesura, it becomes piercingly clear: post-Soviet societies have failed to travel the path of emancipation and to break out of the historical rut of imperialism and colonialism. Russian citizens have betrayed their federation as a guiding idea, a republican model, and an emancipative practice of the early 1990s. Other post-Soviet nations have not been able to break out of the colonial imagination and to present their successful collective sociopolitical projects to the world, preferring to choose between the peripheries of warring geopolitical cores.

The mainstream processes of the post-Soviet tetrad largely faded away as the growing contradictions they exposed ceased to be a source of creative energy for achieving the transition and its goals. Democratization hampered the effectiveness of state institutions, and governments eventually began to perceive the political freedoms of citizens as a challenge to their own security. Authoritarian tendencies were born out of both the failures of democratic experiments and the traditional temptations of subordination. Only at the beginning did the nationalization of the new states proceed in alliance with the development of democracy. The thirst for unification of a population's diversity that the post-Soviet leviathans inherited from the Soviet Union reinforced the inequalities that the new market economies produced. The post-Soviet traumatic knot was tightened by freedom, which was increasingly torn between law and corruption. In the tangle of these conflicting tendencies, Europeanization, which for a time supported increased civil rights and freedoms within political systems, legal and economic integration, and peace among the peoples of the region, soon became an additional factor contributing to regional fragmentation. One Big Europe and its constituent countries underwent a tragic transition, which started on the Dublin-Vladivostok axis but somewhere along the way jumped the track to the Belfast-Magadan axis, a radically alternative pair of symbolic poles of Europe that stretch from eth-noreligiously conflictogenic Ulster to the gulag's Kolyma.

History does try to teach, but it has few students. In this book, I have highlighted only some of the lessons of post-Soviet history — only those that I have been able to identify to date. There is still time to study this era, not just out of academic interest but also for entirely pragmatic reasons. For the sake of the future, which will inevitably come after the Russian-Ukrainian war and the current caesura end, it is necessary to figure out how to put the region's leviathans on the chain of the rule of law, ensure the stability of political and legal systems that respect the divided branches of power, minimize the malignancy of the resulting socioeconomic systems, and build an infrastructure of peace among the peoples of Europe and Eurasia. We must be willing to work through our post-Soviet traumatic experience and be able to undertake many deconstructions — de-Putinization (as well as de-Lukashevization and the like), denuclearization, war crimes tribunals, and the rejection of imperialism and ethnonationalism. The new, post-post-Soviet republics, once under new geopolitical conditions and with little connection to the Soviet experience, will be able to cope with the imperial-colonial ruts and clan structures of their systems and lifeworlds only if they take into account the lessons of post-Soviet history.

Without learning the lessons of our recent history, we are doomed to perpetually go in circles repeating it: from revolutionary traumas to Bolshevik-style experiments, to Stalinist thermidors, to fragile thaws, to Brezhnevite stagnation, to new futile revolutions. This endless spinning undermines and destroys creative achievement. This abortive reversibility indeed characterizes the history of modernity in Eastern Europe and northern Eurasia. But our modernity is also characterized by critical rationality, solidarity, and dedication to the common good. And it is the choice of each human being how to be and who to be, and thus to determine what the world of our presence and becoming will be like after the current caesura ends.

Bibliography

Abdullaev, N., & Saradzhayan, S. (2006). The trade-offs between security and civil liberties in Russia's war on terror: The regional dimension. *Demokratizatsiya, 14*(3), 361–406.

Abdullaev, Y. (2023). Philosophy in post-Soviet Uzbekistan. In M. Minakov (ed.), *Philosophy unchained: Developments in post-Soviet philosophical thought* (pp. 232–242). Stuttgart: ibidem.

Adam, B., Van Loon, J., & Beck, U. (2000). *The risk society and beyond.* London: Sage.

Adorno, T. (1968). Sociology and psychology II. *New Left Review, 47*(1), 79–97.

Ágh, A. (2022). The third wave of autocratization in East-Central Europe. *Journal of Comparative Politics, 15*(2), 72–87.

Ambrosio, T. (2015). Leadership succession in Kazakhstan and Uzbekistan: Regime survival after Nazarbayev and Karimov. *Journal of Balkan and Near Eastern Studies, 17*(1), 49–67.

Antonenko, O. (2008). A war with no winners. *Survival, 50*(5), 23–36.

Antonov, M. (2021). Legal positivism and problems of development of Russian law. *Ideology and Politics Journal, 2*(18), 120–151.

Antonov, M., & Vovk, D. (2021). Soviet and post-Soviet law: Failed transition from socialist legality to rule of law. *Ideology and Politics Journal, 18*(2), 4–9.

Appolonov, A. (2015). Neozhidannye prikljuchenija Hajdeggera v Rossii [Unexpected adventures of Heidegger in Russia]. *Logos* (2), 224–232.

Arel, D. (2018). How Ukraine has become more Ukrainian. *Post-Soviet Affairs* (2–3), 186–189.

Arendt, H. (2006). *On revolution.* New York: Penguin.

Arrighi, G., Silver, B. J., & Brewer, B. D. (2003). Industrial convergence, globalization, and the persistence of the north-south divide. *Studies in Comparative International Development, 38*(1), 3–31.

Åslund, A. (2013). *How capitalism was built: The transformation of Central and Eastern Europe, Russia, the Caucasus, and Central Asia.* Cambridge: Cambridge University Press.

Atlani-Duault, L. (2008). *Humanitarian aid in post-Soviet countries:* An anthropological perspective. London: Routledge.

Bandelin, O. J. (1998). *Return to NEP: The search for a program and ideological rationale for reform in the Gorbachev years,* 1985–1991. Seattle: University of Washington Press.

Barbott, B., & Eff, H. (2019). The genetic basis of creativity: A multivariate approach. In J. C. Kaufman & R. J. Sternberg (eds.), *The Cambridge handbook of creativity* (pp. 132–147). Cambridge: Cambridge University Press.

Barrett, T. (2021). Oligarchs and judges: The political economy of the courts in post-Soviet unconsolidated democracies. *Ideology and Politics, 18*(2), 260–291.

Barshynova, O., & Martynyuk, O. (2021). Ukrainian art of the independence era: Transitions and aspirations. In M. Minakov, G. Kasianov, & M. Rojansky (eds.), *From "The Ukraine" to Ukraine: A contemporary history* (pp. 134–167). Stuttgart: ibidem.

Bartram, D. (2013). Happiness and "economic migration": A comparison of Eastern European migrants and stayers. *Migration Studies, 1*(2), 156–175.

Bassin, M. (2016). *The Gumilev mystique: Biopolitics, Eurasianism, and the construction of community in modern Russia*. Ithaca: Cornell University Press.

Beacháin, D. Ó., & Polese, F. (eds.). (2010). *The colour revolutions in the former Soviet republics*. London: Routledge.

Beck, U. (1992). From industrial society to the risk society: Questions of survival, social structure and ecological enlightenment. *Theory, Culture & Society, 9*(1), 97–123.

Bell, D. S. (1996). Post-Communism in Western Europe. *Journal of Communist Studies and Transition Politics, 12*(2), 247–52.

Bell, D. S., & Dahrendorf, R. (1989). Wir sollten endlich alle Revisionisten sein. *Die Zeit*, December 29.

Berekashvili, B. (2021). Ideological dialectics of post-Soviet nationalism. *Copernicus Journal of Political Studies*, (2), 73–90.

Blackburn, M., & Petersson, B. (2022). Parade, plebiscite, pandemic: Legitimation efforts in Putin's fourth term. *Post-Soviet Affairs, 38*(4), 293–311.

Bod, R., Kursell, J., Maat, J., & Weststeijn, T. (2016). A new field: History of humanities. *History of Humanities, 1*(1), 1–8.

Brill, S. (2020). *Aristotle on the concept of the shared life*. Oxford: Oxford University Press.

Bromley, R. (1990). A new path to development? The significance and impact of Hernando De Soto's ideas on underdevelopment, production, and reproduction. *Economic Geography, 66*(4), 328–348.

Brown, R. T. (1989). Creativity: What are we to measure? In J. A. Glover, R. R. Ronning, & C. R. Reynolds (eds.), *Handbook of creativity* (pp. 3–33). New York: Springer.

Brubaker, R. (1996). *Nationalism reframed: Nationhood and the national question in the New Europe.* Cambridge: Cambridge University Press.

Brubaker, R. (2011). Nationalizing states revisited: Projects and processes of nationalization in post-Soviet states. *Ethnic and Racial Studies, 34*(11), 1785–1814.

Bugaric, B. (2008). Populism, liberal democracy, and the rule of law in Central and Eastern Europe. *Communist and Post-Communist Studies, 41*(2), 191–203.

Calder, K. E. (1995). *Strategic capitalism.* Princeton: Princeton University Press.

Carothers, T. (2002). The end of the transition paradigm. *Journal of Democracy, 13*(1), 5–21.

Chateaubriand, F. R. (2000 [1838]). *Génie du christianisme.* Paris: Lefèvre-Reprint.

Cheterian, V. (2009). From reform and transition to "coloured revolutions." *Journal of Communist Studies and Transition Politics, 25*(2–3), 136–160.

Clapham, C. S. (1985). *Third world politics: An introduction.* Madison: University of Wisconsin Press.

Cohen, J. L., & Arato, A. (1994). *Civil society and political theory.* Cambridge, MA: MIT Press.

Collier, S. J. (2011). *Post-Soviet social: Neoliberalism, social modernity, biopolitics.* Princeton: Princeton University Press.

Coppieters, B., Huysseune, M., Kovziridze, T., Noutcheva, G., Tocci, N., Emerson, M., & Vahl, M. (2004). *Europeanization and conflict resolution: Case studies from the European periphery,* vol. 3. Brussels: Academia Press.

Corbet, J., & Gummich, A. (1990). *The Soviet Union at the crossroads: Facts and figures on the Soviet republics.* Frankfurt am Main: Deutsche Bank.

Cornell, S. E., & Nilsson, N. (2009). Georgian politics since the August 2008 war. *Demokratizatsiya, 17*(3), 251–277.

de Saint-Laurent, C. (2018). Thinking through time: From collective memories to collective futures. In C. de Saint-Laurent, S. Obradović, & K. R. Carriere (eds.), *Imagining collective futures: Perspectives from social, cultural and political psychology* (pp. 2–13). London: Palgrave Macmillan.

De Waal, T. (2018). Uncertain territory. *New Eastern Europe,* (3–4), 7–14.

Deleuze, G. (1994). *Difference and repetition.* New York: Columbia University Press.

Denisenko, M., Strozza, S., & Light, M. (2020). *Migration from the newly independent states: 25 years after the collapse of the USSR.* Cham, CH: Springer.

Derrida, J. (1978). *Writing and difference*. Chicago: University of Chicago Press.

Dewey, J. (1998 [1935]). *Liberalism and social action*. New York: SUNY Press.

Dewey, J. (2021 [1939]). Creative democracy: The task before us. In *America's public philosopher* (pp. 59–66). New York: Columbia University Press.

Dickey, H., Drinkwater, S., & Shubin, S. (2018). Labour market and social integration of Eastern European migrants in Scotland and Portugal. *Environment and Planning A: Economy and Space*, (6), 1250–1268.

Ditrych, O. (2010). Georgia: A state of flux. *Journal of International Relations and Development*, 13(1), 3–25.

Dryzek, J. S., & Holmes, L. (2002). *Post-communist democratization: Political discourses across thirteen countries*. Cambridge: Cambridge University Press.

Dugin, A. (2002). *Filosofija tradicii* [Philosophy of tradition]. Moskva: Arktogeja.

Dugin, A. (2010). *Martin Hajdegger: filosofija drugogo nachala* [from Rus.: Martin Heidegger: The Philosophy of Another Principle]. Moskva: Arktogeja.

Dugin, A. (2015). *Etnosociologija* [Ethnosociology]. Moskva: Arktogeja.

Dugin, A. (2021). Bol'shaja perezagruzka i Velikoe probuzhdenie [The great reset and greater awakening]. *RIA Novosti*, March 15. https://ria.ru/20210215/perezagruzka-1597564983.html?fbclid=IwAR1m-Hz HPOcoA8YUVjiUX0Lo_fQ6_RzTZINFq9KTMEuOVkZ2ZaqPKAgB Rlo.

ECA (European Court of Auditors). (2021). *Reducing grand corruption in Ukraine: Several EU initiatives, but still insufficient results. A special report*. Brussels: ECA.

Esanu, O. (2013). *Transition in post-Soviet art: The Collective Actions Group before and after 1989*. Budapest: CEU Press.

Etkind, A., & Minakov, M. (2020). Post-Soviet ideological creativity. In A. Etkind & M. Minakov (eds.), *Ideology after union* (pp. 9–18). Stuttgart: ibidem.

Fairbanks, C. H. (1990). The suicide of Soviet communism. *Journal of Democracy*, 2(1), 18–26.

Feist, G. J. (2007). An evolutionary model of artistic and musical creativity. In C. Martindale, P. Locher, & V. M. Petrov (eds.), *Evolutionary and neurocognitive approaches to aesthetics, creativity, and the arts* (pp. 15–30). Amityville: Baywood Publishing.

Fisun, O. (2003). Developing democracy or competitive neopatrimonial-ism? The political regime of Ukraine in comparative perspective. In *Institution building and policy making in Ukraine* (pp. 1–7). Toronto: University of Toronto Press.

Fisun, O. (2012). Rethinking post-Soviet politics from a neopatrimonial perspective. *Demokratizatsiya, 20*(2), 87–96.

Forest, J. (1990). *Religion and the new Russia: The impact of perestroika on the varieties of religious life in the Soviet Union.* New York: Crossroads.

Freeden, M. (1996). *Ideologies and political theory: A conceptual approach.* London: Clarendon Press of Oxford University Press.

Freud, S. (2012 [1927]). *The future of an illusion.* New York: Broadview Press.

Fukuyama, F. (1989). The end of history? *National Interest, 16*(1), 3–18.

Galeotti, M. (2017). *Russian and post-Soviet organized crime.* London: Routledge.

Galvan, D. C., Hattam, V. C., & Berk, G. (2013). Introduction: Beyond dualist social science: The mangle of order and change. In G. Berk, D. C. Galvan, & V. C. Hattam (eds.), *Political creativity: Reconfiguring institutional order and change* (pp. 1–28). Philadelphia: University of Pennsylvania Press.

Gans-Morse, J. (2004). Searching for transitologists. *Post-Soviet Affairs, 20*(4), 320–349.

Gaidar, E. (2022). *Gosudarstvo i evoljucija* [State and evolution]. Moskva: Litres.

Gaidar, E., Mau, V., Sinelnikov-Muryliov, S., & Uliukajev, F. (1998). *Ekonomika perekhodnogo perioda* [the economy of the transition]. Moskva: IEPP.

Gel'man, V. (2003). Post-Soviet transitions and democratization: Towards theory-building. *Democratization, 10*(2), 87–104.

Gel'man, V. (2006). From "feckless pluralism" to "dominant power politics"? The transformation of Russia's party system. *Democratization, 13*(4), 545–561.

Gelashvili, T. (2023). Opportunities matter: The evolution of far-right protest in Georgia. *Europe-Asia Studies, 75*(4), 649–674.

Gibbs, J. (1999). *Gorbachev's glasnost: The Soviet media in the first phase of perestroika.* Austin: University of Texas Press.

Gilbert, L., & Mohseni, P. (2018). Disabling dissent: The colour revolutions, autocratic linkages, and civil society regulations in hybrid regimes. *Contemporary Politics, 24*(4), 454–480.

Gill, G. (1994). *The collapse of a single-party system: The disintegration of the Communist Party of the Soviet Union.* Cambridge: Cambridge University Press.

Glaveanu, V. P., & Kaufman, J. C. (2019). Creativity. A historical perspective. In J. C. Kaufman & R. J. Sternberg (eds.), *The Cambridge handbook of creativity* (pp. 9–26). Cambridge: Cambridge University Press.

Golovakha, E., & Panina, N. (1994). *Social'noe bezumie: Istorija, teorija i sovremennaja praktika* [Social madness: History, theory and practice]. Kyiv: Abris.

Grant, T. (2014). The Budapest Memorandum of 5 December 1994: Political engagement or legal obligation? *Polish Yearbook of International Law, 34*(2,) 89–114.

Grigorishin, S. (2023). Wuquf Yelbasy: Islamic mysticism and Kazakh democracy. *Ideology and Politics Journal, 23*(1), 172–218.

Gudkov, L. (2022). *Vozvratnyj totalitarizm* [fThe returning totalitarianism]. Moscow: Novoe literaturnoe obozrenie.

Guihai, G. (2010). The influence of the collapse of the Soviet Union on China's political choices. In T. P. Bernstein & H.-Y. Li (eds.), *China learns from the Soviet Union, 1949–present* (pp. 505–516).Lexington, MA: Lexington Books. 505–516.

Gunitsky, S. (2018). Democratic waves in historical perspective. *Perspectives on Politics, 16*(3), 634–651.

Gurchiani, K. (2017). How Soviet is the religious revival in Georgia: Tactics in everyday religiosity. *Europe-Asia Studies, 69*(3), 508–531.

Habermas, J. (1981). *Theorie des kommunikativen Handelns. Band 1: Handlungsrationalität und gesellschaftliche Rationalisierung. Band 2: Zur Kritik der funktionalistischen Vernunft.* Frankfurt am Main: Suhrkamp.

Habermas, J. (1991). What does socialism mean today? In R. Blackburn (ed.), *After the fall: The failure of communism and the future of socialism* (pp. 25–46). London: Verso.

Hafso, J. P. (2019). The first major reform: Mikhail Gorbachev's anti-alcohol policies in the 1980s. *Constellations, 11*(1), 332–346.

Haggard, S., & Kaufman, R. (2016). Democratization during the third wave. *Annual Review of Political Science, 19*(2), 125–144.

Hale, H. (2005). Regime cycles: Democracy, autocracy, and revolution in post-Soviet Eurasia. *World Politics, 58*(1), 133–165.

Hale, H. (2011). Formal constitutions in informal politics: Institutions and democratization in post-Soviet Eurasia. *World Politics, 63*(4), 581–617.

Hale, H. (2014). *Patronal politics: Eurasian regime change in comparative perspective.* Cambridge: Cambridge University Press.

Havel, V. (1992). Paradise lost. *New York Review of Books, 39*(7), 4.

Havrylyshyn, O. (2006). *Divergent paths in post-communist transformation.* London: Palgrave Macmillan.

Hegel, G. W. F. (2018 [1807]). *The phenomenology of spirit.* Oxford: Oxford University Press.

Heidegger, M. (2010 [1928]). *Being and time.* New York: SUNY Press.

Heidegger, M. (2014). *Introduction to metaphysics.* New Haven: Yale University Press.

Heiss, A. (2019). NGOs and authoritarianism. In T. Davies (ed.), *Routledge handbook of NGOs and international relations* (pp. 557–572). London: Routledge.

Helmke, G., & Levitsky, S. (2004). Informal institutions and comparative politics: A research agenda. *Perspectives on Politics, 4*(2), 725–740.

Hemment, J. (2012). Nashi, youth voluntarism, and Potemkin NGOs: Making sense of civil society in post-Soviet Russia. *Slavic Review, 71*(2), 234–260.

Honneth, A. (1998). Democracy as reflexive cooperation: John Dewey and the theory of democracy today. *Political Theory, 26*(6), 763–783.

Horowitz, S. (2003). Sources of post-communist democratization. *Nationalities Papers, 31*(2), 119–137.

Horvat, P., & Evans, G. (2011). Age, inequality, and reactions to marketization in post-communist Central and Eastern Europe. *European Sociological Review, 27*(6), 708–727.

Huntington, S. P. (1965). Political development and political decay. *World Politics, 17*(3), 386–430.

Huntington, S. P. (1991). Democracy's third wave. *Journal of Democracy, 2*(2), 12–34.

Huntington, S. P. (1993). *The third wave: Democratization in the late twentieth century.* Norman: University of Oklahoma Press.

Huntington, S. P. (2000). *The clash of civilizations?* (99–118). New York: Palgrave Macmillan.

Huss, O. (2020). *How corruption and anti-corruption policies sustain hybrid regimes.* London: ibidem.

Hutcheson, D. S., & Korosteleva, E. A. (2006). Patterns of participation in post-Soviet politics. *Comparative European Politics, 4*(1), 23–46.

IDEA (International Institute for Democracy and Electoral Assistance). (2023). IDEA Voter Turnout Database. https://www.idea.int/data-tools/data/voter-turnout.

Inglehart, R., & Welzel, C. (2005). *Modernization, cultural change and democracy: The human development sequence.* Cambridge: Cambridge University Press.

Isaev, E. (2020). The militarization of the past in Russian popular historical films. In A. Etkind & M. Minakov (eds.), *Ideology after union* (pp. 237–250). Stuttgart: ibidem.

Isakava, V., & Beumers, B. (2017). Reality excess: Chernukha cinema in the late 1980s. In B. Beumers & E. Zvonkine (eds.), *Ruptures and continuities in Soviet/Russian cinema* (pp. 147–165). New York: Routledge.

Jayatilleka, D. (2014). *The fall of global socialism: A counter-narrative from the south.* Basingstoke: Palgrave Macmillan.

Jeffries, I. (2004). *The countries of the former Soviet Union at the turn of the twenty-first century.* London: Routledge.

Jensen, C. B. (2003). Latour and Pickering: Post-human perspectives on science, becoming, and normativity. In D. J. Haraway, A. Pickering, & B. Latour (eds.), *Chasing technoscience: Matrix for materiality* (pp. 225–244). Bloomington: Indiana University Press.

Joas, H. (1996). *The creativity of action.* Cambridge: Polity Press.

Jonson, L. (2015). *Art and protest in Putin's Russia.* London: Routledge.

Judt, T. (1988). The dilemmas of dissidence: The politics of opposition in east-central Europe. *East European Politics and Societies, 2*(2), 185–240.

Judt, T. (1990). The rediscovery of Central Europe. *Daedalus, 119*(1), 23–54.

Kant, I. (2008 [1795]). *Toward perpetual peace and other writings on politics, peace, and history.* New Haven: Yale University Press.

Kasianov, G. (2008). *Ukraina 1991–2007: Ocherki novejshej istorii* [Ukraine 1991–2007: Notes to the contemporary history]. Kyiv: Nash chas.

Kasianov, G. (2022). *Memory crash: Politics of history in and around Ukraine, 1980s–2010s.* Budapest: CEU Press.

Kasianov, G., & Minakov, M. (2020). The image of "the other" in post-socialist societies. *Ideology and Politics Journal, 16*(2), 3–5.

Kavadze, A. (2018). The contemporary authoritarianism in the Post-Soviet space: Case study of Belarus and Georgia under Saakashvili rule. *Journal of Social Sciences, 7*(2), 7–20.

Keynes, J. M. (2010 [1926]). The end of laissez-faire. In *The Keynes reader* (272–294). London: Palgrave Macmillan.

Khomeini, R. M. M. (2001 [1940]). *Forty hadith.* Tehran and Paris: Creative Space.

Kiryukhin, D., & Shcherbak, S. (2022). The people, values, and the state: How Vladimir Putin's views on ideology evolved. *Studia Politica: Romanian Political Science Review, 22*(1), 43–63.

Kolakowski, L. (1990). Uncertainties of a democratic age. *Journal of Democracy, 1*(1), 47–50.

Köllner, T. (2020). Religiosity in Orthodox Christianity: An anthropological perspective on post-Soviet Russia. In S. Demmrich & U. Riegel (eds.), *Religiosity in East and West: Conceptual and methodological challenges from global and local perspectives* (pp. 121–140). Berlin: Springer Nature.

Kolsto, P. (2018). *Political construction sites: Nation building in Russia and the post-Soviet states*. London: Routledge.

Kordonsky, S. (2000). *Rynki vlasti* [Power markets]. Moscow: OGI.

Korobkov, A., & Zaionchkovskaia, Zh. (2004). The changes in the migration patterns in the Post-Soviet States: The first decade. *Communist and Post-Communist Studies, 37*(4), 481–508.

Kubicek, P. (2009). Problems of post-post-Communism: Ukraine after the Orange Revolution. *Democratization, 16*(2), 323–343.

Kudlenko, A. (2015). From colour revolutions to the Arab Spring: The role of civil society in democracy building and transition processes. *Journal of Contemporary Central and Eastern Europe, 23*(2–3), 167–179.

Kupatadze, A. (2012). *Organized crime, political transitions and state formation in post-Soviet Eurasia*. New York: Springer.

Kutuev, P. (2016). *Transformaciji modernu: Instytuciji, ideji, ideologiji* [Transformations of modernity: Institutions, ideas, ideologies]. Kherson: Gel'vetyka.

Kuzio, T. (2002). History, memory and nation building in the post-Soviet colonial space. *Nationalities Papers, 30*(2), 241–264.

Kuzio, T. (2014). Crime, politics and business in 1990s Ukraine. *Communist and Post-Communist Studies, 47*(2), 195–210.

Kuzio, T. (2022). *Russian nationalism and the Russian-Ukrainian war: Autocracy-orthodoxy-nationality*. London: Routledge.

Labanauskas, L. (2019). Highly skilled migration from Lithuania: A critical overview of the period 1990–2018. *İstanbul University Journal of Sociology, 39*(2), 229–248.

Langenbacher, E., & Shain, Y. (2010). Power and the past: Collective memory and international relations. Washington, DC: Georgetown University Press.

Laruelle, M. (2007). Central Asian labor migrants in Russia: The "diasporization" of the Central Asian states? *China & Eurasia Forum Quarterly, 5*(3), 2–4.

Latour, B. (2007). *Reassembling the social: An introduction to actor-network-theory*. Oxford: Oxford University Press.

Lavrukhin, A. (2016). Hajdegger Dugina i nadezhdy na russkuju konservativnuju revoljuciju. *Russkaja Ideja, 17*(6). https://politconservatism.ru /experiences/hajdegger-dugina-i-nadezhdy-na-russkuyu-konserva tivnuyu-revolyutsiyu.

Ledeneva, A. V. (1998). *Russia's economy of favours: Blat, networking and informal exchange*. Cambridge: Cambridge University Press.

Lenin, V. I. (1974). *Polnoe sobranye sochynenyj* [Complete works], vol. 35. Moskva: GIPL.

Levada, Iu. (2000). The Soviet Man ten years later, 1989–1999: Preliminary findings of comparative research. *Sociological Research, 39*(4), 30–54.

Levitsky, S., & Way, L. A. (2010). *Competitive authoritarianism: Hybrid regimes after the Cold War*. Cambridge: Cambridge University Press, 2010.

Li, Hua-Yu. (2010). Political choices. In T. P. Bernstein (ed.), *China learns from the Soviet Union, 1949–present*. Lanham, MD: Rowman & Littlefield, 505–516.

Libanova, E. (2018). External labor migration of Ukrainians: Scale, causes, consequences. *Demografija ta socialna ekonomika, 2*, 11–26.

Long, D., & Wilson, P. (eds.). (1995). *Thinkers of the twenty years' crisis: Interwar idealism reassessed*. Oxford: Clarendon Press of Oxford University Press.

Lough, J. (2021). *Ukraine's system of crony capitalism. The challenge of dismantling "systema."* London: Chatham House.

Love, J. (ed.). (2017). *Heidegger in Russia and Eastern Europe* (annotated edition). Lanham, MD: Rowman & Littlefield.

Lübbe, H. (1981). *Zwischen Trend und Tradition: Überfordert uns die Gegenwart?* West Berlin: Interform.

Luhmann, N., Baecker, D., & Gilgen, P. (2013). *Introduction to systems theory*. Cambridge: Polity.

Lührmann, A., & Lindberg, S. I. (2019). A third wave of autocratization is here: What is new about it? *Democratization, 26*(7), 1095–1113.

Lutsevych, O. (2013). *How to finish a revolution: Civil society and democracy in Georgia, Moldova and Ukraine*. London: Chatham House.

Magyar, B. (2016). *Post-Communist mafia state*. Budapest: CEU Press.

Magyar, B., & Madlovics, B. (2022). *A concise field guide to post-communist regimes: Actors, institutions, and dynamics*. Budapest: CEU Press.

Magyari, L. (2019). The Romanian patronal system of public corruption. In B. Magyar (ed.), *Stubborn structures: Reconceptualizing post-Communist regimes*. Budapest: CEU Press, 275–319.

Maier, C. S. (1999). *Dissolution: The crisis of communism and the end of East Germany*. Princeton: Princeton University Press.

Mälksoo, M. (2009). The memory politics of becoming European: The East European subalterns and the collective memory of Europe. *European Journal of International Relations, 15*(4), 653–680.

Marat, E. (2009). *Labor migration in Central Asia: Implications of the global economic crisis*. Stockholm: Institute for Security and Development Policy.

March, L. (2002). *The Communist Party in post-Soviet Russia*. Manchester: Manchester University Press.

Marx, K. (2004 [1867]). *Capital: Volume I*. London: Penguin.

Men', A. (1997). *Istoria religii v dvukh knigakh* [History of religion in two volumes]. Moscow: Forum-Press.

Minakov, M. (2012). 'Tsvetnyie revoliutsyi' v postsovetskom mire: Prichiny i posledstviia [Color revolutions in the post-Soviet world: Causes and consequences]. *Obshchaia Tetrad, 12*(2–3), 93–111.

Minakov, M. (2017a). Big Europe's Gap: Dynamic Obstacles for Integration between EU and EAU. In A. Di Gregorio & A. Angeli (eds.), *The Eurasian Economic Union and the European Union: Moving toward a greater understanding* (pp. 45–56).The Hague: Eleven International Publishing.

Minakov, M. (2017b). (Not only) Russian Revolution: Centennial mediations. *Kennan Focus Ukraine*, November 7. https://bit.ly/3ErSFAY.

Minakov, M. (2018). The third sector entering the first: Cooperation and competition of civil society, state and oligarchs after Euromaidan in Ukraine. In R. Marchetti (ed.), *Government-NGOs relationship in Africa, Asia, Europe, and MENA* (pp. 123–143). London: Routledge.

Minakov, M. (2019a). Post-Soviet Eastern Europe: Achievements in post-Soviet development in six Eastern European nations. *Ideology and Politics Journal, 3*(14), 171–193.

Minakov, M. (2019b). Republic of clans: The evolution of the Ukrainian political system. In B. Magyar (ed.), *Stubborn structures: Reconceptualizing post-Communist regimes* (pp. 217–245). Budapest: CEU Press.

Minakov, M. (2019c). Democratisation and Europeanisation in the 21st century Ukraine. In M. Emerson (ed.), *The struggle for good governance in Eastern Europe* (2nd ed., pp. 83–121). Brussels: CEPS.

Minakov, M. (2020a). *Dialektika sovremennosti v vostochnoj Evrope* [Dialectics of modernity in Eastern Europe]. Kyiv: Laurus.

Minakov, M. (2020b). Shades of periphery: A typology of states in new Eastern Europe. In: N. Hayoz, J. Herlth, & J. Richers (eds.), *Centres and peripheries in the post-Soviet space* (pp. 63–102). Berlin: Peter Lang.

Minakov, M. (2021a). The sovereigntist turn: Sovereignty as a contested concept again. *Ideology and Politics Journal, 1*(17) 87–114.

Minakov, M. (2021b). The transition of "transition": Assessing the post-Communist experience and its research. In O. Kushnir & O. Pankieiev (eds.), *Meandering in transition: Thirty years of identity building in post-Communist Europe* (pp. 25–41). Lanham, MD: Rowman & Littlefield.

Minakov, M. (2021c). The world-system and post-Soviet de facto states. In M. Minakov, G. Sasse, & D. Isachenko (eds.), *Post-Soviet secessionism* (pp. 59–88). Stuttgart: ibidem.

Minakov, M. (2022a). Ideological creativity. Introduction into post-Soviet ideological processes. In M. Minakov (ed.), *Inventing majorities: Ideological creativity in post-Soviet societies* (pp. 7–26). Stuttgart: ibidem.

Minakov, M. (2022b). Towards an ontology of the caesura: Reflections on the Russian-Ukrainian war. *Κοινή, 2*(2), 67–79.

Minakov, M. (2022c). The protest movements' opportunities and outcomes: The Euromaidan and the Belarusian protest–2020 compared. *Protest, 1*(2), 272–298.

Minakov, M. (2023). War, de-oligarchization, and the possibility of anti-patronal transformation in Ukraine. In B. Madlovics & B. Magyar (eds.), *Ukraine's patronal democracy and the Russian invasion: The Russia-Ukraine war*, vol. 1 (pp. 141–166). Budapest: CEU Press.

Minakov, M., Isachenko, D., & Sasse, G. (eds.). (2021). *Post-Soviet secessionism, nation-building and state-failure after Communism*. Stuttgart: ibidem.

Minakov, M., & Mylovanov, T. (2016). Why the post-Soviet institution of president is flawed. *Vox Ukraine*, June 6.

Mitchell, L. A. (2012). *The color revolutions*. Philadelphia: University of Pennsylvania Press.

Moghadam, V. M. (1990). *Gender and restructuring: Perestroika, the 1989 revolutions, and women*. Helsinki: United Nations University.

Monaghan, A. (2012). The vertikal: Power and authority in Russia. *International Affairs, 88*(1), 1–16.

Muhametov, R. (2018). Rol' dekommunizacii v politicheskom tranzite gosudarstv Vostochnoj Evropy [The role of decommunization in the political transit of East European states]. *Vestnik Omskogo universiteta. Istoricheskie nauki, 1*, 204–210.

Muravska, L. (2002). Assessment / Mapping activities of the Soros Centers for Contemporary Arts. Budapest: Open Society Institute.

Murdoch, J. (2001). Ecologising sociology: Actor-network theory, co-construction and the problem of human exemptionalism. *Sociology, 35*(1), 111–133.

Neumayer, L. (2008). Euroscepticism as a political label. *European Journal of Political Research, 47*(2), 135–160.

Oakeshott, M. (2011). *Lectures in the history of political thought*. London: Andrews UK.

Olson, D. M., & Norton, P. (2007). Post-Communist and post-Soviet parliaments: Divergent paths from transition. *Journal of Legislative Studies, 13*(1), 164–196.

Pain, L. A. (2007). Xenophobia and ethnopolitical extremism in post-Soviet Russia: Dynamics and growth factors. *Nationalities Papers, 35*(5), 895–911.

Panina, N., & Golovakha, Ye. (1994). *Socialnoje bezumije: Istoria, teoria i sovremennaja praktika* [Social madness: History, theory and current practice]. Kyiv: Abris.

Partlett, W. (2018). Postsovetskoe superprezidentstvo [Post-Soviet super-presidentialism]. *Sravnitel'noe konstitutsionnoe obozrenie, 27*(3), 103–123.

Petrov, N. (2019). Putin's neo-nomenklatura system. In B. Magyar (ed.), *Stubborn structures: Reconceptualizing post-Communist regimes* (pp. 179–216). Budapest: CEU Press.

Pickles, J., & Smith, A. (eds.). (2005). *Theorizing transition: The political economy of post-Communist transformations.* London: Routledge.

Pinker, S. (2011). *The better angels of our nature: The decline of violence in history and its causes.* London: Penguin.

Pocheptsov, G. (2017). Transformacii virtualnogo prostransva v processakh vlijanija [Transformations of virtual space in the processes of influence]. *Mediasapiens*, April 4. http://osvita.mediasapiens.ua/trend s/1411978127/transformatsii_virtualnogo_prostranstva_v_protsess akh_vliyaniya.

Pomeranz, W. E. (2016). How "the state" survived the collapse of the Soviet Union. *Kennan Cable, 18*, 1–9.

Pomeranz, W. E. (2021). Russia's perennial search for the rule of law: Origins, detours, revival, impasse. *Ideology and Politics Journal, 18*(2), 10–29.

Popovych, M. (1998). Mifologija v suspil'nij svidomosti postkommunistichnoï Ukraïni [Mythology in the social consciousness of post-communist Ukraine]. *Dukh i litera*, (3–4), 57–69.

Popper, K. (2012 [1945]). *The open society and its enemies.* London: Routledge.

Potter, W. C. (1994). Nuclear insecurity in the post-Soviet states. *Nonproliferation Review, 3*(1), 61–65.

Puglisi, R. (2003). The rise of the Ukrainian oligarchs. *Democratization, 10*(3), 99–123.

Rabinovych, S. (2021). Can the Ukrainian constitutional justice be depoliticized? *Ideology and Politics Journal, 2*(18), 234–259.

Rabkin, Y., & Minakov, M. (eds.). (2019). *Demodernization: Future in the past.* Stuttgart: ibidem.

Radnitz, S. (2010). The color of money: Privatization, economic dispersion, and the post-Soviet "revolutions." *Comparative Politics, 42*(2), 127–146.

Rawls, J. (1971). *A theory of justice*. New York: Belknap Press of Harvard University Press.

Reuter, O. J. (2017). *The origins of dominant parties: Building authoritarian institutions in post-Soviet Russia*. Cambridge: Cambridge University Press.

Ricoeur, P. (1994). Imagination in discourse and in action. In J. Robinson & G. Robinson (eds.), *Rethinking imagination: Culture and creativity* (120–125). London: Routledge.

Rorty, R. (1998). *Truth and progress: Philosophical papers*. Cambridge: Cambridge University Press.

Rorty, R. (1999). *Philosophy and social hope*. London: Penguin.

Rouda, U. (2019). Is Belarus a classic post-Communist Mafia state? In B. Magyar (ed.), *Stubborn structures: Reconceptualizing post-Communist regimes*. Budapest: CEU Press, 247–274.

Round, J., & Williams, C. (2010). Coping with the social costs of "transition": Everyday life in post-Soviet Russia and Ukraine. *European Urban and Regional Studies, 17*(2), 183–196.

Sablin, I. (2022). A spiritual perestroika: Religion in the late Soviet parliaments, 1989–1991. *Entangled Religions, 13*(8), 3–22.

Sakwa, R. (2021). Sad delusions: The decline and rise of Greater Europe. *Journal of Eurasian Studies, 12*(1), 5–18.

Sakwa, R. (ed.). (1999). *The experience of democratization in Eastern Europe*. Berlin: Springer.

Sartre, J. P. (1960). *Existentialism and humanism*. London: Methuen.

Sasse, G. (2018). *The Crimea question: Identity, transition, and conflict*. Cambridge: Cambridge University Press.

Sato, Y., Lundstedt, M., Morrison, K., Boese, V. A., & Lindberg, S. I. (2022). Institutional order in episodes of autocratization. V-Dem Working Paper 133.

Schmahl, S., & Breuer, M. (eds.). (2017). *The Council of Europe: Its law and policies*. Oxford: Oxford University Press.

Schmäing, S. (2021). "Dictatorship of applause"? The rise of direct representation in contemporary Ukraine. *Topos*, (1), 11–31.

Schumpeter, J. A. (2013). *Capitalism, socialism and democracy*. London: Routledge.

Sen, A. (2001). *Development as freedom*. Oxford: Oxford University Press.

Sharlet, R. (2019). Post-Soviet constitutionalism: Politics and constitution-making in Russia and Ukraine. In *Russia and Eastern Europe after communism* (15–34). New York: Routledge.

Sheiko, K. (2012). Nationalist imaginings of the Russian past: Anatolii Fomenko and the rise of alternative history in post-Communist Russia. Stuttgart: ibidem.

Shekhovtsov, A. (2017). *Russia and the Western far right: Tango noir*. London: Routledge.

Shekhovtsov, A., & Umland, A. (2014). The Maidan and beyond: Ukraine's radical right. *Journal of Democracy, 25*(3), 58–63.

Shevtsova, L. (2001). Ten years after the Soviet breakup: Russia's hybrid regime. *Journal of Democracy, 12*(4), 65–70.

Shlapentokh, D. (1992). Lovemaking in the time of "perestroika": Sex in the context of political culture. *Studies in Comparative Communism, 25*(2), 151–176.

Shlikhar, T. (2020). Between history and memory: Cultural war in contemporary Russian and Ukrainian cinema. PhD diss., University of Pittsburgh.

Shnirelman, V. (2022). Race, ethnicity, and cultural racism in Soviet and post-Soviet ideology, communication, and practice. *Oxford research encyclopedia of communication*, July 18, https://oxfordre.com/communication/view/10.1093/acrefore/9780190228613.001.0001/acrefore-9780190228613-e-1323.

Shparaga, O., & Minakov, M. (2019). Ideology and education in post-Soviet countries: Editorial introduction. *Ideology and Politics Journal, 13*(2), 4–8.

Silitski, V. (2010). Survival of the fittest: Domestic and international dimensions of the authoritarian reaction in the former Soviet Union following the colored revolutions. *Communist and Post-Communist Studies, 43*(4), 339–350.

Simmel, G. (1949). The sociology of sociability. *American Journal of Sociology, 55*(3), 254–261.

Sinkkonen, T. (2011). A security dilemma on the boundary line: An EU perspective to Georgian–Russian confrontation after the 2008 war. *Southeast European and Black Sea Studies, 11*(3), 265–278.

Slater, W., & Wilson, A. (eds). (2004). *The legacy of the Soviet Union*. Berlin: Palgrave Macmillan.

Sorokin, V. (2015). Postsovetskij chelovek razocharoval bol'she, chem sovetskij [The Post-Soviet Human has disappointed more than the Soviet Man]. *Kommersant*, August 17.

Steblyna, N., & Dvorak, J. (2021). Reflections on the independent mass media of post-Soviet countries and political competitiveness. *Politics in Central Europe, 17*(3), 565–588.

Sultanova, S. (2014). Challenging the Aliyev regime: Political opposition in Azerbaijan. *Demokratizatsiya, 22*(1) 15–27.

Sundstrom, L. M. I. (2006). *Funding civil society: Foreign assistance and NGO development in Russia*. Stanford: Stanford University Press.

Surkov, V. (2008). *Osnovnye tendencii i perspektivy razvitija sovremennoj Rossii* [Major tendencies and perspectives of the development of contemporary Russia]. Sankt-Petersburg: Izdatelstvo SPBGU.

Surkov, V. (2018). Odinochestvo polukrovki [The loneliness of a half blood]. *Rossija v global'noj politike*, (1–3), 124–129.

Surkov, V. (2019). Dolgoe gosudarstvo Putina [The long state of Putin]. *Novaja gazeta*, February 11. https://www.ng.ru/ideas/2019-02-11/5_75 03_surkov.html.

Szczerbiak, A., & Taggart, P. (eds.). (2008). *Opposing Europe? The comparative party politics of Euroscepticism*. Oxford: Oxford University Press.

Tishkov, V. (1997). *Ethnicity, nationalism and conflict in and after the Soviet Union: The mind aflame*. London: Sage.

Tishkov, V. (2004). *Chechnya: Life in a war-torn society*. Los Angeles: University of California Press.

Tismaneanu, V. (2009). *Fantasies of salvation: Democracy, nationalism, and myth in post-Communist Europe*. Princeton: Princeton University Press.

Treisman, D. (2011). Presidential popularity in a hybrid regime: Russia under Yeltsin and Putin. *American Journal of Political Science, 55*(3), 590–609.

Trochev, A. (2022). Between blaming and naming: Constitutional review of bans on Communist parties in post-Soviet states. In C.-Y. Huang (ed.), *Constitutionalizing transitional justice* (pp. 222–248). New York: Routledge.

Tucker, J. A. (2007). Enough! Electoral fraud, collective action problems, and post-Communist colored revolutions. *Perspectives on Politics, 5*(3), 535–551.

Turovsky, R. (2011). Party systems in post-Soviet states: The shaping of political competition. *Perspectives on European Politics and Society, 12*(2), 197–213.

Uhlin, A. (2006). *Post-Soviet civil society: Democratization in Russia and the Baltic states*. London: Routledge.

Umland, A. (2023). Historical esotericism as a method of cognition: How Russian pseudoscientists contributed to Moscow's anti-Western turn. *Ideology and Politics Journal, 23*(1), 294–308.

V-Dem. (2023a). V-Dem Project / V-Dem methodology, by Kyle Marquardt. Varieties of Democracy, data version 13. https://v-dem.net/about/v-dem-project/methodology/.

V-Dem. (2023b). Research Programs / Varieties of autocratization. Varieties of Democracy, data version 13, February 2023. https://www.v-dem.net/our-work/research-programs/varieties-of-autocratization/.

Vachudova, M. A., & Snyder, T. (1996). Are transitions transitory? Two types of political change in Eastern Europe since 1989. *East European Politics and Societies*, 11(1), 1–35.

Varlamova, N. (2021). Universal legal concepts in the Soviet socio-political context. *Ideology and Politics Journal*, 2(18), 30–56.

Verdery, K. (1998). Transnationalism, nationalism, citizenship, and property: Eastern Europe since 1989. *American Ethnologist*, 25(2), 291–306.

Vorobiyova-Ray, K. (2010). *The capitalist elephant in Kremlin: Surges of chernukha in post-Soviet cinema & television*. PhD diss., Carleton University.

Waller, M. J., & Yasmann, V. J. (1995). Russia's great criminal revolution: The role of the security services. *Journal of Contemporary Criminal Justice*, 11(4), 276–297.

Wallerstein, I. (1984). *The politics of the world-economy: The states, the movements and the civilizations*. Cambridge: Cambridge University Press.

Way, L. A. (2016). The authoritarian threat: Weaknesses of autocracy promotion. *Journal of Democracy*, 27(1), 64–75.

Way, L. A. (2021). The party of power: Authoritarian diaspora and pluralism by default in Ukraine. *Democratization*, 28(3), 484–501.

Wheatley, J. (2017). *Georgia from national awakening to Rose Revolution: Delayed transition in the former Soviet Union*. London: Routledge.

Williamson, J. (1993). "Democracy and the 'Washington Consensus.'" *World Development*, 21(8), 1329–1336.

World Bank. (2023). GDP per capita (constant 2010 US$) — Ukraine. World Bank Official Database. https://data.worldbank.org/indicator/NY. GDP.PCAP.KD?locations=UA.

Youngs, R. (2019). The new patchwork politics of wider Europe. Centre for European Policy Studies, October 28. https://3dcftas.eu/publication s/the-new-patchwork-politics-of-wider-europe.

Yurchak, A. (2013). *Everything was forever, until it was no more*. Princeton: Princeton University Press.

Zabortseva, Y. N. (2018). Niyazov's ideology and its symbolism: The cult of the leader, nationalism and its suppression of critical thinking. *Politics, Religion & Ideology*, 19(4), 510–530.

Index

Abkhazia 48, 54, 60, 67, 79, 80,
    82, 118, 123
actor-network theory 35
Aitmatov, Chingiz 45
Akaev, Askar 75
Alexievich, Svetlana 69
Aliyev, Heydar 146, 150, 177
Alma-Ata Accords / Protocol
    13, 54
Andrukhovych, Yuri 69, 111
anti-Maidan 81
Arendt, Hannah 23, 28, 49, 163
art, contemporary, in post-
    Soviet countries 19, 26, 27,
    30, 37, 45, 71, 84, 85, 105,
    106, 107, 125, 163, 164, 166,
    170, 176, 177, 178
authoritarian belt 155
axis, Belfast-Magadan (see
    Belfast-Magadan axis) 41,
    63, 160
axis, Dublin-Vladivostok (see
    Dublin-Vladivostok axis)
    41, 63, 160
Azerbaijan 17, 34, 48, 53, 54, 66,
    67, 73, 76, 80, 81, 84, 86, 118,
    122, 123, 125, 140, 146, 151,
    154, 157, 177
Bakiyev, Kurmanbek 75, 76
Being as such 19, 20
Being, being 7, 14, 19, 20, 21, 22,
    24, 25, 30, 37, 41, 51, 58, 60,
    66, 73, 78, 81, 97, 105, 108,
    111, 113, 118, 120, 123, 126,
    154, 161, 169

Being-in-the-world 24
Belarus, elections in; suspicion
    of rigged elections in 17,
    34, 41, 43, 48, 54, 59, 60, 61,
    62, 66, 67, 73, 76, 80, 84, 86,
    105, 109, 118, 124, 131, 134,
    139, 140, 146, 147, 154, 157,
    170, 176
Belavezha Accords 13, 54
Belfast-Magadan axis 41, 63,
    160
Bell, Daniel 95, 99, 103, 164
Bolotnaya Square 109
Bolotnaya, protests 109
Bolshevism, Bolshevik 15, 48,
    107, 114, 161
Budapest Memorandum 43, 59,
    60, 124, 168
Bulgakov, Mikhail 45, 56
caesura, defined; caesura, 1989–
    1991 1, 15, 17, 31, 32, 34, 35,
    36, 42, 43, 47, 50, 53, 58, 70,
    72, 79, 84, 85, 89, 91, 92, 93,
    95, 97, 99, 101, 103, 108, 110,
    116, 143, 153, 159, 160, 161,
    174
Castoriadis, Cornelius 30
catastrophe 19, 32
chaos 23, 29, 46, 68, 90, 93, 141,
    143, 144, 145
chernukha 44, 59, 65, 179
civil society organization (CSO)
    75, 131

clan, patronal 67, 73, 105, 144,
146, 147, 148, 157, 161, 172,
174
clientelism 148
Cold War 14, 36, 39, 93, 100, 172
color revolutions (see Orange
Revolution, Rose
Revolution, Tulip
Revolution) 40, 75, 76, 77,
101, 103, 134, 146, 156, 174
Commonwealth of Independent
States (CIS) 54, 59, 103
constitution, of USSR 115
continuity, interwar 14, 15, 35,
36, 41, 43, 94, 113, 143
core, of world-system 15, 38, 44,
47, 59, 69, 72, 74, 79, 90, 92,
99, 102, 107
corruption, grand, systemic 45,
56, 68, 76, 100, 104, 105, 145,
148, 149, 160, 166, 169, 172
Council of Europe 41, 95, 97, 99,
105, 119, 124, 125, 126, 176
creativity, and destruction 91,
94
creativity, autocratic 144, 150,
154, 155, 157
creativity, democratic 87, 113,
114, 124, 128, 134, 136, 140,
144, 155, 157
Crimea, Crimean Peninsula,
annexation of 13, 48, 53, 54,
60, 81, 124, 147, 155, 156,
176
Criminal Code, Russian 51
Darendorf, Ralf 95
de Soto, Hernando 96
decommunization, in post-
Soviet countries 60, 115,
116, 174

deideologization 151
demodernization 64, 87, 155
de-Putinization 161
de-Stalinization 56
Donbas, war in, occupation of
81, 83, 156
Dublin-Vladivostok axis 160
East 28, 39, 93, 95, 96, 97, 100,
102, 103, 104, 108, 163, 170,
171, 172, 174, 179
Eastern Bloc 32, 40, 44, 90, 92,
93, 95, 99, 101, 107, 108
Eastern Neighborhood policy
80
educational system 78
elections 37, 60, 63, 67, 102, 109,
113, 115, 128, 129, 131, 134,
136, 140, 150, 154, 156
elites 32, 41, 43, 52, 54, 55, 56,
57, 58, 59, 60, 63, 64, 66, 70,
73, 74, 75, 76, 77, 78, 90, 103,
111, 119, 128, 129, 134, 139,
141, 150, 153
emancipation 27, 28, 32, 36, 51,
87, 89, 141, 159, 160
ethnonationalism,
ethnonationalist 14, 68, 103,
107, 146, 161
Eurasianism, Eurasianist 71,
107, 164
Euromaidan 80, 83, 109, 157,
173, 174
European integration 96, 103,
105, 125, 140
Europeanization 14, 16, 36, 39,
41, 43, 59, 75, 84, 91, 92, 93,
95, 97, 99, 105, 160, 165
Euroskepticism 100, 104
Fomenkovians 71

Fukuyama, Francis 96, 167

German, Aleksei 84, 85

glasnost 39, 46, 72, 167

Golovakha, Yevhen 98, 141,
168, 175

Gorbachev, Mikhail 32, 39, 46,
63, 73, 74, 117, 148, 163, 167,
168

Gumilevians 71

Habermas, Jürgen 27, 39, 95,
168

Havel, Václav 95, 98, 168

Hegel, Georg Wilhelm Friedrich
24, 169

hegemony, Western, Soviet
state 13, 15, 36, 37, 38, 41,
44, 46, 48, 55, 59, 60, 63, 66,
69, 70, 71, 72, 75, 76, 79, 84,
86, 87, 90, 91, 92, 93, 96, 99,
102, 103, 106, 110, 111, 115,
116, 117, 118, 120, 121, 125,
138, 139, 140, 141, 143, 144,
158, 164, 165, 171, 175, 177,
178

Heidegger, Martin 19, 24, 28,
30, 108, 163, 166, 169, 172

history 14, 15, 19, 20, 21, 22, 24,
25, 30, 32, 35, 36, 40, 44, 45,
48, 54, 56, 67, 71, 89, 92, 93,
108, 111, 150, 159, 161, 164,
167, 170, 174, 175, 177

Huntington, Samuel 28, 29, 37,
40, 83, 96, 169

Husserl, Edmund 30

ideologeme 94

imagery 29, 89, 90, 91, 98, 108,
109

inequality 39, 56, 57, 78, 85, 109,
169

interobjectivity, interobjective
22, 25

intersubjectivity, intersubjective
22, 25, 26

intimacy 48, 117

Islam Karimov 152

jeansa 72

Judt, Tony 92, 95, 170

KGB 56, 60, 115, 150

khozraschet 50

koinônia 22, 31

Kolakowski, Leszek 95, 170

Kuchma, Leonid 63, 73, 75

legitimacy, legitimation 49, 59,
67, 80, 94, 95, 121, 123, 134,
147, 148, 150

Lenin, Vladimir 15, 28, 61, 172

Lukashenka, Aliaksandr 66, 73,
109, 118, 147

Maidan 81, 177

Marxism, Marxist 15, 16, 32, 45,
48, 50, 57, 65, 92, 94, 95, 96,
97, 109, 114

memory, policies; memory,
suppression of 30, 34, 57,
77, 78, 87, 106, 108, 111, 152,
171, 172, 177

Meshkov, Yuriy 60

migration 61, 78, 164, 171, 172,
173

Nagorno-Karabakh 48, 53, 54,
60, 67, 82, 118, 122, 123

narrative, narration 93, 170

national-conservative 77, 108,
111, 157

Nazarbayev, Nursultan 74, 146,
163

neoimperialism, neoimperialist
107

neoliberal 37, 46, 55, 56, 57, 58,
59, 64, 94, 96, 102, 107, 144
neopatrimonialism 105, 149,
167
neo-Sovietism 150
neotraditionalism 152
Niyazov, Saparmurat 146, 147,
152, 179
nongovernmental organization
(NGO) 137, 138, 139, 150,
169, 173, 178
nonprofit organization (NGO)
137, 138, 139, 150, 169, 173,
178
North Caucasus 54, 60, 79, 124,
154
Nothing, Nothingness 24, 31,
32, 47
oligarchization 146, 147, 174
One Big Europe 39, 93, 99, 160
Orange Revolution (Ukraine,
2004) 76, 103, 156, 171
Ossetia 54, 60, 67, 79, 80, 82,
119, 123
Ostalgie 59, 65, 150
Panina, Natalia 71, 98, 141, 168,
175
Panslavism, Panslavist 107
patrimonial 105
Pelevin, Viktor 69, 85
perestroika 32, 34, 39, 44, 46, 48,
49, 50, 51, 55, 57, 58, 64, 68,
72, 74, 86, 116, 143, 167, 176,
177
periphery, of world-system 44,
53, 59, 72, 78, 79, 81, 82, 85,
90, 99, 110, 165, 173

political freedom 37, 61, 73, 74,
76, 86, 114, 125, 128, 131,
136, 140, 141, 147, 148, 160
polyarchy 67
Popovych, Myroslav 109, 111,
175
power vertical 74, 145
presidentialism 148, 157, 175
press freedom 134
public sphere, enlargement of
during communism 46, 49,
53, 58, 92, 114, 115, 116, 134,
136, 144
Putin, Vladimir 13, 74, 84, 109,
131, 134, 147, 150, 151, 152,
155, 156, 164, 170, 175, 178
pyramid, of power, patronal 74,
146, 147
reideologization 151
religion 48, 52, 58, 62, 65, 80,
137, 173
religious freedom 52, 117, 150
revolution 15, 23, 28, 29, 32, 47,
49, 50, 51, 54, 55, 76, 85, 89,
95, 141, 159, 163, 168, 172,
179
Revolution, 1991 7, 44, 50, 52,
55, 56, 58, 59, 64, 65, 69, 73,
76, 78, 93, 97, 116, 159
revolution, entrepreneurial 50
Revolution, February (Russia,
2017) 47
Revolution, October, Great
Socialist (Russia, 2017) 47
Revolution, Orange 76, 103,
156, 171
revolution, religious 50
Revolution, Rose 75, 103, 179
revolution, sexual 50, 51

Revolution, Tulip 75, 76, 103
Ricoeur, Paul 30, 176
rule of law 37, 86, 94, 105, 116, 122, 125, 126, 132, 140, 141, 145, 151, 156, 161, 163, 165, 175
Rus' 52, 71
Russian-Ukrainian war 87, 108, 161, 171, 174
Russo-Georgian War 79, 80, 104, 155
Saakashvili, Mikhail 75, 76, 79, 154, 155, 170
Salnikov, Alexey 85
Sartre, Jean-Paul 24, 30, 176
Schumpeter, Joseph 91, 176
Schütz, Alfred 30
Second Karabakh War (2020) 82
Serebrennikov, Kirill 84, 85
sexuality 48, 58, 117
Shevardnadze, Eduard 75
Sorokin, Vladimir 45, 85, 159, 177
South Caucasus, de facto states in 49, 54, 57, 64, 75, 90, 123
Soviet Man 15, 48, 50, 51, 53, 65, 69, 70, 117, 143, 159, 172, 177
Supreme Soviet, state/central, republican 55, 115, 117, 118, 122, 127, 128, 129

terrorism [inflicted by who on whom?] 74
tetrad, post-Soviet 14, 16, 36, 41, 43, 84, 86, 129, 141, 160
Thaw 56
The Master and Margarita, novel by Mikhail Bulgakov 45, 56
transgressive 25, 26, 29, 31
transit 90, 174
transition 15, 47, 58, 59, 64, 65, 66, 73, 89, 90, 91, 92, 93, 94, 95, 96, 97, 98, 99, 100, 101, 102, 103, 104, 105, 106, 107, 110, 111, 143, 160, 163, 165, 167, 171, 173, 175, 176, 179
transitology 104, 110
Tymoshenko, Yulia 109, 154
Union Treaty 53, 117
Varieties of Democracy 37, 113, 178
Vasyanovych, Valentyn 84, 85
Washington Consensus 96, 179
world-system 44, 59, 72, 74, 78, 79, 90, 92, 99, 174
Yanukovych, Viktor 76
Yeltsin, Boris 54, 63, 67, 74, 117, 118, 178
Yushchenko, Viktor 75, 76
Zelensky, Volodymyr (president of Ukraine, 2019–) 119
Zhirinovsky, Vladimir 109, 154

SOVIET AND POST-SOVIET POLITICS AND SOCIETY

Edited by Dr. Andreas Umland | ISSN 1614-3515

1   *Андреас Умланд (ред.)* | Воплощение Европейской конвенции по правам человека в России. Философские, юридические и эмпирические исследования | ISBN 3-89821-387-0

2   *Christian Wipperfürth* | Russland – ein vertrauenswürdiger Partner? Grundlagen, Hintergründe und Praxis gegenwärtiger russischer Außenpolitik | Mit einem Vorwort von Heinz Timmermann | ISBN 3-89821-401-X

3   *Manja Hussner* | Die Übernahme internationalen Rechts in die russische und deutsche Rechtsordnung. Eine vergleichende Analyse zur Völkerrechtsfreundlichkeit der Verfassungen der Russländischen Föderation und der Bundesrepublik Deutschland | Mit einem Vorwort von Rainer Arnold | ISBN 3-89821-438-9

4   *Matthew Tejada* | Bulgaria's Democratic Consolidation and the Kozloduy Nuclear Power Plant (KNPP). The Unattainability of Closure | With a foreword by Richard J. Crampton | ISBN 3-89821-439-7

5   *Марк Григорьевич Меерович* | Квадратные метры, определяющие сознание. Государственная жилищная политика в СССР. 1921 – 1941 гг | ISBN 3-89821-474-5

6   *Andrei P. Tsygankov, Pavel A.Tsygankov (Eds.)* | New Directions in Russian International Studies | ISBN 3-89821-422-2

7   *Марк Григорьевич Меерович* | Как власть народ к труду приучала. Жилище в СССР – средство управления людьми. 1917 – 1941 гг. | С предисловием Елены Осокиной | ISBN 3-89821-495-8

8   *David J. Galbreath* | Nation-Building and Minority Politics in Post-Socialist States. Interests, Influence and Identities in Estonia and Latvia | With a foreword by David J. Smith | ISBN 3-89821-467-2

9   *Алексей Юрьевич Безугольный* | Народы Кавказа в Вооруженных силах СССР в годы Великой Отечественной войны 1941-1945 гг. | С предисловием Николая Бугая | ISBN 3-89821-475-3

10 *Вячеслав Лихачев и Владимир Прибыловский (ред.)* | Русское Национальное Единство, 1990-2000. В 2-х томах | ISBN 3-89821-523-7

11 *Николай Бугай (ред.)* | Народы стран Балтии в условиях сталинизма (1940-е – 1950-е годы). Документированная история | ISBN 3-89821-525-3

12 *Ingmar Bredies (Hrsg.)* | Zur Anatomie der Orange Revolution in der Ukraine. Wechsel des Elitenregimes oder Triumph des Parlamentarismus? | ISBN 3-89821-524-5

13 *Anastasia V. Mitrofanova* | The Politicization of Russian Orthodoxy. Actors and Ideas | With a foreword by William C. Gay | ISBN 3-89821-481-8

14 *Nathan D. Larson* | Alexander Solzhenitsyn and the Russo-Jewish Question | ISBN 3-89821-483-4

15 *Guido Houben* | Kulturpolitik und Ethnizität. Staatliche Kunstförderung im Russland der neunziger Jahre | Mit einem Vorwort von Gert Weisskirchen | ISBN 3-89821-542-3

16 *Leonid Luks* | Der russische „Sonderweg"? Aufsätze zur neuesten Geschichte Russlands im europäischen Kontext | ISBN 3-89821-496-6

17 *Евгений Мороз* | История «Мёртвой воды» – от страшной сказки к большой политике. Политическое неоязычество в постсоветской России | ISBN 3-89821-551-2

18 *Александр Верховский и Галина Кожевникова (ред.)* | Этническая и религиозная интолерантность в российских СМИ. Результаты мониторинга 2001-2004 гг. | ISBN 3-89821-569-5

19 *Christian Ganzer* | Sowjetisches Erbe und ukrainische Nation. Das Museum der Geschichte des Zaporoger Kosakentums auf der Insel Chortycja | Mit einem Vorwort von Frank Golczewski | ISBN 3-89821-504-0

20 *Эльза-Баир Гучинова* | Помнить нельзя забыть. Антропология депортационной травмы калмыков | С предисловием Кэролайн Хамфри | ISBN 3-89821-506-7

21 *Юлия Лидерман* | Мотивы «проверки» и «испытания» в постсоветской культуре. Советское прошлое в российском кинематографе 1990-х годов | С предисловием Евгения Марголита | ISBN 3-89821-511-3

22 *Tanya Lokshina, Ray Thomas, Mary Mayer (Eds.)* | The Imposition of a Fake Political Settlement in the Northern Caucasus. The 2003 Chechen Presidential Election | ISBN 3-89821-436-2

23 *Timothy McCajor Hall, Rosie Read (Eds.)* | Changes in the Heart of Europe. Recent Ethnographies of Czechs, Slovaks, Roma, and Sorbs | With an afterword by Zdeněk Salzmann | ISBN 3-89821-606-3

24   *Christian Autengruber* | Die politischen Parteien in Bulgarien und Rumänien. Eine vergleichende Analyse seit Beginn der 90er Jahre | Mit einem Vorwort von Dorothée de Nève | ISBN 3-89821-476-1

25   *Annette Freyberg-Inan with Radu Cristescu* | The Ghosts in Our Classrooms, or: John Dewey Meets Ceauşescu. The Promise and the Failures of Civic Education in Romania | ISBN 3-89821-416-8

26   *John B. Dunlop* | The 2002 Dubrovka and 2004 Beslan Hostage Crises. A Critique of Russian Counter-Terrorism | With a foreword by Donald N. Jensen | ISBN 3-89821-608-X

27   *Peter Koller* | Das touristische Potenzial von Kam''janec'–Podil's'kyj. Eine fremdenverkehrsgeographische Untersuchung der Zukunftsperspektiven und Maßnahmenplanung zur Destinationsentwicklung des „ukrainischen Rothenburg" | Mit einem Vorwort von Kristiane Klemm | ISBN 3-89821-640-3

28   *Françoise Daucé, Elisabeth Sieca-Kozlowski (Eds.)* | Dedovshchina in the Post-Soviet Military. Hazing of Russian Army Conscripts in a Comparative Perspective | With a foreword by Dale Herspring | ISBN 3-89821-616-0

29   *Florian Strasser* | Zivilgesellschaftliche Einflüsse auf die Orange Revolution. Die gewaltlose Massenbewegung und die ukrainische Wahlkrise 2004 | Mit einem Vorwort von Egbert Jahn | ISBN 3-89821-648-9

30   *Rebecca S. Katz* | The Georgian Regime Crisis of 2003-2004. A Case Study in Post-Soviet Media Representation of Politics, Crime and Corruption | ISBN 3-89821-413-3

31   *Vladimir Kantor* | Willkür oder Freiheit. Beiträge zur russischen Geschichtsphilosophie | Ediert von Dagmar Herrmann sowie mit einem Vorwort versehen von Leonid Luks | ISBN 3-89821-589-X

32   *Laura A. Victoir* | The Russian Land Estate Today. A Case Study of Cultural Politics in Post-Soviet Russia | With a foreword by Priscilla Roosevelt | ISBN 3-89821-426-5

33   *Ivan Katchanovski* | Cleft Countries. Regional Political Divisions and Cultures in Post-Soviet Ukraine and Moldova| With a foreword by Francis Fukuyama | ISBN 3-89821-558-X

34   *Florian Mühlfried* | Postsowjetische Feiern. Das Georgische Bankett im Wandel | Mit einem Vorwort von Kevin Tuite | ISBN 3-89821-601-2

35   *Roger Griffin, Werner Loh, Andreas Umland (Eds.)* | Fascism Past and Present, West and East. An International Debate on Concepts and Cases in the Comparative Study of the Extreme Right | With an afterword by Walter Laqueur | ISBN 3-89821-674-8

36   *Sebastian Schlegel* | Der „Weiße Archipel". Sowjetische Atomstädte 1945-1991 | Mit einem Geleitwort von Thomas Bohn | ISBN 3-89821-679-9

37   *Vyacheslav Likhachev* | Political Anti-Semitism in Post-Soviet Russia. Actors and Ideas in 1991-2003 | Edited and translated from Russian by Eugene Veklerov | ISBN 3-89821-529-6

38   *Josette Baer (Ed.)* | Preparing Liberty in Central Europe. Political Texts from the Spring of Nations 1848 to the Spring of Prague 1968 | With a foreword by Zdeněk V. David | ISBN 3-89821-546-6

39   *Михаил Лукьянов* | Российский консерватизм и реформа, 1907-1914 | С предисловием Марка Д. Стейнберга | ISBN 3-89821-503-2

40   *Nicola Melloni* | Market Without Economy. The 1998 Russian Financial Crisis | With a foreword by Eiji Furukawa | ISBN 3-89821-407-9

41   *Dmitrij Chmelnizki* | Die Architektur Stalins | Bd. 1: Studien zu Ideologie und Stil | Bd. 2: Bilddokumentation | Mit einem Vorwort von Bruno Flierl | ISBN 3-89821-515-6

42   *Katja Yafimava* | Post-Soviet Russian-Belarussian Relationships. The Role of Gas Transit Pipelines | With a foreword by Jonathan P. Stern | ISBN 3-89821-655-1

43   *Boris Chavkin* | Verflechtungen der deutschen und russischen Zeitgeschichte. Aufsätze und Archivfunde zu den Beziehungen Deutschlands und der Sowjetunion von 1917 bis 1991 | Ediert von Markus Edlinger sowie mit einem Vorwort von Leonid Luks | ISBN 3-89821-756-6

44   *Anastasija Grynenko in Zusammenarbeit mit Claudia Dathe* | Die Terminologie des Gerichtswesens der Ukraine und Deutschlands im Vergleich. Eine übersetzungswissenschaftliche Analyse juristischer Fachbegriffe im Deutschen, Ukrainischen und Russischen | Mit einem Vorwort von Ulrich Hartmann | ISBN 3-89821-691-8

45   *Anton Burkov* | The Impact of the European Convention on Human Rights on Russian Law. Legislation and Application in 1996-2006 | With a foreword by Françoise Hampson | ISBN 978-3-89821-639-5

46   *Stina Torjesen, Indra Overland (Eds.)* | International Election Observers in Post-Soviet Azerbaijan. Geopolitical Pawns or Agents of Change? | ISBN 978-3-89821-743-9

47   *Taras Kuzio* | Ukraine – Crimea – Russia. Triangle of Conflict | ISBN 978-3-89821-761-3

48   *Claudia Šabić* | „Ich erinnere mich nicht, aber L'viv!" Zur Funktion kultureller Faktoren für die Institutionalisierung und Entwicklung einer ukrainischen Region | Mit einem Vorwort von Melanie Tatur | ISBN 978-3-89821-752-1

49 *Marlies Bilz* | Tatarstan in der Transformation. Nationaler Diskurs und Politische Praxis 1988-1994 | Mit einem Vorwort von Frank Golczewski | ISBN 978-3-89821-722-4

50 *Марлен Ларюэль (ред.)* | Современные интерпретации русского национализма | ISBN 978-3-89821-795-8

51 *Sonja Schüler* | Die ethnische Dimension der Armut. Roma im postsozialistischen Rumänien | Mit einem Vorwort von Anton Sterbling | ISBN 978-3-89821-776-7

52 *Галина Кожевникова* | Радикальный национализм в России и противодействие ему. Сборник докладов Центра «Сова» за 2004-2007 гг. | С предисловием Александра Верховского | ISBN 978-3-89821-721-7

53 *Галина Кожевникова и Владимир Прибыловский* | Российская власть в биографиях I. Высшие должностные лица РФ в 2004 г. | ISBN 978-3-89821-796-5

54 *Галина Кожевникова и Владимир Прибыловский* | Российская власть в биографиях II. Члены Правительства РФ в 2004 г. | ISBN 978-3-89821-797-2

55 *Галина Кожевникова и Владимир Прибыловский* | Российская власть в биографиях III. Руководители федеральных служб и агентств РФ в 2004 г.| ISBN 978-3-89821-798-9

56 *Ileana Petroniu* | Privatisierung in Transformationsökonomien. Determinanten der Restrukturierungs-Bereitschaft am Beispiel Polens, Rumäniens und der Ukraine | Mit einem Vorwort von Rainer W. Schäfer | ISBN 978-3-89821-790-3

57 *Christian Wipperfürth* | Russland und seine GUS-Nachbarn. Hintergründe, aktuelle Entwicklungen und Konflikte in einer ressourcenreichen Region| ISBN 978-3-89821-801-6

58 *Togzhan Kassenova* | From Antagonism to Partnership. The Uneasy Path of the U.S.-Russian Cooperative Threat Reduction | With a foreword by Christoph Bluth | ISBN 978-3-89821-707-1

59 *Alexander Höllwerth* | Das sakrale eurasische Imperium des Aleksandr Dugin. Eine Diskursanalyse zum postsowjetischen russischen Rechtsextremismus | Mit einem Vorwort von Dirk Uffelmann | ISBN 978-3-89821-813-9

60 *Олег Рябов* | «Россия-Матушка». Национализм, гендер и война в России XX века | С предисловием Елены Гощило | ISBN 978-3-89821-487-2

61 *Ivan Maistrenko* | Borot'bism. A Chapter in the History of the Ukrainian Revolution | With a new Introduction by Chris Ford | Translated by George S. N. Luckyj with the assistance of Ivan L. Rudnytsky | Second, Revised and Expanded Edition ISBN 978-3-8382-1107-7

62 *Maryna Romanets* | Anamorphosic Texts and Reconfigured Visions. Improvised Traditions in Contemporary Ukrainian and Irish Literature | ISBN 978-3-89821-576-3

63 *Paul D'Anieri and Taras Kuzio (Eds.)* | Aspects of the Orange Revolution I. Democratization and Elections in Post-Communist Ukraine | ISBN 978-3-89821-698-2

64 *Bohdan Harasymiw in collaboration with Oleh S. Ilnytzkyj (Eds.)* | Aspects of the Orange Revolution II. Information and Manipulation Strategies in the 2004 Ukrainian Presidential Elections | ISBN 978-3-89821-699-9

65 *Ingmar Bredies, Andreas Umland and Valentin Yakushik (Eds.)* | Aspects of the Orange Revolution III. The Context and Dynamics of the 2004 Ukrainian Presidential Elections | ISBN 978-3-89821-803-0

66 *Ingmar Bredies, Andreas Umland and Valentin Yakushik (Eds.)* | Aspects of the Orange Revolution IV. Foreign Assistance and Civic Action in the 2004 Ukrainian Presidential Elections | ISBN 978-3-89821-808-5

67 *Ingmar Bredies, Andreas Umland and Valentin Yakushik (Eds.)* | Aspects of the Orange Revolution V. Institutional Observation Reports on the 2004 Ukrainian Presidential Elections | ISBN 978-3-89821-809-2

68 *Taras Kuzio (Ed.)* | Aspects of the Orange Revolution VI. Post-Communist Democratic Revolutions in Comparative Perspective | ISBN 978-3-89821-820-7

69 *Tim Bohse* | Autoritarismus statt Selbstverwaltung. Die Transformation der kommunalen Politik in der Stadt Kaliningrad 1990-2005 | Mit einem Geleitwort von Stefan Troebst | ISBN 978-3-89821-782-8

70 *David Rupp* | Die Rußländische Föderation und die russischsprachige Minderheit in Lettland. Eine Fallstudie zur Anwaltspolitik Moskaus gegenüber den russophonen Minderheiten im „Nahen Ausland" von 1991 bis 2002 | Mit einem Vorwort von Helmut Wagner | ISBN 978-3-89821-778-1

71 *Taras Kuzio* | Theoretical and Comparative Perspectives on Nationalism. New Directions in Cross-Cultural and Post-Communist Studies | With a foreword by Paul Robert Magocsi | ISBN 978-3-89821-815-3

72 *Christine Teichmann* | Die Hochschultransformation im heutigen Osteuropa. Kontinuität und Wandel bei der Entwicklung des postkommunistischen Universitätswesens | Mit einem Vorwort von Oskar Anweiler | ISBN 978-3-89821-842-9

73 *Julia Kusznir* | Der politische Einfluss von Wirtschaftseliten in russischen Regionen. Eine Analyse am Beispiel der Erdöl- und Erdgasindustrie, 1992-2005 | Mit einem Vorwort von Wolfgang Eichwede | ISBN 978-3-89821-821-4

74   *Alena Vysotskaya* | Russland, Belarus und die EU-Osterwelterung. Zur Minderheitenfrage und zum Problem der Freizügigkeit des Personenverkehrs | Mit einem Vorwort von Katlijn Malfliet | ISBN 978-3-89821-822-1

75   *Heiko Pleines (Hrsg.)* | Corporate Governance in post-sozialistischen Volkswirtschaften | I3BN 970-3-09021-700-0

76   *Stefan Ihrig* | Wer sind die Moldawier? Rumänismus versus Moldowanismus in Historiographie und Schulbüchern der Republik Moldova, 1991-2006 | Mit einem Vorwort von Holm Sundhaussen | ISBN 978-3-89821-466-7

77   *Galina Kozhevnikova in collaboration with Alexander Verkhovsky and Eugene Veklerov* | Ultra-Nationalism and Hate Crimes in Contemporary Russia. The 2004-2006 Annual Reports of Moscow's SOVA Center | With a foreword by Stephen D. Shenfield | ISBN 978-3-89821-868-9

78   *Florian Küchler* | The Role of the European Union in Moldova's Transnistria Conflict | With a foreword by Christopher Hill | ISBN 978-3-89821-850-4

79   *Bernd Rechel* | The Long Way Back to Europe. Minority Protection in Bulgaria | With a foreword by Richard Crampton | ISBN 978-3-89821-863-4

80   *Peter W. Rodgers* | Nation, Region and History in Post-Communist Transitions. Identity Politics in Ukraine, 1991-2006 | With a foreword by Vera Tolz | ISBN 978-3-89821-903-7

81   *Stephanie Solywoda* | The Life and Work of Semen L. Frank. A Study of Russian Religious Philosophy | With a foreword by Philip Walters | ISBN 978-3-89821-457-5

82   *Vera Sokolova* | Cultural Politics of Ethnicity. Discourses on Roma in Communist Czechoslovakia | ISBN 978-3-89821-864-1

83   *Natalya Shevchik Ketenci* | Kazakhstani Enterprises in Transition. The Role of Historical Regional Development in Kazakhstan's Post-Soviet Economic Transformation | ISBN 978-3-89821-831-3

84   *Martin Malek, Anna Schor-Tschudnowskaja (Hgg.)* | Europa im Tschetschenienkrieg. Zwischen politischer Ohnmacht und Gleichgültigkeit | Mit einem Vorwort von Lipchan Basajewa | ISBN 978-3-89821-676-0

85   *Stefan Meister* | Das postsowjetische Universitätswesen zwischen nationalem und internationalem Wandel. Die Entwicklung der regionalen Hochschule in Russland als Gradmesser der Systemtransformation | Mit einem Vorwort von Joan DeBardeleben | ISBN 978-3-89821-891-7

86   *Konstantin Sheiko in collaboration with Stephen Brown* | Nationalist Imaginings of the Russian Past. Anatolii Fomenko and the Rise of Alternative History in Post-Communist Russia | With a foreword by Donald Ostrowski | ISBN 978-3-89821-915-0

87   *Sabine Jenni* | Wie stark ist das „Einige Russland"? Zur Parteibindung der Eliten und zum Wahlerfolg der Machtpartei im Dezember 2007 | Mit einem Vorwort von Klaus Armingeon | ISBN 978-3-89821-961-7

88   *Thomas Borén* | Meeting-Places of Transformation. Urban Identity, Spatial Representations and Local Politics in Post-Soviet St Petersburg | ISBN 978-3-89821-739-2

89   *Aygul Ashirova* | Stalinismus und Stalin-Kult in Zentralasien. Turkmenistan 1924-1953 | Mit einem Vorwort von Leonid Luks | ISBN 978-3-89821-987-7

90   *Leonid Luks* | Freiheit oder imperiale Größe? Essays zu einem russischen Dilemma | ISBN 978-3-8382-0011-8

91   *Christopher Gilley* | The 'Change of Signposts' in the Ukrainian Emigration. A Contribution to the History of Sovietophilism in the 1920s | With a foreword by Frank Golczewski | ISBN 978-3-89821-965-5

92   *Philipp Casula, Jeronim Perovic (Eds.)* | Identities and Politics During the Putin Presidency. The Discursive Foundations of Russia's Stability | With a foreword by Heiko Haumann | ISBN 978-3-8382-0015-6

93   *Marcel Viëtor* | Europa und die Frage nach seinen Grenzen im Osten. Zur Konstruktion ‚europäischer' Identität' in Geschichte und Gegenwart | Mit einem Vorwort von Albrecht Lehmann | ISBN 978-3-8382-0045-3

94   *Ben Hellman, Andrei Rogachevskii* | Filming the Unfilmable. Casper Wrede's 'One Day in the Life of Ivan Denisovich' | Second, Revised and Expanded Edition | ISBN 978-3-8382-0044-6

95   *Eva Fuchslocher* | Vaterland, Sprache, Glaube. Orthodoxie und Nationenbildung am Beispiel Georgiens | Mit einem Vorwort von Christina von Braun | ISBN 978-3-89821-884-9

96   *Vladimir Kantor* | Das Westlertum und der Weg Russlands. Zur Entwicklung der russischen Literatur und Philosophie | Ediert von Dagmar Herrmann | Mit einem Beitrag von Nikolaus Lobkowicz | ISBN 978-3-8382-0102-3

97   *Kamran Musayev* | Die postsowjetische Transformation im Baltikum und Südkaukasus. Eine vergleichende Untersuchung der politischen Entwicklung Lettlands und Aserbaidschans 1985-2009 | Mit einem Vorwort von Leonid Luks | Ediert von Sandro Henschel | ISBN 978-3-8382-0103-0

98   *Tatiana Zhurzhenko* | Borderlands into Bordered Lands. Geopolitics of Identity in Post-Soviet Ukraine | With a foreword by Dieter Segert | ISBN 978-3-8382-0042-2

99 *Кирилл Галушко, Лидия Смола (ред.)* | Пределы падения – варианты украинского буду-
щего. Аналитико-прогностические исследования | ISBN 978-3-8382-0148-1

100 *Michael Minkenberg (Ed.)* | Historical Legacies and the Radical Right in Post-Cold War Central
and Eastern Europe | With an afterword by Sabrina P. Ramet | ISBN 978-3-8382-0124-5

101 *David-Emil Wickström* | Rocking St. Petersburg. Transcultural Flows and Identity Politics in the St. Petersburg
Popular Music Scene | With a foreword by Yngvar B. Steinholt | Second, Revised and Expanded Edition |
ISBN 978-3-8382-0100-9

102 *Eva Zabka* | Eine neue „Zeit der Wirren"? Der spät- und postsowjetische Systemwandel 1985-2000 im Spiegel
russischer gesellschaftspolitischer Diskurse | Mit einem Vorwort von Margareta Mommsen | ISBN 978-3-8382-0161-0

103 *Ulrike Ziemer* | Ethnic Belonging, Gender and Cultural Practices. Youth Identitites in Contemporary Russia |
With a foreword by Anoop Nayak | ISBN 978-3-8382-0152-8

104 *Ksenia Chepikova* | ‚Einiges Russland' - eine zweite KPdSU? Aspekte der Identitätskonstruktion einer post-
sowjetischen „Partei der Macht" | Mit einem Vorwort von Torsten Oppelland | ISBN 978-3-8382-0311-9

105 *Леонид Люкс* | Западничество или евразийство? Демократия или идеократия? Сборник статей
об исторических дилеммах России | С предисловием Владимира Кантора | ISBN 978-3-8382-0211-2

106 *Anna Dost* | Das russische Verfassungsrecht auf dem Weg zum Föderalismus und zurück. Zum
Konflikt von Rechtsnormen und -wirklichkeit in der Russländischen Föderation von 1991 bis 2009 | Mit einem Vorwort von Ale-
xander Blankenagel | ISBN 978-3-8382-0292-1

107 *Philipp Herzog* | Sozialistische Völkerfreundschaft, nationaler Widerstand oder harmloser Zeit-
vertreib? Zur politischen Funktion der Volkskunst im sowjetischen Estland | Mit einem Vorwort von Andreas Kappeler | ISBN
978-3-8382-0216-7

108 *Marlène Laruelle (Ed.)* | Russian Nationalism, Foreign Policy, and Identity Debates in Putin's
Russia. New Ideological Patterns after the Orange Revolution | ISBN 978-3-8382-0325-6

109 *Michail Logvinov* | Russlands Kampf gegen den internationalen Terrorismus. Eine kritische Bestands-
aufnahme des Bekämpfungsansatzes | Mit einem Geleitwort von Hans-Henning Schröder und einem Vorwort von Eckhard Jesse
| ISBN 978-3-8382-0329-4

110 *John B. Dunlop* | The Moscow Bombings of September 1999. Examinations of Russian Terrorist Attacks at
the Onset of Vladimir Putin's Rule | Second, Revised and Expanded Edition | ISBN 978-3-8382-0388-1

111 *Андрей А. Ковалёв* | Свидетельство из-за кулис российской политики I. Можно ли делать добро
из зла? (Воспоминания и размышления о последних советских и первых послесоветских годах) | With a foreword by Peter
Reddaway | ISBN 978-3-8382-0302-7

112 *Андрей А. Ковалёв* | Свидетельство из-за кулис российской политики II. Угроза для себя и окру-
жающих (Наблюдения и предостережения относительно происходящего после 2000 г.) | ISBN 978-3-8382-0303-4

113 *Bernd Kappenberg* | Zeichen setzen für Europa. Der Gebrauch europäischer lateinischer Sonderzeichen in der
deutschen Öffentlichkeit | Mit einem Vorwort von Peter Schlobinski | ISBN 978-3-89821-749-1

114 *Ivo Mijnssen* | The Quest for an Ideal Youth in Putin's Russia I. Back to Our Future! History, Modernity, and
Patriotism according to Nashi, 2005-2013 | With a foreword by Jeronim Perović | Second, Revised and Expanded Edition |
ISBN 978-3-8382-0368-3

115 *Jussi Lassila* | The Quest for an Ideal Youth in Putin's Russia II. The Search for Distinctive Conformism in
the Political Communication of Nashi, 2005-2009 | With a foreword by Kirill Postoutenko | Second, Revised and Expanded Edi-
tion | ISBN 978-3-8382-0415-4

116 *Valerio Trabandt* | Neue Nachbarn, gute Nachbarschaft? Die EU als internationaler Akteur am Beispiel ihrer
Demokratieförderung in Belarus und der Ukraine 2004-2009 | Mit einem Vorwort von Jutta Joachim | ISBN 978-3-8382-0437-6

117 *Fabian Pfeiffer* | Estlands Außen- und Sicherheitspolitik I. Der estnische Atlantizismus nach der wiedererlang-
ten Unabhängigkeit 1991-2004 | Mit einem Vorwort von Helmut Hubel | ISBN 978-3-8382-0127-6

118 *Jana Podßuweit* | Estlands Außen- und Sicherheitspolitik II. Handlungsoptionen eines Kleinstaates im Rah-
men seiner EU-Mitgliedschaft (2004-2008) | Mit einem Vorwort von Helmut Hubel | ISBN 978-3-8382-0440-6

119 *Karin Pointner* | Estlands Außen- und Sicherheitspolitik III. Eine gedächtnispolitische Analyse estnischer Ent-
wicklungskooperation 2006-2010 | Mit einem Vorwort von Karin Liebhart | ISBN 978-3-8382-0435-2

120 *Ruslana Vovk* | Die Offenheit der ukrainischen Verfassung für das Völkerrecht und die europäi-
sche Integration | Mit einem Vorwort von Alexander Blankenagel | ISBN 978-3-8382-0481-9

121 *Mykhaylo Banakh* | Die Relevanz der Zivilgesellschaft bei den postkommunistischen Transformationsprozessen in mittel- und osteuropäischen Ländern. Das Beispiel der spät- und postsowjetischen Ukraine 1986-2009 | Mit einem Vorwort von Gerhard Simon | ISBN 978-3-8382-0499-4

122 *Michael Moser* | Language Policy and the Discourse on Languages in Ukraine under President Viktor Yanukovych (25 February 2010–28 October 2012) | ISBN 978-3-8382-0497-0 (Paperback edition) | ISBN 978-3-8382-0507-6 (Hardcover edition)

123 *Nicole Krome* | Russischer Netzwerkkapitalismus Restrukturierungsprozesse in der Russischen Föderation am Beispiel des Luftfahrtunternehmens „Aviastar" | Mit einem Vorwort von Petra Stykow | ISBN 978-3-8382-0534-2

124 *David R. Marples* | 'Our Glorious Past'. Lukashenka's Belarus and the Great Patriotic War | ISBN 978-3-8382-0574-8 (Paperback edition) | ISBN 978-3-8382-0675-2 (Hardcover edition)

125 *Ulf Walther* | Russlands „neuer Adel". Die Macht des Geheimdienstes von Gorbatschow bis Putin | Mit einem Vorwort von Hans-Georg Wieck | ISBN 978-3-8382-0584-7

126 *Simon Geissbühler (Hrsg.)* | Kiew – Revolution 3.0. Der Euromaidan 2013/14 und die Zukunftsperspektiven der Ukraine | ISBN 978-3-8382-0581-6 (Paperback edition) | ISBN 978-3-8382-0681-3 (Hardcover edition)

127 *Andrey Makarychev* | Russia and the EU in a Multipolar World. Discourses, Identities, Norms | With a foreword by Klaus Segbers | ISBN 978-3-8382-0629-5

128 *Roland Scharff* | Kasachstan als postsowjetischer Wohlfahrtsstaat. Die Transformation des sozialen Schutzsystems | Mit einem Vorwort von Joachim Ahrens | ISBN 978-3-8382-0622-6

129 *Katja Grupp* | Bild Lücke Deutschland. Kaliningrader Studierende sprechen über Deutschland | Mit einem Vorwort von Martin Schulz | ISBN 978-3-8382-0552-6

130 *Konstantin Sheiko, Stephen Brown* | History as Therapy. Alternative History and Nationalist Imaginings in Russia, 1991-2014 | ISBN 978-3-8382-0665-3

131 *Elisa Kriza* | Alexander Solzhenitsyn: Cold War Icon, Gulag Author, Russian Nationalist? A Study of the Western Reception of his Literary Writings, Historical Interpretations, and Political Ideas | With a foreword by Andrei Rogatchevski | ISBN 978-3-8382-0589-2 (Paperback edition) | ISBN 978-3-8382-0690-5 (Hardcover edition)

132 *Serghei Golunov* | The Elephant in the Room. Corruption and Cheating in Russian Universities | ISBN 978-3-8382-0570-0

133 *Manja Hussner, Rainer Arnold (Hgg.)* | Verfassungsgerichtsbarkeit in Zentralasien I. Sammlung von Verfassungstexten | ISBN 978-3-8382-0595-3

134 *Nikolay Mitrokhin* | Die „Russische Partei". Die Bewegung der russischen Nationalisten in der UdSSR 1953-1985 | Aus dem Russischen übertragen von einem Übersetzerteam unter der Leitung von Larisa Schippel | ISBN 978-3-8382-0024-8

135 *Manja Hussner, Rainer Arnold (Hgg.)* | Verfassungsgerichtsbarkeit in Zentralasien II. Sammlung von Verfassungstexten | ISBN 978-3-8382-0597-7

136 *Manfred Zeller* | Das sowjetische Fieber. Fußballfans im poststalinistischen Vielvölkerreich | Mit einem Vorwort von Nikolaus Katzer | ISBN 978-3-8382-0757-5

137 *Kristin Schreiter* | Stellung und Entwicklungspotential zivilgesellschaftlicher Gruppen in Russland. Menschenrechtsorganisationen im Vergleich | ISBN 978-3-8382-0673-8

138 *David R. Marples, Frederick V. Mills (Eds.)* | Ukraine's Euromaidan. Analyses of a Civil Revolution | ISBN 978-3-8382-0660-8

139 *Bernd Kappenberg* | Setting Signs for Europe. Why Diacritics Matter for European Integration | With a foreword by Peter Schlobinski | ISBN 978-3-8382-0663-9

140 *René Lenz* | Internationalisierung, Kooperation und Transfer. Externe bildungspolitische Akteure in der Russischen Föderation | Mit einem Vorwort von Frank Ettrich | ISBN 978-3-8382-0751-3

141 *Juri Plusnin, Yana Zausaeva, Natalia Zhidkevich, Artemy Pozanenko* | Wandering Workers. Mores, Behavior, Way of Life, and Political Status of Domestic Russian Labor Migrants | Translated by Julia Kazantseva | ISBN 978-3-8382-0653-0

142 *David J. Smith (Eds.)* | Latvia – A Work in Progress? 100 Years of State- and Nation-Building | ISBN 978-3-8382-0648-6

143 *Инна Чувычкина (ред.)* | Экспортные нефте- и газопроводы на постсоветском пространстве. Анализ трубопроводной политики в свете теории международных отношений | ISBN 978-3-8382-0822-0

144 *Johann Zajaczkowski* | Russland – eine pragmatische Großmacht? Eine rollentheoretische Untersuchung russischer Außenpolitik am Beispiel der Zusammenarbeit mit den USA nach 9/11 und des Georgienkrieges von 2008 | Mit einem Vorwort von Siegfried Schieder | ISBN 978-3-8382-0837-4

145 *Boris Popivanov* | Changing Images of the Left in Bulgaria. The Challenge of Post-Communism in the Early 21st Century | ISBN 978-3-8382-0667-7

146 *Lenka Krátká* | A History of the Czechoslovak Ocean Shipping Company 1948-1989. How a Small, Landlocked Country Ran Maritime Business During the Cold War | ISBN 978-3-8382-0666-0

147 *Alexander Sergunin* | Explaining Russian Foreign Policy Behavior. Theory and Practice | ISBN 978-3-8382-0752-0

148 *Darya Malyutina* | Migrant Friendships in a Super-Diverse City. Russian-Speakers and their Social Relationships in London in the 21st Century | With a foreword by Claire Dwyer | ISBN 978-3-8382-0652-3

149 *Alexander Sergunin, Valery Konyshev* | Russia in the Arctic. Hard or Soft Power? | ISBN 978-3-8382-0753-7

150 *John J. Maresca* | Helsinki Revisited. A Key U.S. Negotiator's Memoirs on the Development of the CSCE into the OSCE | With a foreword by Hafiz Pashayev | ISBN 978-3-8382-0852-7

151 *Jardar Østbø* | The New Third Rome. Readings of a Russian Nationalist Myth | With a foreword by Pål Kolstø | ISBN 978-3-8382-0870-1

152 *Simon Kordonsky* | Socio-Economic Foundations of the Russian Post-Soviet Regime. The Resource-Based Economy and Estate-Based Social Structure of Contemporary Russia | With a foreword by Svetlana Barsukova | ISBN 978-3-8382-0775-9

153 *Duncan Leitch* | Assisting Reform in Post-Communist Ukraine 2000–2012. The Illusions of Donors and the Disillusion of Beneficiaries | With a foreword by Kataryna Wolczuk | ISBN 978-3-8382-0844-2

154 *Abel Polese* | Limits of a Post-Soviet State. How Informality Replaces, Renegotiates, and Reshapes Governance in Contemporary Ukraine | With a foreword by Colin Williams | ISBN 978-3-8382-0845-9

155 *Mikhail Suslov (Ed.)* | Digital Orthodoxy in the Post-Soviet World. The Russian Orthodox Church and Web 2.0 | With a foreword by Father Cyril Hovorun | ISBN 978-3-8382-0871-8

156 *Leonid Luks* | Zwei „Sonderwege"? Russisch-deutsche Parallelen und Kontraste (1917-2014). Vergleichende Essays | ISBN 978-3-8382-0823-7

157 *Vladimir V. Karacharovskiy, Ovsey I. Shkaratan, Gordey A. Yastrebov* | Towards a New Russian Work Culture. Can Western Companies and Expatriates Change Russian Society? | With a foreword by Elena N. Danilova | Translated by Julia Kazantseva | ISBN 978-3-8382-0902-9

158 *Edmund Griffiths* | Aleksandr Prokhanov and Post-Soviet Esotericism | ISBN 978-3-8382-0963-0

159 *Timm Beichelt, Susann Worschech (Eds.)* | Transnational Ukraine? Networks and Ties that Influence(d) Contemporary Ukraine | ISBN 978-3-8382-0944-9

160 *Mieste Hotopp-Riecke* | Die Tataren der Krim zwischen Assimilation und Selbstbehauptung. Der Aufbau des krimtatarischen Bildungswesens nach Deportation und Heimkehr (1990-2005) | Mit einem Vorwort von Swetlana Czerwonnaja | ISBN 978-3-89821-940-2

161 *Olga Bertelsen (Ed.)* | Revolution and War in Contemporary Ukraine. The Challenge of Change | ISBN 978-3-8382-1016-2

162 *Natalya Ryabinska* | Ukraine's Post-Communist Mass Media. Between Capture and Commercialization | With a foreword by Marta Dyczok | ISBN 978-3-8382-1011-7

163 *Alexandra Cotofana, James M. Nyce (Eds.)* | Religion and Magic in Socialist and Post-Socialist Contexts. Historic and Ethnographic Case Studies of Orthodoxy, Heterodoxy, and Alternative Spirituality | With a foreword by Patrick L. Michelson | ISBN 978-3-8382-0989-0

164 *Nozima Akhrarkhodjaeva* | The Instrumentalisation of Mass Media in Electoral Authoritarian Regimes. Evidence from Russia's Presidential Election Campaigns of 2000 and 2008 | ISBN 978-3-8382-1013-1

165 *Yulia Krasheninnikova* | Informal Healthcare in Contemporary Russia. Sociographic Essays on the Post-Soviet Infrastructure for Alternative Healing Practices | ISBN 978-3-8382-0970-8

166 *Peter Kaiser* | Das Schachbrett der Macht. Die Handlungsspielräume eines sowjetischen Funktionärs unter Stalin am Beispiel des Generalsekretärs des Komsomol Aleksandr Kosarev (1929-1938) | Mit einem Vorwort von Dietmar Neutatz | ISBN 978-3-8382-1052-0

167 *Oksana Kim* | The Effects and Implications of Kazakhstan's Adoption of International Financial Reporting Standards. A Resource Dependence Perspective | With a foreword by Svetlana Vlady | ISBN 978-3-8382-0987-6

168 *Anna Sanina* | Patriotic Education in Contemporary Russia. Sociological Studies in the Making of the Post-Soviet Citizen | With a foreword by Anna Oldfield | ISBN 978-3-8382-0993-7

169 *Rudolf Wolters* | Spezialist in Sibirien Faksimile der 1933 erschienenen ersten Ausgabe | Mit einem Vorwort von Dmitrij Chmolnizki | ISBN 078 3 8382 0616 1

170 *Michal Vít, Magdalena M. Baran (Eds.)* | Transregional versus National Perspectives on Contemporary Central European History. Studies on the Building of Nation-States and Their Cooperation in the 20th and 21st Century | With a foreword by Petr Vágner | ISBN 978-3-8382-1015-5

171 *Philip Gamaghelyan* | Conflict Resolution Beyond the International Relations Paradigm. Evolving Designs as a Transformative Practice in Nagorno-Karabakh and Syria | With a foreword by Susan Allen | ISBN 978-3-8382-1057-5

172 *Maria Shagina* | Joining a Prestigious Club. Cooperation with Europarties and Its Impact on Party Development in Georgia, Moldova, and Ukraine 2004–2015 | With a foreword by Kataryna Wolczuk | ISBN 978-3-8382-1084-1

173 *Alexandra Cotofana, James M. Nyce (Eds.)* | Religion and Magic in Socialist and Post-Socialist Contexts II. Baltic, Eastern European, and Post-USSR Case Studies | With a foreword by Anita Stasulane | ISBN 978-3-8382-0990-6

174 *Barbara Kunz* | Kind Words, Cruise Missiles, and Everything in Between. The Use of Power Resources in U.S. Policies towards Poland, Ukraine, and Belarus 1989–2008 | With a foreword by William Hill | ISBN 978-3-8382-1065-0

175 *Eduard Klein* | Bildungskorruption in Russland und der Ukraine. Eine komparative Analyse der Performanz staatlicher Antikorruptionsmaßnahmen im Hochschulsektor am Beispiel universitärer Aufnahmeprüfungen | Mit einem Vorwort von Heiko Pleines | ISBN 978-3-8382-0995-1

176 *Markus Soldner* | Politischer Kapitalismus im postsowjetischen Russland. Die politische, wirtschaftliche und mediale Transformation in den 1990er Jahren | Mit einem Vorwort von Wolfgang Ismayr | ISBN 978-3-8382-1222-7

177 *Anton Oleinik* | Building Ukraine from Within. A Sociological, Institutional, and Economic Analysis of a Nation-State in the Making | ISBN 978-3-8382-1150-3

178 *Peter Rollberg, Marlene Laruelle (Eds.)* | Mass Media in the Post-Soviet World. Market Forces, State Actors, and Political Manipulation in the Informational Environment after Communism | ISBN 978-3-8382-1116-9

179 *Mikhail Minakov* | Development and Dystopia. Studies in Post-Soviet Ukraine and Eastern Europe | With a foreword by Alexander Etkind | ISBN 978-3-8382-1112-1

180 *Aijan Sharshenova* | The European Union's Democracy Promotion in Central Asia. A Study of Political Interests, Influence, and Development in Kazakhstan and Kyrgyzstan in 2007–2013 | With a foreword by Gordon Crawford | ISBN 978-3-8382-1151-0

181 *Andrey Makarychev, Alexandra Yatsyk (Eds.)* | Boris Nemtsov and Russian Politics. Power and Resistance | With a foreword by Zhanna Nemtsova | ISBN 978-3-8382-1122-0

182 *Sophie Falsini* | The Euromaidan's Effect on Civil Society. Why and How Ukrainian Social Capital Increased after the Revolution of Dignity | With a foreword by Susann Worschech | ISBN 978-3-8382-1131-2

183 *Valentyna Romanova, Andreas Umland (Eds.)* | Ukraine's Decentralization. Challenges and Implications of the Local Governance Reform after the Euromaidan Revolution | ISBN 978-3-8382-1162-6

184 *Leonid Luks* | A Fateful Triangle. Essays on Contemporary Russian, German and Polish History | ISBN 978-3-8382-1143-5

185 *John B. Dunlop* | The February 2015 Assassination of Boris Nemtsov and the Flawed Trial of his Alleged Killers. An Exploration of Russia's "Crime of the 21st Century" | ISBN 978-3-8382-1188-6

186 *Vasile Rotaru* | Russia, the EU, and the Eastern Partnership. Building Bridges or Digging Trenches? | ISBN 978-3-8382-1134-3

187 *Marina Lebedeva* | Russian Studies of International Relations. From the Soviet Past to the Post-Cold-War Present | With a foreword by Andrei P. Tsygankov | ISBN 978-3-8382-0851-0

188 *Tomasz Stępniewski, George Soroka (Eds.)* | Ukraine after Maidan. Revisiting Domestic and Regional Security | ISBN 978-3-8382-1075-9

189 *Petar Cholakov* | Ethnic Entrepreneurs Unmasked. Political Institutions and Ethnic Conflicts in Contemporary Bulgaria | ISBN 978-3-8382-1189-3

190 *A. Salem, G. Hazeldine, D. Morgan (Eds.)* | Higher Education in Post-Communist States. Comparative and Sociological Perspectives | ISBN 978-3-8382-1183-1

191 *Igor Torbakov* | After Empire. Nationalist Imagination and Symbolic Politics in Russia and Eurasia in the Twentieth and Twenty-First Century | With a foreword by Serhii Plokhy | ISBN 978-3-8382-1217-3

192 *Aleksandr Burakovskiy* | Jewish-Ukrainian Relations in Late and Post-Soviet Ukraine. Articles, Lectures and Essays from 1986 to 2016 | ISBN 978-3-8382-1210-4

193 *Natalia Shapovalova, Olga Burlyuk (Eds.)* | Civil Society in Post-Euromaidan Ukraine. From Revolution to Consolidation | With a foreword by Richard Youngs | ISBN 978-3-8382-1216-6

194 *Franz Preissler* | Positionsverteidigung, Imperialismus oder Irredentismus? Russland und die „Russischsprachigen", 1991–2015 | ISBN 978-3-8382-1262-3

195 *Marian Madeła* | Der Reformprozess in der Ukraine 2014-2017. Eine Fallstudie zur Reform der öffentlichen Verwaltung | Mit einem Vorwort von Martin Malek | ISBN 978-3-8382-1266-1

196 *Anke Giesen* | „Wie kann denn der Sieger ein Verbrecher sein?" Eine diskursanalytische Untersuchung der russlandweiten Debatte über Konzept und Verstaatlichungsprozess der Lagergedenkstätte „Perm'-36" im Ural | ISBN 978-3-8382-1284-5

197 *Victoria Leukavets* | The Integration Policies of Belarus and Ukraine vis-à-vis the EU and Russia. A Comparative Analysis Through the Prism of a Two-Level Game Approach | ISBN 978-3-8382-1247-0

198 *Oksana Kim* | The Development and Challenges of Russian Corporate Governance I. The Roles and Functions of Boards of Directors | With a foreword by Sheila M. Puffer | ISBN 978-3-8382-1287-6

199 *Thomas D. Grant* | International Law and the Post-Soviet Space I. Essays on Chechnya and the Baltic States | With a foreword by Stephen M. Schwebel | ISBN 978-3-8382-1279-1

200 *Thomas D. Grant* | International Law and the Post-Soviet Space II. Essays on Ukraine, Intervention, and Non-Proliferation | ISBN 978-3-8382-1280-7

201 *Slavomír Michálek, Michal Štefansky* | The Age of Fear. The Cold War and Its Influence on Czechoslovakia 1945–1968 | ISBN 978-3-8382-1285-2

202 *Iulia-Sabina Joja* | Romania's Strategic Culture 1990–2014. Continuity and Change in a Post-Communist Country's Evolution of National Interests and Security Policies | With a foreword by Heiko Biehl | ISBN 978-3-8382-1286-9

203 *Andrei Rogatchevski, Yngvar B. Steinholt, Arve Hansen, David-Emil Wickström* | War of Songs. Popular Music and Recent Russia-Ukraine Relations | With a foreword by Artemy Troitsky | ISBN 978-3-8382-1173-2

204 *Maria Lipman (Ed.)* | Russian Voices on Post-Crimea Russia. An Almanac of Counterpoint Essays from 2015–2018 | ISBN 978-3-8382-1251-7

205 *Ksenia Maksimovtsova* | Language Conflicts in Contemporary Estonia, Latvia, and Ukraine. A Comparative Exploration of Discourses in Post-Soviet Russian-Language Digital Media | With a foreword by Ammon Cheskin | ISBN 978-3-8382-1282-1

206 *Michal Vít* | The EU's Impact on Identity Formation in East-Central Europe between 2004 and 2013. Perceptions of the Nation and Europe in Political Parties of the Czech Republic, Poland, and Slovakia | With a foreword by Andrea Pető | ISBN 978-3-8382-1275-3

207 *Per A. Rudling* | Tarnished Heroes. The Organization of Ukrainian Nationalists in the Memory Politics of Post-Soviet Ukraine | ISBN 978-3-8382-0999-9

208 *Kaja Gadowska, Peter Solomon (Eds.)* | Legal Change in Post-Communist States. Progress, Reversions, Explanations | ISBN 978-3-8382-1312-5

209 *Pawel Kowal, Georges Mink, Iwona Reichardt (Eds.)* | Three Revolutions: Mobilization and Change in Contemporary Ukraine I. Theoretical Aspects and Analyses on Religion, Memory, and Identity | ISBN 978-3-8382-1321-7

210 *Pawel Kowal, Georges Mink, Adam Reichardt, Iwona Reichardt (Eds.)* | Three Revolutions: Mobilization and Change in Contemporary Ukraine II. An Oral History of the Revolution on Granite, Orange Revolution, and Revolution of Dignity | ISBN 978-3-8382-1323-1

211 *Li Bennich-Björkman, Sergiy Kurbatov (Eds.)* | When the Future Came. The Collapse of the USSR and the Emergence of National Memory in Post-Soviet History Textbooks | ISBN 978-3-8382-1335-4

212 *Olga R. Gulina* | Migration as a (Geo-)Political Challenge in the Post-Soviet Space. Border Regimes, Policy Choices, Visa Agendas | With a foreword by Nils Muižnieks | ISBN 978-3-8382-1338-5

213 *Sanna Turoma, Kaarina Aitamurto, Slobodanka Vladiv-Glover (Eds.)* | Religion, Expression, and Patriotism in Russia. Essays on Post-Soviet Society and the State. ISBN 978-3-8382-1346-0

214 *Vasif Huseynov* | Geopolitical Rivalries in the "Common Neighborhood". Russia's Conflict with the West, Soft Power, and Neoclassical Realism | With a foreword by Nicholas Ross Smith | ISBN 978-3-8382-1277-7

215 *Mikhail Suslov* | Geopolitical Imagination. Ideology and Utopia in Post-Soviet Russia | With a foreword by Mark Bassin | ISBN 978-3-8382-1361-3

216 *Alexander Etkind, Mikhail Minakov (Eds.)* | Ideology after Union. Political Doctrines, Discourses, and Debates in Post-Soviet Societies | ISBN 978-3-8382-1388-0

217 *Jakob Mischke, Oleksandr Zabirko (Hgg.)* | Protestbewegungen im langen Schatten des Kreml. Aufbruch und Resignation in Russland und der Ukraine | ISBN 978-3-8382-0926-5

218 *Oksana Huss* | How Corruption and Anti-Corruption Policies Sustain Hybrid Regimes. Strategies of Political Domination under Ukraine's Presidents in 1994-2014 | With a foreword by Tobias Debiel and Andrea Gawrich | ISBN 978-3-8382-1430-6

219 *Dmitry Travin, Vladimir Gel'man, Otar Marganiya* | The Russian Path. Ideas, Interests, Institutions, Illusions | With a foreword by Vladimir Ryzhkov | ISBN 978-3-8382-1421-4

220 *Gergana Dimova* | Political Uncertainty. A Comparative Exploration | With a foreword by Todor Yalamov and Rumena Filipova | ISBN 978-3-8382-1385-9

221 *Torben Waschke* | Russland in Transition. Geopolitik zwischen Raum, Identität und Machtinteressen | Mit einem Vorwort von Andreas Dittmann | ISBN 978-3-8382-1480-1

222 *Steven Jobbitt, Zsolt Bottlik, Marton Berki (Eds.)* | Power and Identity in the Post-Soviet Realm. Geographies of Ethnicity and Nationality after 1991 | ISBN 978-3-8382-1399-6

223 *Daria Buteiko* | Erinnerungsort. Ort des Gedenkens, der Erholung oder der Einkehr? Kommunismus-Erinnerung am Beispiel der Gedenkstätte Berliner Mauer sowie des Soloveckij-Klosters und -Museumsparks | ISBN 978-3-8382-1367-5

224 *Olga Bertelsen (Ed.)* | Russian Active Measures. Yesterday, Today, Tomorrow | With a foreword by Jan Goldman | ISBN 978-3-8382-1529-7

225 *David Mandel* | "Optimizing" Higher Education in Russia. University Teachers and their Union "Universi-tetskaya solidarnost'" | ISBN 978-3-8382-1519-8

226 *Mikhail Minakov, Gwendolyn Sasse, Daria Isachenko (Eds.)* | Post-Soviet Secessionism. Nation-Building and State-Failure after Communism | ISBN 978-3-8382-1538-9

227 *Jakob Hauter (Ed.)* | Civil War? Interstate War? Hybrid War? Dimensions and Interpretations of the Donbas Conflict in 2014–2020 | With a foreword by Andrew Wilson | ISBN 978-3-8382-1383-5

228 *Tima T. Moldogaziev, Gene A. Brewer, J. Edward Kellough (Eds.)* | Public Policy and Politics in Georgia. Lessons from Post-Soviet Transition | With a foreword by Dan Durning | ISBN 978-3-8382-1535-8

229 *Oxana Schmies (Ed.)* | NATO's Enlargement and Russia. A Strategic Challenge in the Past and Future | With a foreword by Vladimir Kara-Murza | ISBN 978-3-8382-1478-8

230 *Christopher Ford* | Ukapisme – Une Gauche perdue. Le marxisme anti-colonial dans la révolution ukrainienne 1917-1925 | Avec une préface de Vincent Présumey | ISBN 978-3-8382-0899-2

231 *Anna Kutkina* | Between Lenin and Bandera. Decommunization and Multivocality in Post-Euromaidan Ukraine | With a foreword by Juri Mykkänen | ISBN 978-3-8382-1506-8

232 *Lincoln E. Flake* | Defending the Faith. The Russian Orthodox Church and the Demise of Religious Pluralism | With a foreword by Peter Martland | ISBN 978-3-8382-1378-1

233 *Nikoloz Samkharadze* | Russia's Recognition of the Independence of Abkhazia and South Ossetia. Analysis of a Deviant Case in Moscow's Foreign Policy | With a foreword by Neil MacFarlane | ISBN 978-3-8382-1414-6

234 *Arve Hansen* | Urban Protest. A Spatial Perspective on Kyiv, Minsk, and Moscow | With a foreword by Julie Wilhelmsen | ISBN 978-3-8382-1495-5

235 *Eleonora Narvselius, Julie Fedor (Eds.)* | Diversity in the East-Central European Borderlands. Memories, Cityscapes, People | ISBN 978-3-8382-1523-5

236 *Regina Elsner* | The Russian Orthodox Church and Modernity. A Historical and Theological Investigation into Eastern Christianity between Unity and Plurality | With a foreword by Mikhail Suslov | ISBN 978-3-8382-1568-6

237 *Bo Petersson* | The Putin Predicament. Problems of Legitimacy and Succession in Russia | With a foreword by J. Paul Goode | ISBN 978-3-8382-1050-6

238 *Jonathan Otto Pohl* | The Years of Great Silence. The Deportation, Special Settlement, and Mobilization into the Labor Army of Ethnic Germans in the USSR, 1941–1955 | ISBN 978-3-8382-1630-0

239 *Mikhail Minakov (Ed.)* | Inventing Majorities. Ideological Creativity in Post-Soviet Societies | ISBN 978-3-8382-1641-6

240 *Robert M. Cutler* | Soviet and Post-Soviet Foreign Policies I. East-South Relations and the Political Economy of the Communist Bloc, 1971–1991 | With a foreword by Roger E. Kanet | ISBN 978-3-8382-1654-6

241 *Izabella Agardi* | On the Verge of History. Life Stories of Rural Women from Serbia, Romania, and Hungary, 1920–2020 | With a foreword by Andrea Pető | ISBN 978-3-8382-1602-7

242 *Sebastian Schäffer (Ed.)* | Ukraine in Central and Eastern Europe. Kyiv's Foreign Affairs and the International Relations of the Post-Communist Region | With a foreword by Pavlo Klimkin and Andreas Umland| ISBN 978-3-8382-1615-7

243 *Volodymyr Dubrovskyi, Kalman Mizsei, Mychailo Wynnyckyj (Eds.)* | Eight Years after the Revolution of Dignity. What Has Changed in Ukraine during 2013–2021? | With a foreword by Yaroslav Hrytsak | ISBN 978-3-8382-1560-0

244 *Rumena Filipova* | Constructing the Limits of Europe Identity and Foreign Policy in Poland, Bulgaria, and Russia since 1989 | With forewords by Harald Wydra and Gergana Yankova-Dimova | ISBN 978-3-8382-1649-2

245 *Oleksandra Keudel* | How Patronal Networks Shape Opportunities for Local Citizen Participation in a Hybrid Regime A Comparative Analysis of Five Cities in Ukraine | With a foreword by Sabine Kropp | ISBN 978-3-8382-1671-3

246 *Jan Claas Behrends, Thomas Lindenberger, Pavel Kolar (Eds.)* | Violence after Stalin Institutions, Practices, and Everyday Life in the Soviet Bloc 1953–1989 | ISBN 978-3-8382-1637-9

247 *Leonid Luks* | Macht und Ohnmacht der Utopien Essays zur Geschichte Russlands im 20. und 21. Jahrhundert | ISBN 978-3-8382-1677-5

248 *Iuliia Barshadska* | Brüssel zwischen Kyjiw und Moskau Das auswärtige Handeln der Europäischen Union im ukrainisch-russischen Konflikt 2014-2019 | Mit einem Vorwort von Olaf Leiße | ISBN 978-3-8382-1667-6

249 *Valentyna Romanova* | Decentralisation and Multilevel Elections in Ukraine Reform Dynamics and Party Politics in 2010–2021 | With a foreword by Kimitaka Matsuzato | ISBN 978-3-8382-1700-0

250 *Alexander Motyl* | National Questions. Theoretical Reflections on Nations and Nationalism in Eastern Europe | ISBN 978-3-8382-1675-1

251 *Marc Dietrich* | A Cosmopolitan Model for Peacebuilding. The Ukrainian Cases of Crimea and the Donbas | With a foreword by Rémi Baudouï | ISBN 978-3-8382-1687-4

252 *Eduard Baidaus* | An Unsettled Nation. Moldova in the Geopolitics of Russia, Romania, and Ukraine | With forewords by John-Paul Himka and David R. Marples | ISBN 978-3-8382-1582-2

253 *Igor Okunev, Petr Oskolkov (Eds.)* | Transforming the Administrative Matryoshka. The Reform of Autonomous Okrugs in the Russian Federation, 2003–2008 | With a foreword by Vladimir Zorin | ISBN 978-3-8382-1721-5

254 *Winfried Schneider-Deters* | Ukraine's Fateful Years 2013–2019. Vol. I: The Popular Uprising in Winter 2013/2014 | ISBN 978-3-8382-1725-3

255 *Winfried Schneider-Deters* | Ukraine's Fateful Years 2013–2019. Vol. II: The Annexation of Crimea and the War in Donbas | ISBN 978-3-8382-1726-0

256 *Robert M. Cutler* | Soviet and Post-Soviet Russian Foreign Policies II. East-West Relations in Europe and the Political Economy of the Communist Bloc, 1971–1991 | With a foreword by Roger E. Kanet | ISBN 978-3-8382-1727-7

257 *Robert M. Cutler* | Soviet and Post-Soviet Russian Foreign Policies III. East-West Relations in Europe and Eurasia in the Post-Cold War Transition, 1991–2001 | With a foreword by Roger E. Kanet | ISBN 978-3-8382-1728-4

258 *Paweł Kowal, Iwona Reichardt, Kateryna Pryshchepa (Eds.)* | Three Revolutions: Mobilization and Change in Contemporary Ukraine III. Archival Records and Historical Sources on the 1990 Revolution on Granite | ISBN 978-3-8382-1376-7

259 *Mikhail Minakov (Ed.)* | Philosophy Unchained. Developments in Post-Soviet Philosophical Thought. | With a foreword by Christopher Donohue | ISBN 978-3-8382-1768-0

260 *David Dalton* | The Ukrainian Oligarchy After the Euromaidan. How Ukraine's Political Economy Regime Survived the Crisis | With a foreword by Andrew Wilson | ISBN 978-3-8382-1740-6

261 *Andreas Heinemann-Grüder (Ed.)* | Who Are the Fighters? Irregular Armed Groups in the Russian-Ukrainian War since 2014 | ISBN 978-3-8382-1777-2

262 *Taras Kuzio (Ed.)* | Russian Disinformation and Western Scholarship. Bias and Prejudice in Journalistic, Expert, and Academic Analyses of East European, Russian and Eurasian Affairs | ISBN 978-3-8382-1685-0

263 *Darius Furmonavicius* | LithuaniaTransforms the West. Lithuania's Liberation from Soviet Occupation and the Enlargement of NATO (1988–2022) | With a foreword by Vytautas Landsbergis | ISBN 978-3-8382-1779-6

264 *Dirk Dalberg* | Politisches Denken im tschechoslowakischen Dissens. Egon Bondy, Miroslav Kusý, Milan Šimečka und Petr Uhl (1968-1989) | ISBN 978-3-8382-1318-5

265 *Леонид Люкс* | К столетию «философского парохода». Мыслители «первой» русской эмиграции о русской революции и о тоталитарных соблазнах XX века | ISBN 978-3-8382-1775-8

266 *Daviti Mtchedlishvili* | The EU and the South Caucasus. European Neighborhood Policies between Eclecticism and Pragmatism, 1991-2021 | With a foreword by Nicholas Ross Smith | ISBN 978-3-8382-1735-2

267 *Bohdan Harasymiw* | Post-Euromaidan Ukraine. Domestic Power Struggles and War of National Survival in 2014–2022 | ISBN 978-3-8382-1798-7

268 *Nadiia Koval, Denys Tereshchenko (Eds.)* | Russian Cultural Diplomacy under Putin. Rossotrudnichestvo, the "Russkiy Mir" Foundation, and the Gorchakov Fund in 2007–2022 | ISBN 978-3-8382-1801-4

269 *Izabela Kazejak* | Jews in Post-War Wrocław and L'viv. Official Policies and Local Responses in Comparative Perspective, 1945-1970s | ISBN 978-3-8382-1802-1

270 *Jakob Hauter* | Russia's Overlooked Invasion. The Causes of the 2014 Outbreak of War in Ukraine's Donbas | With a foreword by Hiroaki Kuromiya | ISBN 978-3-8382-1803-8

271 *Anton Shekhovtsov* | Russian Political Warfare. Essays on Kremlin Propaganda in Europe and the Neighbourhood, 2020-2023 | With a foreword by Nathalie Loiseau | ISBN 978-3-8382-1821-2

272 *Андреа Пето* | Насилие и Молчание. Красная армия в Венгрии во Второй Мировой войне | ISBN 978-3-8382-1636-2

273 *Winfried Schneider-Deters* | Russia's War in Ukraine. Debates on Peace, Fascism, and War Crimes, 2022–2023 | With a foreword by Klaus Gestwa | ISBN 978-3-8382-1876-2

274 *Rasmus Nilsson* | Uncanny Allies. Russia and Belarus on the Edge, 2012-2024 | ISBN 978-3-8382-1288-3

275 *Anton Grushetskyi, Volodymyr Paniotto* | War and the Transformation of Ukrainian Society (2022–23). Empirical Evidence | ISBN 978-3-8382-1944-8

276 *Christian Kaunert, Alex MacKenzie, Adrien Nonjon (Eds.)* | In the Eye of the Storm. Origins, Ideology, and Controversies of the Azov Brigade, 2014–23 | ISBN 978-3-8382-1750-5

277 *Gian Marco Moisé* | The House Always Wins. The Corrupt Strategies that Shaped Kazakh Oil Politics and Business in the Nazarbayev Era | With a foreword by Alena Ledeneva | ISBN 978-3-8382-1917-2

278 *Mikhail Minakov* | The Post-Soviet Human | Philosophical Reflections on Social History after the End of Communism | ISBN 978-3-8382-1943-1

279 *Natalia Kudriavtseva, Debra A. Friedman (Eds.)* | Language and Power in Ukraine and Kazakhstan. Essays on Education, Ideology, Literature, Practice, and the Media | With a foreword by Laada Bilaniuk | ISBN 978-3-8382-1949-3

280 *Paweł Kowal, Georges Mink, Iwona Reichardt (Eds.)* | The End of the Soviet World? Essays on Post-Communist Political and Social Change | With a foreword by Richardt Butterwick-Pawlikowski | ISBN 978-3-8382-1961-5

281 *Kateryna Zarembo, Michèle Knodt, Maksym Yakovlyev (Eds.)* | Teaching IR in Wartime. Experiences of University Lecturers during Russia's Full-Scale Invasion of Ukraine | ISBN 978-3-8382-1954-7

282 *Oleksiy V. Kresin* | The United Nations General Assembly Resolutions. Their Nature and Significance in the Context of the Russian War Against Ukraine | Edited by William E. Butler | ISBN 978-3-8382-1967-2

283 *Jakob Hauter* | Russlands unbemerkte Invasion. Die Ursachen des Kriegsausbruchs im ukrainischen Donbas im Jahr 2014 | Mit einem Vorwort von Hiroaki Kuromiya | ISBN 978-3-8382-2003-1

ibidem.eu